PART 2
MARKETING TO AMERICAN LATINOS

MARKETING BOOKS FROM PMP

The Kids Market: Myths & Realities

Marketing to American Latinos, Part I

Marketing to American Latinos, Part II

*The Mirrored Window: Focus Groups
from a Moderator's Point of View*

The Great Tween Buying Machine

Marketing Insights to Help Your Business Grow

Why People Buy Things They Don't Need

PART 2

MARKETING TO AMERICAN LATINOS

A Guide to the In-Culture Approach™

M. Isabel Valdés

PARAMOUNT MARKET PUBLISHING, INC.

Paramount Market Publishing, Inc.
301 S. Geneva Street, Suite 109
Ithaca, NY 14850
www.paramountbooks.com
Telephone: 607-275-8100; 888-787-8100   Facsimile: 607-275-8101

Publisher: James Madden
Editorial Director: Doris Walsh

Library of Congress Catalog Number:
Cataloging in Publication Data available
ISBN 0-9671439-2-6

Book design and composition: Paperwork

To see the creative materials associated with case studies in this book,
go to www.incultureapproach.com

User ID: Latino
Password: paramount

To Raul Yzaguirre

A dear leader whose 30 years of community work

has left clear tracks for generations to follow!

Contents

Acknowledgments   ix

Introduction   xiii

Section 1   Hispanics in the United States, A Current Look   1

    Chapter 1.   A growth market   3

    Chapter 2.   Hispanics are young   8

    Chapter 3.   Diversity within the Latino community   10

    Chapter 4.   Geographic distribution   16

    Chapter 5.   Hispanic buying power   22

    Chapter 6.   Hispanic households   30

    Chapter 7.   The acculturation factor   33

    Chapter 8.   Educational attainment   35

    Chapter 9.   Hispanics in the labor force, business, and politics   41

Section 2 Targeting to the Hearts and Minds of U.S. Latinos   53

    Chapter 10.   Segmenting Latinos for profits   55

    Chapter 11.   Segmenting by place of birth and generation   58

    Chapter 12.   Segmenting by language   64

    Chapter 13.   Segmenting by country of origin   71

    Chapter 14.   *In-culture* age segments   77

Section 3   Hispanics as Customers   141

    Chapter 15.   Using *in-culture* household intelligence   143

    Chapter 16.   What Latinos buy   153

    Chapter 17.   How to get your products in front of Latinos   179

Section 4 Latino Lifestyles   215

    Chapter 18.   Healthcare and Latinos today   219

    Chapter 19.   Hispanic travel: an uncharted frontier   228

    Chapter 20.   Digital Marketing to U.S. Latinos   233

    Chapter 21.   The Hispanic media scene   253

Section 5   An Integrated Strategy for Hispanic Markets   303

    Chapter 22.   The integrated *in-culture* marketing strategy   305

Online resources   329

Index   339

Author's bio   352

ACKNOWLEDGMENTS

This book is truly the work of many people, and I am deeply indebted to each and every one of them.

Two people stand out very specially and I will be eternally indebted to them: Doris Walsh, publisher, editor, and writer, Paramount Market Publishing, whose unwavering support and genius went far beyond what a writer can dream of from a publisher! Doris, you not only enriched the book with your direction and contributions, but you were also a friend who helped mold my creative muses and dreams into a cohesive and round book. My gratitude is deep and sincere. Carlos Santiago, partner, client, colleague, and friend of many years, who supported my dedication to this demanding project through an intense year of work at Santiago & Valdés Solutions (SVS), our joint venture, now The Santiago Solutions Group. Carlos provided original ideas and material to include in specific sections of the book and also generously gave me free access to all SVS papers to include in the book. Carlos, no words can do justice to what it is like to have a partner like you, willing to go the extra mile to support somebody else's dream! Doris and Carlos, *Muchas gracias!*

Many contributed much to the richness of the book and I want to acknowledge you very specially:

From AARP, Dawn Sweeney and Nancy Franklin, together with AARP's Hispanic marketing team. Thanks for the opportunity to work with you and more thanks for sharing your experience by contributing a case study! Thanks to Horacio Gomes, HeadQuarters Advertising, AARP's agency of record, who also contributed a second case study.

To Loreto Caro Valdés, who compiled most of the website information in the Online Resources section, *mil gracias,* my dear cyber-niece! and to Derene Allen, friend and partner, many thanks for your contribution to the Online section.

To Ken Greenberg, Nick Sorvillo and Matt Bell from the ACNielsen Homescan Panel, thanks for your generous contribution and support of many years and for the data for Section 3. And to Madalyn Friedman, who sifted through a million data bits from the ACNielsen Homescan Hispanic Panel to find "the best cases" to illustrate usage and applications. Many thanks!

To Neil Comber, thanks for preparing the P&G case study days before retiring—what an honor! To Xavier Saucedo (Gamesa), great advice, many thanks!

Thanks to Jennifer Lynch, Karin Navarro, Jannet Torres, Macuqui Robau-Garcia, Beth Broderson, Lady Delgado, Gil Bugarin and Jacqueline Gumucio, dear friends and colleagues from the days at CAG, who graciously extended an unselfish hand to their former boss—many thanks!

To Monica Lozano, (*La Opinión* and *La Opinión* Online) thanks for many years of friendship and for contributing case studies for both parts of this book! To Victoria Varela (The Cartel Creativo) for your on-going support, friendship and case studies for both books, many thanks! To Dr. Aliza Lipsich and Deborah Rosado Shaw, (authors). To Tom Maney, (Fox Sports Español) Jon Munoz (Bank One) Giuseppi D'Alessandro, (PepsiCo), Becky Johnson (Frito-Lay), Tony Dieste and Victor Arroyo (Dieste, Harmel & Partners). To Linda Crowly, and Tom Gee (Kraft) and Jorge Calvachi (now at NFO) for the Oscar Mayer case study prepared with support from The Bravo Group.

Many thanks to Eva May (Español Marketing & Communications), for your suggestions and the Franklin Electronics case study. Also to Ana Maria Fernández Haar (The IAC Group), for taking time to prepare two case studies (Zoloft and Dolphin Malls), *gracias*. To Michelle Aragon and Roberto Fois, PhD (Aragon Advertising), Liz Castells Heald (Ad Americas). To Jorge Flores and Dolores Kunda (Lapiz), for helping to make the Kellogg's case study a reality! To Marta Pero (now at :30 Segundos), Anita Santiago and Climara Santos (Anita Santiago Advertising), and Carl Kravetz (cruz/kravetz IDEAS), so many thanks for your case study contributions!

To Dr. Rosa Maria Gil, Pfizerz (board member), for the "Sana la Rana" materials! To Ingrid Otero Smart, Hector and Norma Orci (La Agencia de Orci & Asociados), Guillermo Paz (Lopito, Ileana & Howie), Peggy Goff (Al Punto Advertising), and Alex Lopez Negrete (Lopez Negrete Advertising), for preparing case studies that even though they did not get to see the light, required your time and dedication! So many thanks!

Many thanks to Arturo Villar (*Hispanic Market Weekly*), Eugenio (Gene) Bryan (Hispanic Ad.com), Harry Pachon (Tomás Rivera Policy Institute), Jesus Chavarria and Jim Medina (*Hispanic Business* Magazine), Zeke Montes (national Association of Hispanic Publications) Tom Exter (TGE Demographics), Geo-Scape, and *American Demographics,* for the data contributed to enrich many sections throughout the book.

To Lisa Quiroz (*People en Español*), David Morse (Cultural Access Group), Peter Roslow (Roslow Research Group), Felipe Korzenny (Cheskin Research), *Hispanic Web Monitor,* Karen Plount (Nielsen Media Research), thanks for making your data and reports available.

Thanks to the many corporations and organizations that contributed a case studies, data ,and insights.

Finally, many thanks to Jenice Mariano, for your terrific work deciphering and transcribing my notes into a clean and neat manuscript, to Marisa Rivera-Allbert, and Art Ruiz, for your friendship and inspiration to invest more in our growing community, and to Dr. Celia Correas my wonderful *madrina*, thanks for your ongoing support and for finding Jorge Luis Borges' poem for my "peace of mind"—*gracias!*

My last words of gratitude for those closest to my heart; to my parents, Rodolfo Valdés and Maria Echenique de Valdés, for teaching me the true meaning of "We are all created equal;" and many many thanks to my children, Gabriel and Clara Aranovich, and to Julio Aranovich, my life partner. Thanks for your love, for feeding me delicious "homemade lattes" and meals, and for your patience with a mom who cannot seem to be able to live and travel around the world without manuscripts, laptops, and all night productions.

My sincere hope is that the wonderful contributions made by so many to this work will benefit future generations of Latinos, Latinas, and *in-culture* marketers in the U.S. and abroad. I apologize for not mentioning many others who I am sure I would have wished to thank, had my memory been in better shape. Please consider yourself acknowledged and thanked as I do in my heart.

May you be as blessed as I have been over the years by the only Love, Truth and Power that counts, you know What I am talking about!

Enjoy!

AUGUST 4, 2002
PALO ALTO, CALIFORNIA

To see the creative materials associated with case studies in this book, go to

www.incultureapproach.com

User ID: Latino

Password: paramount

INTRODUCTION

Politicians are well aware of how the 2000 Census results are reshaping their home districts and in many cases, their political futures. However, many CEOs, boards of directors, and marketing executives are still largely unaware of what the census numbers may mean for their bottom lines and their shareholders.

Is corporate America investing enough in the Hispanic market to fully maximize shareholder value? A few companies are "right spending" on the Hispanic market compared with their spending on other market segments. However, even companies that are "right spending" tens of millions of dollars to market to Hispanics are under investing to take advantage of the immense opportunity that exists.

It is estimated that corporate America spends about $0.03 in the general media to attract every non-Hispanic purchase dollar available. Conversely, corporate America spent a hundred times less or about $0.004 to $0.005 in Hispanic media for every available Hispanic purchase dollar in 1998. Based on share of the total population and language preference, consumer driven organizations should invest, on average, a minimum of 8 percent of their total marketing dollars toward the Spanish and bilingual Hispanic markets. Santiago & Valdés Solutions (now Santiago Solutions Group) estimated that American corporations are underspending by about $14 billion in their efforts to tap into Hispanic pocketbooks.

The business community seems somewhat surprised by the

size of the Hispanic population in the United States. At 42 million, including the population of Puerto Rico and the undercount, it is larger than Canada and most Spanish-speaking nations of the world.

Population of Selected Countries in 2000

in millions

Mexico	99.6
Hispanic United States	**42.0***
Spain	39.5
Argentina	37.0
Canada	30.8
Peru	27.1
Venezuela	24.2
Chile	15.2

*Includes 3.8 million population of Puerto Rico and the undercount.

Source: Population Reference Bureau and U.S. Census Bureau

One of the most surprising findings of the 2000 Census has been how much Hispanics have penetrated into states and counties that never before considered themselves to have a Hispanic constituency.

Over the last 10 years, many field sales personnel, franchisees and retailers have asked their headquarters for corporate-wide, aggressive Hispanic initiatives. They have asked for increased marketing spending aimed at Hispanics to increase brand awareness, create custom promotions including loyalty and rewards incentives, improve retail presence, develop unique merchandise, hire more bilingual personnel, and create targeted direct-response programs. Increased spending is needed to keep up with the Latinization of America's largest metro areas and in counties throughout the United States. Experts on the 2000 Census have remarked that one of the most surprising findings has been how much Hispanics have penetrated into states and counties that never before considered themselves to have a Hispanic constituency.

Historically, the more astute market segmentation specialists have not relied even on the census high-series population projections for the Hispanic market. Hispanic marketing pioneers still remember that throughout the 1980s the census forecasts of the size of the Hispanic market for 1990 ended up missing about 6 percent of the market. The middle level projections, the ones most businesses rely on, were 15 percent under the actual count in 1990.

In 2000, forecasters were again surprised. The high-series census projections were off by 4.3 million or 12 percent of the actual size of the Latino market. That is like missing as many Hispanic consumers as there are in the entire New York Tri-State region. In fact, corporations that made strategic investments such as opening additional stores based on the census low series now know that they undersized the market by 17 percent or 6.1 million Hispanic consumers.

Few corporations in the new millennium can afford to disbelieve the recent census numbers. Those who do are losing opportunity and donating precious time to smarter competitors. In the 12 months of 2001, 1.7 million new Hispanic consumers were added to the U. S. economy. There were $224 million in additional expenditures, and half a million new households formed. It is simply too much growth to ignore.

Although this book is written primarily for a corporate audience, corporations are not the only ones who pay attention to the 2000 census. A survey of government agencies in 1992 found that $185 billion in government spending was affected in some way by the 1990 census. The Department of Commerce uses census data to help set congressional districts. The Department of Justice uses racial and ethnic data from the census to make sure that every segment of the population is equally represented in legislative districts, national as well as local. As another example, the Associated Press has reported on what it calls the "Hot Sauce Factor," in which the Agriculture Department can waive requirements to purchase only American-made food if immigrant children who eat in school cafeterias prefer products from their native lands. Census data helps the Agriculture Department track the areas that might qualify for this wavier.

State school administrators use census data to help them determine the need for teachers of English as a second language. Other agencies use it to guide groups who distribute grants based on race or ethnic identity. Public health officials are often big users of the racial component of census data.

This book is designed to help believers further understand—and profit from—the true opportunities in the Hispanic market and to help persuade those who don't believe what they are missing.

Section one provides an up-to-date statistical portrait of the Hispanic population in the United States, including Puerto Rico. It includes data on political involvement of Hispanics and on Hispanic businesses.

Section two details the Hispanic market segments that have been created by the maturity and growth in the Hispanic marketplace, including some new, age-based segments never before revealed in such detail.

Section three provides numerous case studies of product use and implications for repositioning based on volumetric data from the ACNielsen Homescan Hispanic Panel of households that has never before been publicly available. This section alone will help you put numbers on the dollar and volume market potential of the Hispanic market segments in section one.

To see the creative materials associated with case studies in this book, go to www.incultureapproach.com

User ID: Latino
Password: paramount

Section four provides a snapshot of Hispanic lifestyles, including the exploding Hispanic media sector, from online to print, TV, radio and more. Separate chapters take a brief look at two frontiers for Hispanic marketers, healthcare and travel.

Section five puts it all together, focusing on an integrated Hispanic marketing strategy and providing you with a model guide for integrated marketing to this diverse consumer market. This section also includes a detailed case study to help you understand how an integrated Hispanic market strategy actually worked for the AARP.

Throughout the book I have incorporated actual case studies, generously prepared by corporate Hispanic business and marketing leaders, to illustrate the new millennium's Hispanic market experience and drive home the point that some businesses have already grabbed the opportunity at hand.

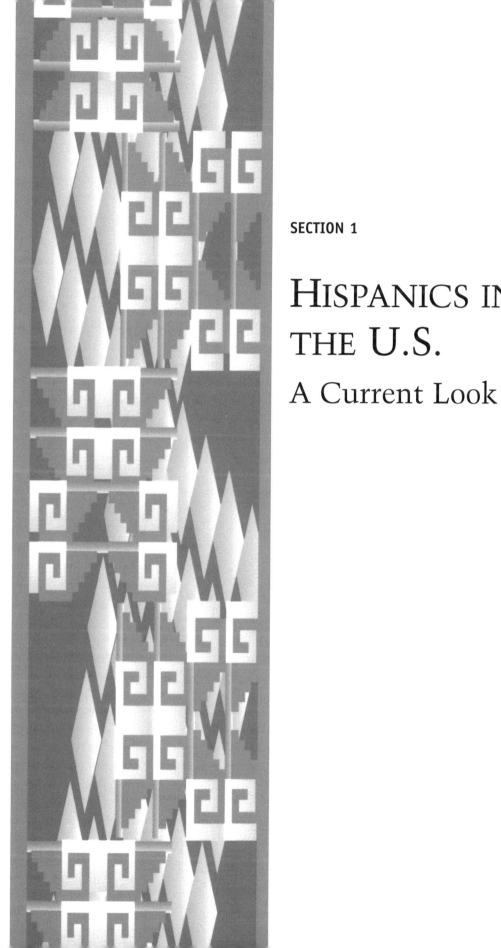

SECTION 1

HISPANICS IN THE U.S.

A Current Look

Chapter 1

A Growth Market

The most important news from the 2000 United States Census was the growth in the Hispanic market. With a surge of 13 million people between 1990 and 2000, Hispanics grew faster than any other ethnic group—a record 57.9 percent. By contrast, the number of non-Hispanic whites increased by only about 5.3 percent. The total population increased by 13.5 percent in the same period.

No longer can any business afford to ignore this prominent consumer group. For more than four decades, a significant number of emigrants from every country in Latin America have become active members of the U.S. consumer market. In less than 40 years, the total Hispanic market has more than quadrupled in size, a trend projected to continue for the near future. Between 1960 and 2001, the number of Hispanic consumers in the continental United States increased from 6.9 million to 35.3 million, representing 12.5 percent of the total U.S. population, a share similar to that of blacks.

In 2000, when I published Part I of *Marketing to American Latinos: A Guide to the In-Culture Approach,* no one knew how the actual

FIGURE 1.1

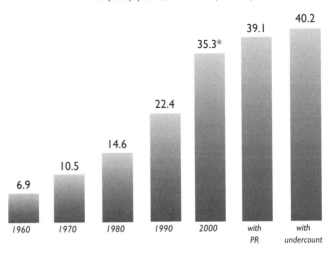

The True Size of the Hispanic Market
U.S. Hispanic population, 1960–2000 (in millions)

1960	1970	1980	1990	2000	with PR	with undercount
6.9	10.5	14.6	22.4	35.3*	39.1	40.2

* 2000 does not include the population of Puerto Rico nor the undercount.
Source: U.S. Bureau of the Census

As a whole, the Hispanic market adds about half a million new households per year and an estimated $163 billion in additional spending, based on current averages.

count from the 2000 census would compare with the best estimates available. As I write this book, data from the 2000 Census are in, and the numbers of Latinos are even higher than expected by the most optimistic forecasts. The U.S. government estimated that 32.8 million Hispanics would be counted in 2000, but the actual count showed they had underestimated the number by about 2.5 million.

TRUE SIZE OF THE HISPANIC MARKET OPPORTUNITY

Census 2000 also counted 3.8 million people living in the Commonwealth of Puerto Rico, people not included in the 35.3 million mentioned above. When the 3.8 million people residing in Puerto Rico are taken into consideration, we are talking about just over 39 million people who claim Hispanic origin. In addition, if you assume a 2.85 percent undercount (just over 1 million Hispanics), there are now just over 40.2 million Latinos in the U.S.

At the present rate of growth, the "true size" of the Hispanic market for marketing purposes was closer to 42 million in 2002 and is expected to reach 44.6 million by summer 2005.

FIGURE 1.2

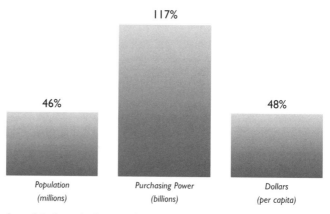

Growth Trends 1990–2001
Hispanic income gains outpace population growth.

117%

46%

48%

Population (millions) Purchasing Power (billions) Dollars (per capita)

Source: Selig Center for Economic Growth, University of Georgia, 1998 & 2000

From a marketing perspective, growth in the Hispanic market presents a unique business opportunity since the Hispanic population also experienced sustained income growth. About a half million Hispanic households are added each year, all with more money. At current rates, these households represent additional spending of about $163.7 billion per year.

UNIQUE BUSINESS VALUE

Why is this growth in the Latino population so important to U.S. business? Population growth overall is fairly flat and the population is aging. However, in many states and in the United States in general, the Hispanic population continues to grow and contribute population growth particularly to the younger age groups. All indications and projections show that the Hispanic market growth will continue for several reasons:

- *Immigration from South America continues to be strong* and immigrants are usually younger than the general population.

- *Latinos have higher fertility rates than non-Hispanic women,* with an average of 2.4 births per woman. White, non-Hispanic women have a fertility rate of 1.8 children per woman of childbearing age.

- *Latinos are younger than the population in general,* with a median age of just 26.6 years, compared with 30.8 for the population in general. In 2000, 35.7

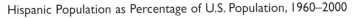

FIGURE 1.3

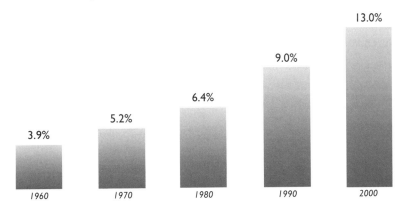

Hispanic Population as Percentage of U.S. Population, 1960–2000

13.0%

9.0%

6.4%

5.2%

3.9%

1960   1970   1980   1990   2000

Does not include the population of Puerto Rico nor the undercount.

Source: U.S. Bureau of the Census 2000

percent of Hispanics were younger than age 18, compared with 23.5 percent of non-Hispanic whites.

Although Latinos are just 12.5 percent of the total U.S. population, within certain geographic areas and age groups their prevalence is more significant. We will take a closer look at the new Latino consumer segments in Section 2.

HOW THE TERM HISPANICS AND LATINOS ARE USED IN THIS BOOK

The terms "Hispanic" and "Latino" are used interchangeably in this book and reflect both modern terminology and new standards being used by the Office of Management and Budget which are to be implemented by January 1, 2003.

According to the U.S. Census Bureau, "In Census 2000, people of Spanish/Hispanic/Latino origin could identify themselves as Mexican, Puerto Rican, Cuban, or other Spanish/Hispanic/Latino. The term Latino appeared for the first time in 2000. People who marked "other Spanish/Hispanic/Latino" had additional space to write Hispanic origins, such as Salvadoran or Dominican, a practice started in the 1990 Census.

Hispanic is not a "race"

In 1990, census respondents could select their race from one of only five categories: "white," "black," "American Indian, Eskimo or Aleutian," "Asian or Pacific Islander," or "some other race."

For the first time in Census 2000, respondents could chose from one of 63 options about race, including more than one race. Despite these options, only about 2 percent of respondents chose more than one race.

Although many people think of Hispanic or Latino as a being a racial designation, it is not. People who consider themselves among the ethnic group called Hispanic or Latino can be of any race—black, white, Asian, Mestizo Indian, etc. Because Hispanics may be of any race, the Census Bureau usually refers to non-Hispanic whites—people who have said they are white, but have not indicated they are Hispanic. For marketers and advertisers, the fact to remember is that Hispanics and Latinos may represent many different racial backgrounds.

FIGURE 1.4

Reproduction of the Question on Hispanic Origin from Census 2000

> **5. Is this person Spanish/Hispanic/Latino?** *Mark* ☒ *the* "**No**" *box if* **not** *Spanish/Hispanic/Latino.*
>
> ☐ **No**, not Spanish/Hispanic/Latino   ☐ Yes, Puerto Rican
> ☐ Yes, Mexican, Mexican Am., Chicano   ☐ Yes, Cuban
> ☐ Yes, other Spanish/Hispanic/Latino — Print group. ➘
>
> | | | | | | | | | | | | | | | | | | | |

Source: U.S. Census Bureau, Census 2000 questionnaire

Presently, Hispanic consumers in some areas such as California and Texas tend to prefer Latino. When you refer to a particular Hispanic group, however, the name of the country of origin is usually used. In current usage, the term Latino refers more specifically to the peoples born in Latin American countries, regardless of race.

There is currently no consensus within the Hispanic community as to how to refer to its members collectively. The term Hispanic is neither offensive nor preferable.

What do people of Hispanic origin prefer? In a Gallup poll in mid-2001, Americans of Spanish origin overwhelmingly said they preferred "Hispanic" rather than "Latino," by 67 percent to 13 percent. However, regardless of which term they favor, few Hispanics say they are significantly bothered by the use of either term. Most immigrants use their country of origin to refer to themselves e.g. I am Mexican, or Puerto Rican, or Salvadoran.

Chapter 2

Hispanics Are Young

On average, Hispanics are much younger than the non-Hispanic white population in the United States. More than 35 percent of Hispanics were younger than age 18 in 2001 compared with nearly 24 percent of non-Hispanic whites. Fifty-nine percent of Hispanics fall into the group aged 18 to 64, compared with 62.4 percent of non-Hispanic

FIGURE 2.1

The Hispanic population is younger than the non-Hispanic white population.

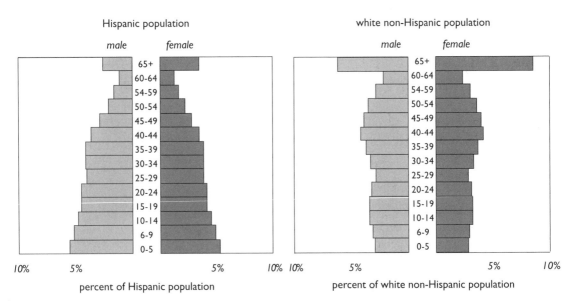

Source: Population pyramids based on U.S. Census Bureau projections of the population for July 1, 2002

whites. Just over 5 percent of Hispanics are aged 65 and over, compared with 14 percent of non-Hispanic whites.

The median age of Hispanics in 2000 was 25.9 years, compared with the median age for the entire U.S. population of 35.3 years.

Based on age alone, we know that in the coming decades, Hispanics will be more likely to be forming new households and bearing children than will non-Hispanic whites. We also know that as the baby boom ages, the educational system and the labor force will become more diversified, and many more Hispanics will be paying into the social security system.

The population pyramids shown at left illustrate the age and sex differences in the Hispanic and non-Hispanic white populations in 2001.

Chapter 3

Diversity Within the Hispanic Community

Hispanics in the United States come from every Spanish-speaking country in the world, but primarily from Mexico, Central American, and South American countries (Figure 3.1). People of Mexican origin, by far the largest segment, now make up 58.5 percent of the Hispanic population in the United States, compared with 65 percent in 1999. That decrease can be attributed to the growth of other groups, especially those from Central America who now represent nearly 10 percent of Hispanics in the U.S.

Because most Hispanics come from Mexico, Central and South America, it is important to determine not only how they are different from non-Hispanics, but also how they are different from each other. For example, when micro-targeting via direct mail, you can identify zip codes with high concentrations of Cubans or Mexicans or Puerto Ricans using geo-segmentation and adapt the visuals and the copy of your direct mail piece to the specific sub-group.

Marketing to American Latinos: A Guide to the In-Culture Approach, Part I, addresses the differences and similarities—in a cultural context—what I call an *in-culture* approach to marketing to Hispanics of all different origins. It answers many questions marketers must ask about the differences among these groups.

Hispanic immigration started long before the Pilgrims arrived on the North American continent and continues to

FIGURE 3.1

Hispanic Population by Country of Origin, 2000

This table shows the numbers of people who claimed specific Hispanic origins on the 2000 Census and the percent of the Hispanic population they represent.

	Number	Percent
Total U.S. Population	**281,421,906**	**100%**
Hispanic or Latino, of any race	35,305,818*	12.5*
Not Hispanic or Latino	246,116,088	87.5
Hispanic or Latino by Country of Origin (Total)	**35,305,818***	**100**
Mexican	20,640,711	58.5
Puerto Rican	3,406,178	9.6
Cuban	1,241,685	3.5
Other Hispanic or Latino	**10,017,244**	**28.4**
Dominican	764,945	2.2
Central American	1,686,937	4.8
Costa Rican	68,588	0.2
Guatemalan	372,487	1.1
Honduran	217,569	0.6
Nicaraguan	177,684	0.5
Panamanian	91,723	0.3
Salvadoran	655,165	1.9
Other Central American	103,721	0.3
South American	1,353,562	3.8
Argentinean	100,864	0.3
Bolivian	42,068	0.1
Chilean	68,849	0.2
Colombian	470,684	1.3
Ecuadorian	260,559	0.7
Paraguayan	8,769	0.0
Peruvian	233,926	0.7
Uruguayan	18,804	0.1
Venezuelan	91,507	0.3
Other South American	57,532	0.2
Spaniard	100,135	0.3
All other Hispanic or Latino	**6,111,665**	**17.3**
Checked box only, "Other Hispanic"	1,733,274	4.9
Wrote-in Spanish	686,004	1.9
Wrote-in Hispanic	2,454,529	7.0
Wrote-in Latino	450,769	1.3
Not elsewhere classified	787,089	2.2

*Does not include the population of the island of Puerto Rico, 3.8 million, nor the about 1 million undercount.

Source: U.S. Census Bureau, Census 2000 Summary File 1.

take place today. During the past two decades, the Hispanic market has become a major factor for businesses looking for new markets and to grow market share. The largest ongoing contributor of new immigrants is Mexico (see Figure 3.1) followed in order by the Caribbean countries, Central America, and South America.

With the maturation of globalization and internet marketing opportunities, it is helpful to marketers to know exactly where immigrants come from. Many companies based in the U.S. that sell across boundaries by the internet or by sales representation can improve their targeting and product development by understanding more about the origins of their Hispanic customers. The same is true, of course, for companies developing products and marketing to any foreign-born populations in this country.

Marketers interested in "cross-border" transactions such as money transfers and telephone services will benefit by knowing that Mexican immigrants come from a handful of states. (Figure 3.2) Below are the state and "micro-regions" with the highest immigration from Mexico into the United States.

FIGURE 3.2

Immigration Sources from Mexico

States and "micro-regions" with the highest immigration from Mexico into the U.S.

Coahuila

Jiménez

Colima

Cuauhtémoc

Chihuahua

Balleza

Batopilas

Guadalupe y Calvo

Durango

Mezquital

Otaez

Estado de Mexico

Sultepec

Guanajuato

Allende

Moroleón

Ocampo

Santiago Maravatio

Uriangato

Guerrero

Ajuchitlan del Progreso

General Canuto A. Neri

Olinala

Pedro Ascencio Alquisiras

San Miguel Totolapan

Michoacán

Aguililla

Aguila

Carácuaro

Jiménez

Jiquilpan

Nocupetaro

Susupuato

Tangancicuaro

Tepalcatepec

Tinguindin

Tzitzio

Villamar

Nayarit

Ixtlán del Rio

El Nayar

Nuevo León

Agualeguas

General Bravo

Oaxaca

Coicoyan de las Flores

San Miguel Tlacotepec

San Pedro Mártir

Yucuxaco

San Simón Zahuatlán

Santiago Juxtlahuaca

Santiago Tilantongo

Santa Inés de Zaragoza

Veracruz

Chicontepec

Soteapan

Tantoyuca

Zongolica

Zacatecas

Sultepec

Apulco

Atolingua

Trinidad

Garcia de la Cadena

General Joaquin Amaro

Huanusco

Juchipita

Tepetongo

Valparaiso

Villanueva

Source: Prepared by Fundación Solidaridad Mexicana-Americana and the Consulate of Mexico, San Francisco, July 2001

Median age of all Hispanics is 26.6 years compared with 36.2 years for non-Hispanic whites.

DEMOGRAPHIC DIFFERENCES TO CONSIDER

Marketers must be aware of the significant demographic differences among Hispanic sub-groups that are relevant to marketing. For example, Mexicans, the largest Hispanic sub-group, have the highest share of people under age 18 at 38.2 percent, compared to Hispanics of Cuban origin who have only 19.2 percent. Cubans are the oldest group among Hispanics, with 21 percent aged 65 and older. Only 4.5 percent of Mexicans and Central and South Americans fell into this age group.

FIGURE 3.3

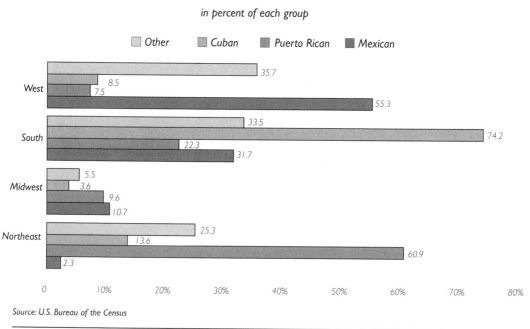

Distribution of Hispanics by U.S. Region and Origin, 2000

in percent of each group

Source: U.S. Bureau of the Census

Among Latino groups, Puerto Ricans and other Hispanics are most likely to live in a downtown area within metropolitan areas, whereas Cubans are most likely to live outside the downtown within a metropolitan area. Latinos of Mexican origin are more likely to live in the West (56.8 percent) and

South (32.6 percent). Puerto Ricans are most likely to live in the Northeast, reflecting their easy access to the East Coast and the large Puerto Rican population in and around New York City. Central and South Americans are almost equally distributed among three regions: the Northeast (32.3 percent), the South (34.6 percent), and the West (28.2 percent).

In addition, remember the Census Bureau counts only documented Hispanics. Due to the existing immigration laws, poor labor conditions in Latin America, and labor demands in the United States, the number of undocumented Hispanic immigrants continues to grow. This undocumented immigration contributes 160,000 to 180,000 people to the U.S. Hispanic market annually, a number partially included in projections from the U.S. Census Bureau. Anecdotal evidence indicates that whereas in the mid-1990s, most undocumented immigrants came from Mexico, presently more seem to come from Central American countries such as El Salvador. Late in 2001, the U.S. Congress, and the Presidents of both the United States and Mexico were discussing solutions to this issue, including the possibility of amnesty for undocumented immigrants. Perhaps if that happens, we will know more about these additional potential customers.

FIGURE 3.4

Median Age by Country of Origin

Country	Median Age in Years
Mexico	24.2
Puerto Rico	27.3
Central America	29.2
Dominican Republic	33.1
Spain	36.4
Cuba	40.7
All other	24.7

Source: U.S. Bureau of the Census

Chapter 4

Geographic Distribution

Presently, Hispanics are more likely than non-Hispanic whites to live in the West and less likely to live in the Northeast and Midwest.

FIGURE 4.1

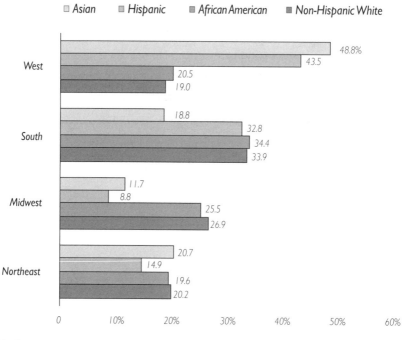

Distribution by Race in Percent of Racial Group, 2000

Of all U.S. Hispanics, 43.5 percent live in the West

☐ Asian   ▧ Hispanic   ▨ African American   ■ Non-Hispanic White

West
- 48.8%
- 43.5
- 20.5
- 19.0

South
- 18.8
- 32.8
- 34.4
- 33.9

Midwest
- 11.7
- 8.8
- 25.5
- 26.9

Northeast
- 20.7
- 14.9
- 19.6
- 20.2

0   10%   20%   30%   40%   50%   60%

Source: U.S. Bureau of the Census

Latinos are responsible for the vast majority of the population growth between 1990 and 2000 in seven states: California, New Jersey, Texas, Illinois, New Mexico, New York, and Pennsylvania. Hispanics represent one-third or more of the total growth in Florida, Washington, Massachusetts, Arizona, and Nevada.

It is clear that diversity is growing in the United States. Although this book focuses on growth among people of Hispanic origin, the 2000 Census also found about 6.8 million people who identified themselves as multi-racial. As mentioned earlier, this was the first census that allowed respondents to choose more than one racial identity. The six racial categories offered 126 multi-ethnic combinations. The new U.S. portrait is a challenge for marketers, advertisers, and retailers, many of whom have been slow to pay attention to any community of a different cultural background.

FIGURE 4. 2

Hispanic or Latino U.S. State, District, and Territory Populations

Ranked in order of size of Hispanic population, highest to lowest

	Total Population	Hispanic or Latino (of any race)	Percent of state population
1. California	33,871,648	10,966,556	32.4
2. Texas	20,851,820	6,669,666	32.0
3. New York	18,976,457	2,867,583	15.1
4. Florida	15,982,378	2,682,715	16.8
5. Illinois	12,419,293	1,530,262	12.3
6. Arizona	5,130,632	1,295,617	25.3
7. New Jersey	8,414,350	1,117,191	13.3
8. New Mexico	1,819,046	765,386	42.1
9. Colorado	4,301,261	735,601	17.1
10. Washington	5,894,121	441,509	7.5
11. Georgia	8,186,453	435,227	5.3
12. Massachusetts	6,349,097	428,729	6.8
13. Pennsylvania	12,281,054	394,088	3.2
14. Nevada	1,998,257	393,970	19.7
15. North Carolina	8,049,313	378,963	4.7
16. Virginia	7,078,515	329,540	4.7
17. Michigan	9,938,444	323,877	3.3
18. Connecticut	3,405,565	320,323	9.4
19. Oregon	3,421,399	275,314	8.0
20. Maryland	5,296,486	227,916	4.3

Latinos contributed the vast majority of the population growth in the largest states in the nation between 1990 and 2000.

continues . . .

State	Total Population	Hispanic or Latino (of any race)	Percent of state population
21. Ohio	11,353,140	217,123	1.9
22. Indiana	6,080,485	214,536	3.5
23. Utah	2,233,169	201,559	9.0
24. Wisconsin	5,363,675	192,921	3.6
25. Kansas	2,688,418	188,252	7.0
26. Oklahoma	3,450,654	179,304	5.2
27. Minnesota	4,919,479	143,382	2.9
28. Tennessee	5,689,283	123,838	2.2
29. Missouri	5,595,211	118,592	2.1
30. Louisiana	4,468,976	107,738	2.4
31. Idaho	1,293,953	101,690	7.9
32. South. Carolina	4,012,012	95,076	2.4
33. Nebraska	1,711,263	94,425	5.5
34. Rhode Island	1,048,319	90,820	8.7
35. Hawaii	1,211,537	87,699	7.2
36. Arkansas	2,673,400	86,866	3.2
37 Iowa	2,926,324	82,473	2.8
38. Alabama	4,447,100	75,830	1.7
39. Kentucky	4,041,769	59,939	1.5
40. Mississippi	2,844,658	39,569	1.4
41. Delaware	783,600	37,277	4.8
42. Wyoming	493,782	31,669	6.4
43. Alaska	626,932	25,852	4.1
44. New Hampshire	1,235,786	20,489	1.7
45. Montana	902,195	18,081	2.0
46. West Virginia	1,808,344	12,279	0.7
47. South. Dakota	754,844	10,903	1.4
48. Maine	1,274,923	9,360	0.7
49. North Dakota	642,200	7,786	1.2
50. Vermont	608,827	5,504	0.9
District of Columbia	572,059	44,953	7.9
Puerto Rico (Territory)	3,808,610	3,762,746	98.8

Traditional states where Hispanics are largest "cultural" population

  Arizona
  California
  New Mexico
  Texas
  Washington
  Commonwealth of Puerto
    Rico

New states states where Hispanics are largest "cultural" population

  Colorado
  Florida
  Kansas
  New Jersey
  New York

Future states where Hispanics will become the largest "cultural" population

  Illinois
  Oklahoma
  Wisconsin

Source: *Profiles of General Demographic Characteristics 2000 Census of Population and Housing United States 2000* Issued May 2001

In 1990, Hispanics were the largest cultural segment in a handful of states—California, New Mexico, Texas, Arizona, and Washington, and the Commonwealth of Puerto Rico. However by 2000, Hispanics were the largest cultural segment or ethnic group in the United States overall, and in the states of Florida, New York, New Jersey, Connecticut, and Kansas, in addition to the previously named states. By the next census, projections show that Hispanics will have become the largest cultural segment in Illinois, Oklahoma, and Wisconsin as well. Overall, the Hispanic population grew by 4.4 percent annually from 1990 to 2000 in the United States whereas the non-Hispanic population grew at only 3.1 percent.

URBAN GROWTH

It is not surprising that Hispanics have flocked to the nation's largest cities where they are more likely to find jobs, better educational opportunities, and more diversity in general, along with friends and relatives.

As shown in Figure 4.3 below, the share of the population that is Hispanic in the ten largest cities in the country ranges from nearly 59 percent in San Antonio to just 5 percent in Detroit. Note that many of these cities would have seen almost no growth in the past decade if the Hispanic population had not been growing so rapidly.

FIGURE 4.3

Ten Largest Places, Total Population and Hispanic Population, 1990–2000

percent growth

Place	Census count 1990	Census count 2000	Population growth 1990-2000	Hispanic population in 1990	Hispanic population in 2000	Growth in Hispanics 1990-2000
New York, NY	7,323,000	8,008,278	9.4%	24.4%	27.0%	21.0%
Los Angeles, CA	3,486,000	3,694,820	6.0	39.9	46.5	23.5
Chicago, IL	2,784,000	2,896,016	4.0	19.6	26.0	38.0
Houston, TX	1,631,000	1,953,631	19.8	27.6	37.4	62.3
Philadelphia, PA	1,586,000	1,517,550	- 4.3	5.6	8.5	45.2
Phoenix, AZ	984,000	1,321,045	34.2	20.0	34.1	128.9
San Diego, CA	1,111,000	1,223,400	10.1	20.7	25.4	35.1
Dallas, TX	1,008,000	1,188,580	17.9	20.9	35.6	101.0
San Antonio, TX	935,000	1,144,646	22.4	55.6	58.7	29.2
Detroit, MI	1,028,000	951,270	-7.5	2.8	5.0	68.7

Sources: Statistical Abstract of the United States, 1997; U.S. Census Bureau, Census 2000 Summary File 1

NO LONGER A "MINORITY"
Growth in Suburbs

The growth among Hispanics is in suburbs as well as cities. For example, in East Los Angeles (a census-designated place), Hispanics were 96.8 percent of the population, the highest for any place outside the Commonwealth of Puerto Rico with 100,000 or more total population. Hispanics were also the majority of the population in the 19 other cities as shown below.

During the 1990s, the Hispanic population became the largest cultural segment in the United States

FIGURE 4.4 _____

Cities and Suburbs with Majority Hispanic Population

City	Total population	Hispanic population	Hispanic share of total
East Los Angeles, CA	124,283	120,307	96.8
Laredo, TX	176,576	166,216	94.1
Brownsville, TX	139,722	127,535	91.3
Hialeah, TX	226,419	204,543	90.3
McAllen, TX	106,414	85,427	80.3
El Paso, TX	563,662	431,875	76.6
Santa Ana, CA	337,977	257,097	76.1
El Monte, CA	115,965	83,945	72.4
Oxnard, CA	170,358	112,807	66.2
Miami, FL	362,470	238,351	65.8
Pomona, CA	149,473	96,370	64.5
Salinas, CA	151,060	96,880	64.1
Norwalk, CA	103,298	64,965	62.9
Ontario, CA	158,007	94,610	59.9
San Antonio, TX	1,144,646	671,394	58.7
Downey, CA	107,323	62,089	57.9
Fontana, CA	128,929	74,424	57.7
Corpus Christi, TX	277,454	150,737	54.3
Paterson, NJ	149,222	74,774	50.1

Source: U.S. Bureau of the Census, 2000

FIGURE 4.5

Concentrations of Hispanics in U.S. Cities by Country of Origin

Although you can find Hispanics in almost every city in the United States, concentrations by country of origin are still high in most cities. The table below shows some cities where you will find concentrations by country of origin.

Mexican	Chicago	**Central American**	Houston
	Houston		Los Angeles
	Los Angeles		Miami
	Phoenix		New York
	San Antonio		San Francisco
Puerto Rican	Chicago	**South American**	Chicago
	New York		Los Angeles
	Philadelphia		Miami
			New York
Cuban	Hialeah		
	Los Angeles		
	Miami		
	New York		
	Tampa		

Chapter 5

Hispanic Buying Power

The huge economic clout wielded by Hispanics today can help businesses determine how much spending on marketing and new business development should be directed to this segment.

Buying power is defined as the total personal (after-tax) income that consumers have to spend on goods and services, or disposable personal income. The U.S. government, academia, and other organizations use different criteria and econometric tools to estimate buying power. I believe that, for marketing purposes, the Selig Center for Economic Growth at the University of Georgia's Terry College of Business provides the most comprehensive estimates. The Selig Center estimates the total buying power of all market segments, regardless of race, for 1990 to 2002, using national and regional econometric models, univariate forecasting techniques, and data from various U.S. government sources. Selig allocates the total buying power based on population distributions by the Census Bureau's estimates of the population of states by age, sex, race and Hispanic origin.

According to the Selig Center, Hispanic buying power is increasing faster nationwide than that of any other minority group. "In terms of sheer dollar power," said a Selig press release on July 11, 2002, "Hispanics' economic clout nationally rose from $223 billion in 1990 to $490.7 billion in 2000 to $580.5 billion in 2002." By 2007, Jeff Humphreys, director of the center, projects that Hispanic buying power will top $926.1 billion. He noted that the U.S. Hispanic market is already larger than the entire economies of all but 11 countries in the world. By 2007, it may exceed the GDP of Canada, the eighth largest economy in the world.

Santiago & Valdés Solutions (SVS), now The Santiago Solutions Group, believes that even the Selig estimates may be slightly low because they are based on census data and the census has undercounted Hispanics. For example, I believe that the 2002 number may be closer to $630 billion.

In contrast, the U.S. Bureau of Labor Statistics estimates Hispanic buying power at about $311 billion, much lower than either Selig's or SVS' estimates. This does not include spending by the population of Puerto Rico, nor the undercount, nor several economic variables and corrections made by the Selig Center Team.

FIGURE 5.1

Household Income, 1998

in dollars

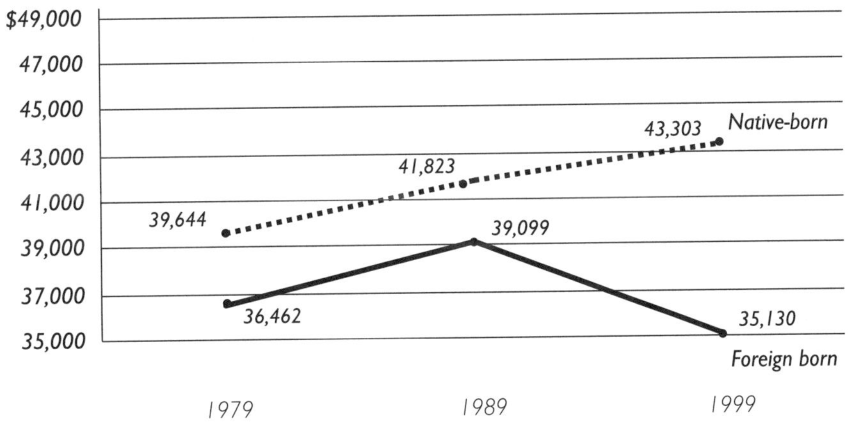

Source: U.S. Bureau of Labor Statistics

MEDIAN INCOME

According to the U.S. Bureau of Labor Statistics, the median income of Hispanic households reached $32,735 in 2000, up from $28,330 in 1998. However, it is important to notice the difference between full- and part-time workers. In households where the primary earner worked full-time, year-round, median income in 1999 was $40,420, up from $37,152 in 1998.

FIGURE 5.2

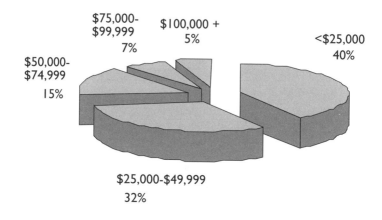

Income Distribution, Hispanic Households, 2000

in percentage of households in each income category

$75,000-
$99,999
7%

$100,000 +
5%

<$25,000
40%

$50,000-
$74,999
15%

$25,000-$49,999
32%

Source: U.S. Bureau of Labor Statistics

*New emerging,
Hispanic
markets are
quickly grow-
ing their
Hispanic buy-
ing power.*

DIFFERENT REGIONS, DIFFERENT INCOMES

When it comes to Hispanic buying power, not all states are equal. The five states with the largest Hispanic population account for 71 percent of Hispanic buying power. By contrast, the five states with the largest total U.S. consumer markets account for only 38 percent of total Hispanic buying power, according to The Selig Center. It estimates that California Hispanics had the highest buying power in 2002, $170.7 billion, almost twice that of number-two ranked Texas.

The three figures below show the states with the most Hispanic buying power in 2001, the states with the highest shares of Hispanic buying power, and the states where Hispanic buying power grew the fastest from 1990 to 2001. These charts underscore that although Hispanic-buying power is concentrated in a few states, many more are beginning to feel the impact of an increasing Hispanic population and should be considered for marketing purposes.

FIGURE 5.3

Ten States with the Highest Estimated Hispanic Buying Power, 2002

Hispanic buying power in billion US$

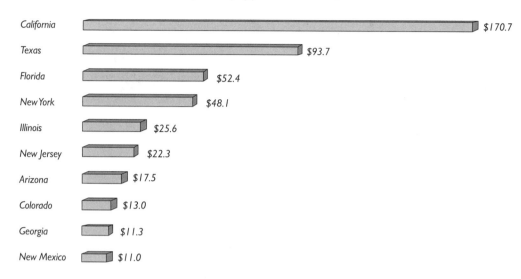

California $170.7
Texas $93.7
Florida $52.4
New York $48.1
Illinois $25.6
New Jersey $22.3
Arizona $17.5
Colorado $13.0
Georgia $11.3
New Mexico $11.0

Source: Selig Center for Economic Growth, Terry College of Business, The University of Georgia, July 2002

FIGURE 5.4

Ten States with the Most Concentrated Hispanic Buying Power, 2001 Estimated

in percent of total buying power in the state

State	Hispanic share of total buying power
New Mexico	28.8%
California	17.4
Texas	16.4
Arizona	14.3
Nevada	13.6
Florida	12.6
Colorado	9.8
New York	8.2
New Jersey	7.9
Illinois	7.1

Source: Selig Center for Economic Growth, Terry College of Business, The University of Georgia, July 2002

Hispanic women make up the fastest-growing segment of new entrants to the U.S. labor force. This fact contributes greatly to the growth of purchasing power of the Hispanic market.

FIGURE 5.5

Fast-growing Hispanic Consumer Markets

Ten states with the highest percentage change in Hispanic buying power, 1990–2001

State	Percentage change in Hispanic buying power, 1990-2001
North Carolina	912.2%
Arkansas	777.6
Georgia	711.2
Tennessee	654.9
Alabama	466.0
South Carolina	463.2
Nevada	442.5
Minnesota	417.7
Kentucky	415.4
Iowa	369.8

Source: Selig Center for Economic Growth, Terry College of Business, The University of Georgia, July 2002

An important point for marketers to factor in is that the gain in Hispanic buying power stems from more than the natural increase and immigration growth. Selig attributes many forces supporting this substantial and continued growth of Hispanic buying power. Most important, according to Selig, is better employment opportunities, enhanced by the highest number ever of young Hispanics pursuing higher education, who are entering the workforce better prepared than ever before. This results in higher salaries, and more families with higher incomes.

With this much population growth and buying power at stake, corporations need to better understand and manage the new consumer market segments that are appearing among Latinos.

The following case study targeting upscale Hispanics shows how Ford Motor Company has focused in on the traveling Hispanic to market its Lincoln LS and Navigator.

Ford Motor Company

For more detail on this case and creative

materials, go to www.incultureapproach.com

Brand or product: Lincoln LS and Navigator

BACKGROUND

During a California market field visit, Carl Kravetz, president of cruz/kravetz:IDEAS, was approached by a Corporate Vice President from the Ford Motor Company. "Why," he was asked, "is it that in Mexico our products are looked up to as aspirational, while here they are seen by Hispanics as merely affordable?" Kravetz answered, "Look at your advertising. In Mexico, you tell people you are elite and high quality. Here you sell Hispanics on affordable family transportation. Your problem is that people *believe* what you tell them . . ."

The Ford Motor Company is a pioneer in Hispanic marketing, with well over 20 years aggressive spending in the category. However, as a result of the notion that Hispanics couldn't afford anything else, Ford had always concentrated its efforts on its most economical vehicles. This was consistent throughout its subsidiaries, including at Lincoln Mercury where Hispanic marketing programs concentrated on the Tracer and the Mystique.

In 1998, the Southern California Lincoln Mercury Dealers' Association (SCLMDA) hired its first-ever Hispanic agency, cruz/kravetz:IDEAS. In 1999, it showed double-digit growth in Mercury sales. Not surprisingly, an additional consequence of the increased dealer traffic was a spike in Lincoln sales as well.

With some nudging from the agency and a solid commitment from Lincoln Mercury's Regional Director, a Lincoln test was put into place for 2000. A total of $3 million was available for the test.

MEDIA STRATEGIES

In the Southern California Hispanic automotive category, $3 million is not a lot of money. Several dealer associations spend *three times* as much, not including spill in from national advertising. This meant that a successful program would require *focus and concentration*—Lincoln could not be everywhere all the time.

The key decision was to focus on Latino households with an annual income of $75,000+. Because many affluent Hispanic households prefer English, the program was to be bilingual.

The advertising retained the global "American Luxury" positioning, but American Luxury was redefined. While to the Anglo market it meant "old money"—understated white-linen-on-the-beach type luxury, to Hispanics it was positioned as "new money"—glamorous, a bit show-off, emblematic of success, of having made it. Therefore, it was decided to focus on the younger, more forward looking models—Lincoln LS and Navigator, rather than the older, more traditional cars in the line.

Research showed that the Spanish-language television programming most likely to cross-over into bilingual or English-dominant households was the news. So, a decision was made to "own" the news, rather than spreading relatively meager dollars throughout the broadcast day. Ownership of the news also gave Lincoln a high-quality image. By concentrating television dollars in the early and late news, a 40-week schedule was achieved. Radio spots emphasized sales events and filled in the missing weeks.

Cruz/kravetz:IDEAS also worked closely with the SCLMDA's general market agency, to ensure that the Spanish-language ads would run in the appropriate English-language programming. Some examples of this are the broadcasts of the Latin Grammys and the Alma Awards. The agencies also collaborated on bilingual inserts in *The Los Angeles Times*.

PROMOTIONAL STRATEGIES

Event marketing was the major "medium" used to target bilingual and English-dominant Hispanics. Events were carefully selected to reflect the redefinition of "American Luxury" and to target affluent Latinos. It was equally important to decide which events not to sponsor. For example, it was decided not to get involved with Fiesta Broadway, which draws 600,000 to the streets of downtown Los Angeles, but rather to sponsor its VIP Gala at the Getty Center. This way 2,000 "influentials" would have a close-up, hands-on experience with the vehicles prominently on display.

The events program emphasized the interests of the affluent and successful consumers most likely to buy Lincoln vehicles. Events included entertainment awards ceremonies like the Latin Entertainment Media Institute Gala, Latin Grammys, Imágen Awards and the Nosotros Golden Eagle Awards; the Los Angeles and San Diego Latino Film Festivals; business association galas; Latino golf tournaments like the Eduardo Quezada Golf Tournament, the HOPE Golf Classic, the USC Mexican-American Alumni Golf Tournament and the LBA Golf Tournament; and the Hispanic Designers Gala. A special relationship with Paul Rodriguez included loaning him a vehicle "to be seen in," sponsorship of his Latino Comedy Nights at the Conga Room and special media appearances.

RESULTS

The results of the program were spectacular! As measured by Polk, Lincoln sales showed a 170 percent increase between 1998 and 2000. In that same time period, Lincoln sales grew from 29 percent to 45 percent of Lincoln Mercury's product mix. The Lincoln Navigator (at $50,000+, the company's most profitable product) became the largest selling model in the line to Southern California Hispanics.

Most importantly, the test proved to Ford Motor Company not only that "Affluent Latinos" exist, but that they will purchase luxury cars and SUVs if they are marketed to in a manner relevant to their lifestyles and aspirations.

AGENCY: cruz/kravets:Ideas, www.ckideas.com

Chapter 6

Hispanic Households

Population growth estimates show that Hispanics form about one-half million new households each year, contributing to their strength as consumers of all kinds of household goods and services as well as to their visibility in the new homeowners and financial communities. In 2001, more than 9 million households were headed by someone of Hispanic origin.

FIGURE 6.1

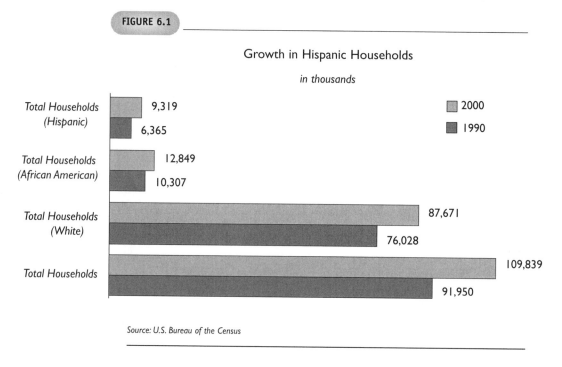

Growth in Hispanic Households

in thousands

| | 2000 |
| | 1990 |

Total Households (Hispanic): 9,319 / 6,365

Total Households (African American): 12,849 / 10,307

Total Households (White): 87,671 / 76,028

Total Households: 109,839 / 91,950

Source: U.S. Bureau of the Census

Hispanic households continue to be, on average, larger than non-Hispanic households are. In 2000, the Current Population Survey found that 30.6 percent of Hispanic family households consisted of five or more people. Only 11.8 percent of non-Hispanic white households were this large.

Mexican households were most likely to have five or more people. Family households with only two people represented 21.7 percent of Hispanic family households compared with 46 percent of non-Hispanic white households. Among Hispanic family households, 41.3 percent of Cuban households had only two people, the largest share among all Hispanics. However, an analysis of the trend shows that Hispanic households are also becoming smaller, albeit at a much slower pace than non-Hispanic white households.

FIGURE 6.2

Consumer Expenditure, 2000

This table compares the average expenditure of Hispanic households in many different categories with those of non-Hispanic whites and blacks.

	Non-Hispanic whites	Black	Hispanic
Average annual expenditures	$38,549	$28,152	$32,735
Food	5,139	4,095	5,362
Food at home	2,977	2,691	3,496
Cereals bakery products	152	159	201
Bakery products	298	234	290
Beef	230	236	326
Pork	163	199	213
Other meats	99	106	116
Poultry	141	185	190
Fish and seafood	108	139	136
Eggs	33	43	55
Fresh milk and cream	128	102	170
Other dairy products	194	143	189
Fresh fruits	157	131	228
Fresh vegetables	152	129	228
Processed fruits	114	118	125
Processed vegetables	83	76	89
Sugar and other sweets	118	89	110
Fats and oils	82	83	100
Miscellaneous foods	440	316	405
Nonalcoholic beverages	246	186	292
Food prepared by consumer on out-of-town trips	40	17	34
Food away from home	2,162	1,404	1,865
Alcoholic beverages	380	211	285
Tobacco products and smoking supplies	332	243	173

Continues . . .

	Non-Hispanic whites	Black	Hispanic
Housing	12,458	9,906	10,850
Utilities, including water and telephone	2,519	2,571	2,170
Household operations	705	468	465
Housekeeping supplies	483	303	474
Household furnishings and equipment	1,572	887	1,303
Apparel and services	1,836	1,695	2,076
Transportation, including fuel and vehicles	7,484	5,214	6,719
Public transportation	431	268	385
Healthcare	2,144	1,107	1,243
Entertainment	1,928	1,014	1,186
Personal care products and services	564	627	564
Reading	155	72	59
Education	657	383	363
Miscellaneous	792	572	602
Cash contributions	1,244	700	645
Personal insurance and pensions	3,437	2,313	2,608

Source: Table 7, Consumer Expenditure Survey, 2000, Bureau of Labor Statistics, U.S. Department of Commerce

Chapter 7

The Acculturation Factor

From a marketing perspective, it makes a big difference whether consumers are born in the United States or in Latin American. Foreign and native-born Hispanics differ considerably in terms of language use, marketing maturity, media consumption, purchase patterns, and cultural traits—all of which affect marketing, advertising strategies, and consumer research. The significance of the number of foreign-born Hispanics is hard to ignore. In 2000, 39 percent (or 12.8 million) of the Hispanic population in the United States was foreign-born. Of this group 43 percent entered the United States in the 1990s. Nearly 30 percent came in the 1980s, and the remainder (27 percent) entered before 1980.

FIGURE 7.1

Hispanics Are a Growing Share of Immigrants

region of origin of total immigrants in percent

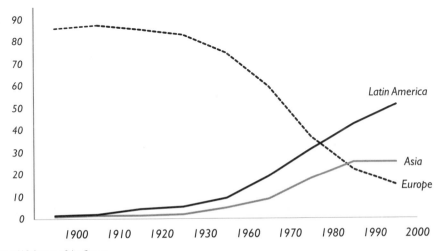

Source: U.S. Bureau of the Census

It is also important to keep in mind that immigrants tend to be adults. Thus, from a marketing perspective, new immigrants are "instant" new shoppers in the basic categories. The longer Hispanics have lived in the United States, the more likely they are to have become naturalized citizens. Among those who entered the U.S. before 1970, 74.2 percent had obtained citizenship by 2000. Only 6.7 percent of those who entered in the 1990s had become citizens by 2000.

The acculturation process kicks in as soon as the immigrant consumer is in juxtaposition with the new, host-country's culture. The longer consumers have lived in the new country's cultural milieu, the greater the chances they will adopt behaviors, values, and expectations from the new country. The acculturation process is not linear. It varies drastically by personal characteristics, such as the ability to accept change. Other factors include:

Acculturation is the process of integration of the immigrant consumers' values, beliefs, attitudes, dreams, likes, and dislikes from his or her country of origin with those of the new host country.
—*I. Valdés, 1987*

- Socio-economics can make a difference because more-educated consumers tend to speak English and hence interact and absorb more from the host country's culture.

- The geographic region where the immigrant settles is a factor. The higher the concentration of Hispanics, the lower the opportunities to interact with—and learn from—the new culture.

- Finally, the attitude of the host country's population toward a particular immigrant group is also a factor. If they are accepting of the immigrant, there is a greater chance for interaction, and again for more learning from the new culture.

Section 3 of this book provides specific examples of the way that acculturation affects food preferences and choice of retail channels.

Throughout this book you will find examples of how the acculturation process impacts every aspect of marketing to American Latinos.

Chapter 8

Educational Attainment

In October 2000 (latest available data), there were 10.2 million Hispanic children or 32.6 percent of the Hispanic population enrolled in school, including nursery, kindergarten, elementary, high school, and college. Of those enrolled, 12.3 percent were enrolled in a nursery or kindergarten program, 51 percent in elementary school, 22 percent in high school, and 14 percent in college. This distribution of enrollment is very similar to that of the population in general. However, Hispanic children are more likely to be enrolled in public schools than are white, non-Hispanic children.

Among Hispanic school-age children in 1999, 65 percent had at least one foreign-born parent, including 17.5 percent of elementary and high school students who are themselves foreign-born.

FIGURE 8.1

Enrollment of Hispanics (aged 3 to 55+) in School, October 2000

in millions

Nursery or kindergarten	1.3
Elementary	5.2
High School	2.3
College	1.4
Total	10.2

Source: U.S. Census Bureau, Current Population Survey, October 2000

The share of Hispanic children in the educational system is rising for two reasons: higher fertility rates among Hispanic women (tied to cultural background and religion) and ongoing immigration. Of these, immigration has the greatest effect. Among Hispanic school-age children in 1999, 65 percent had at least one foreign-born parent, including 17.5 percent of elementary and high school students who are themselves foreign born.

Most Hispanic children aged 7 to 15 are enrolled in school, but there is a noticeable drop-off after age 16 when children in most school districts are legally allowed to leave school.

MORE IS NEEDED

Despite improvements in educational attainment, high school students of Hispanic origin continue to have more problems in school. According to the U.S. Census Bureau, 36.5 percent of Hispanic high school students aged 15 to 17 are below their grade level. The annual dropout rate of 7.1 percent for Hispanics in the tenth to twelfth grades is higher than among any other ethnic group.

FIGURE 8.2

High School and Beyond

Hispanics aged 18 to 24 still lag behind their peers of other ethnic groups in attaining a college degree.

Percent of 18-24-year-olds	High School graduate	Some college	College graduate
Hispanic	29.7	22.3	4.6
Asian	19.9	43.4	20.0
Black	34.2	29.4	7.5
White Non Hispanic	30.2	38.0	13.5

Source: Educational Attainment of the Population 15 Years and Over, March 2000. Released December 2000, U.S. Census Bureau

Among Hispanics aged 18 to 24 in 2000, nearly 30 percent were high school graduates. Another 22 percent received some college education, including 4.6 percent who had already earned their college degrees. However, Hispanic students are still less likely to go directly to college than are their white non-Hispanic peers. Government and business members of the Hispanic community are concerned about this low enrollment level. Scholarships—provided most often by American corporations—have become increasingly available to ease the financial burden for Hispanic high school graduates who want to enter college.

HISPANICS IN COLLEGE

Of the 15.3 million college students enrolled in the U.S. in 2000, only 9.3 percent were Hispanic. If you consider that few of these students' parents had the opportunity to go to school beyond a few grades, it is miraculous that so many Hispanic children manage to make it through the school system at all. As a parent of one teenager and one young adult who recently graduated from college, I am aware of how difficult it is to help in some school homework. I often asked myself, "How do less advantaged families cope in trying to help their children comply and get good grades?" Hence, it is encouraging to see improvements in Hispanic school attainments. However, much more help is obviously needed.

FIGURE 8.3

College Enrollments for Hispanics Aged 15+, October 2000

	Enrollment	Percent female
Two year college	543,000	52.5%
Four-year college	883,000	59.1
Year enrolled		
First	453,000	54.5
Second	348,000	58.9
Third	228,000	53.9
Fourth	200,000	59.0
Fifth	67,000	61.2
Sixth or higher	131,000	55.0

Source: U.S. Census Bureau, Current Population Survey, 2000

Despite the challenges, there are noticeable improvements and most Hispanics have gotten the message that college is important to success in the U.S. employment market.

There are significant differences among Hispanic sub-groups with regard to educational attainment. Among all groups of Hispanic origin, Cuban adults

Despite improvements in educational attainment, much help is needed to ensure that the future generations are able to face the challenge of the computer-based economy.

aged 25 and over were the most likely to have graduated from high school (73 percent) or attained a bachelor's degree (23 percent), compared with Mexicans (51 percent high-school graduates, 6.9 percent bachelor's degrees). Among Puerto Ricans and people from Central and South America, 64.3 percent of adults aged 25 and older have obtained at least a high school education.

DIVERSITY IS A FACT

Diversity is an important issue in the educational system. The U.S. Census Bureau reports, "Elementary and high school students today are more racially and ethnically diverse than the baby-boom generation of students. In 1972, when the crest of the baby-boom was enrolled in elementary and high school, 79 percent of the student population was white, non-Hispanic, 14 percent black, and the remaining 1 percent Asian/Pacific Islander and other races. Only 6 percent were Hispanic. In 1999, 64 percent of elementary and high school students were white non-Hispanic, 16 percent black, 5 percent Asian and Pacific Islander and other races, and 15 percent Hispanic. Moreover, the Census Bureau's projections indicate that the school-age population (aged 6 to 17) will become even more diverse in future years."

LATINO COLLEGE STUDENTS

About 65 percent of Hispanics who were in college in October 2000 were aged 16 to 24, considered "traditional" ages for higher education. However, more Hispanics are also enrolling in college at later ages. Nearly 22 percent of Hispanic college enrollees were aged 25 to 29 in 2000, up from about 15 percent in 1999; 9.9 percent were aged 30 to 34, and 13.6 percent were aged 35 and older. These shares are similar to those of blacks and non-Hispanic whites, indicating that Hispanics are taking advantage of educational opportunities. Of the 1.4 million Hispanic students aged 15 and over who are enrolled in college, 38.7 percent were enrolled part-time in 2000. Sixty percent of full-time students were also employed either full or part time while going to school. Among part-time students, nearly 87 percent are employed, the majority full time. Full-time employment of Hispanic students was the highest among any cultural group attending college.

FIGURE 8.4

College Enrollment by Race

Enrolled in college full or part-time, October 2000

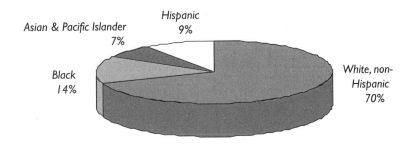

Asian & Pacific Islander
7%

Hispanic
9%

Black
14%

White, non-
Hispanic
70%

Source: U.S. Bureau of the Census

A COMMUNITY THAT CARES

Hispanic leaders are concerned about the state of Hispanic education. Programs as well as corporate sponsorships emerge daily. For example, in May 2001, the Association of Hispanic Advertising Agencies (ahaa) launched "FuturaMente," to promote early childhood education and to encourage Hispanic youth to pursue careers in teaching. An impressive $50 million in media commitments at its launch backed the pro bono media and advertising campaign. It targeted two groups:

- Parents of 3- to 4-year-olds—to help them understand the importance of early childhood education and how to create a learning environment in the home,

• Hispanic senior high school students—to acquaint them with the need for teachers that understand Spanish and can help reach Hispanic youth in a cultural context.

A website, www.futuramente.yahoo.com features links to education sites, quarterly chats with education experts and role models, clubs for mothers to get support on pre-schools from other parents, and links to relevant sites for high school students interested in pursuing higher education.

Many corporations are building "share of heart" with the Hispanic market by contributing to scholarship funds and providing support for schools and colleges to create solutions to the educational challenges facing the Latino community.

Share of heart, *now a popular marketing term, was created by Norma Orci, one of the pioneers of U.S. Hispanic marketing (La Agencia de Orci & Asociados).*

Chapter 9

Labor Force

The Bureau of Labor Statistics reports that Hispanics now account for just over 11 percent of the civilian labor force, compared with just 7.4 percent in 1988. Hispanic men participate in the labor force at rates similar to white and black men. However, Hispanic women are slightly less likely than either white or black women to be employed outside the home.

FIGURE 9. 1

Labor Force Status of the Population by Age and
Hispanic Origin, Annual Average, 2000

in percent of each age and origin group in the labor force

Age group	Hispanic		White		Black	
	Male	*Female*	*Male*	*Female*	*Male*	*Female*
16-19	50.9%	41.4%	56.6%	54.7%	39.0%	39.4%
20-24	89.2	64.9	85.0	74.7	73.4	70.5
25-54	92.3	67.7	92.7	76.9	84.4	78.9
55-64	69.4	41.3	68.2	52.3	57.1	48.4
65 +	18.2	7.7	17.7	9.4	14.2	9.9

Source: Bureau of Labor Statistics, Current Population Survey, 2001

Hispanics have broadened their work force participation moving into more management and professional positions, however as mentioned earlier, they still lag behind African-Americans and whites because of limited education. Among Hispanic men in the labor force in 2000, 30.9 percent of those aged 25 and older had more than a high school diploma, compared with 57.8 percent of white men and 49.2 percent of black men. Among women in the labor force in

2000, 38 percent of Hispanic women aged 25 or older had more than a high school diploma, compared with 60 percent of white women and 54.2 percent of black women. Note that among all groups, women in the labor force, aged 25 and older are more likely than men in the same age group to have more than a high school diploma.

LATINOS IN MANAGEMENT

Full-time employment of Hispanic students was the highest among any cultural group attending college.

Among Hispanic men in the labor force, 11.5 percent hold managerial or professional positions, compared with 29.2 percent of white men and 18.5 percent of black men. Among women, 27.8 percent of Hispanics are managers or professionals, compared with 33.4 percent of whites, and 24.8 percent of blacks.

As expected, education has an impact on earnings. In 2000, according to the Bureau of Labor Statistics, among full-time wage and salary workers, the median weekly earnings of Hispanics was $396, compared with $468 for blacks and $591 for whites. The earnings gap is also higher for Hispanic men than for Hispanic women, probably reflecting the higher educational levels of Hispanic women. Hispanic men earned about 62 percent of what their white counterparts earned, whereas Hispanic women earned about 72 percent of what their white counterparts earned. Since 1986, the earnings gap between Hispanics and their white counterparts has widened. Among workers paid hourly rates, there was little difference among Hispanics, whites, and blacks in the proportion who worked at or below the prevailing minimum federal wage in 2000.

Growth in the Hispanic labor force is projected by the Bureau of Labor Statistics to continue for the near future. By 2008, the Hispanic labor force is projected to overtake the black labor force in size, primarily as a result of continued immigration. Labor force participation rates for Hispanics are projected to remain virtually the same.

FIGURE 9.2

Civilian Labor Force by Race and Hispanic Origin, 1998, and Projected 2008

numbers in thousands

Characteristic	Civilian labor force		Change 1998–2008
Total, 16 and older	1998	2008 projected	
Black	15,982	19,101	19.5%
Hispanic origin	14,317	19,585	36.8
Asian and other	6,278	8,809	40.3
White	115,415	126,665	9.7

Source: Table 2 in Howard N. Fullerton, "Labor force projections to 2008: Steady growth and changing composition," Monthly Labor Review, November 1999, p. 20

HISPANICS IN BUSINESS AND POLITICS

Along with the impressive growth in the population and buying power of American Latinos, there has also been significant growth in their business involvement. Not only are Hispanics consumers of mass market goods, but they also contribute greatly to the marketplace as entrepreneurs and producers of goods and services, and as employers and employees. The Tomás Rivera Policy Institute reports that the 1997 output of Latino-owned firms, as measured by annual sales receipts, was nearly $200 billion. This contribution by Latino-owned firms was larger than the individual gross product of 38 states including Washington, Colorado, Arizona, Kansas, Nevada, and New Hampshire.

When I wrote Part I of *Marketing to American Latinos* (Paramount Market Publishing, 2000) the only data available on Hispanic-owned businesses was from the 1992 Economic Census. In this book I am able to use data from 1997, which are the most current available. The Census Bureau will conduct a 2002 Economic Census and new data on Hispanic businesses may be available in 2003. In sum, the best data available now are the 1997 data, presented here as a benchmark.

FIGURE 9.3

Growth of Hispanic-owned Firms, Revenues and Employees

Survey year	Number of businesses	Revenue in billions US$	Number of employees
1969	100,212	$3.6	126,296
1972	120,108	5.3	149,656
1977	219,355	10.4	206,054
1982	233975	11.8	154,791
1987	422373	24.7	264,846
1992	862605	76.8	691,056
1997	1,199,896	186.3	1,388,746

Source: U.S. Bureau of the Census, Economic Surveys. Growth percentages are expressed as compound annual rates. Data for surveys before 1982 reflect some differences from current methodology. However, the apparent slow growth between 1977 and 1982, including the decrease in employment, was real and reflects general economic conditions at that time.

In 1997, there were 1.2 million Hispanic-owned businesses in the United States, up from 862,605 in 1992, a 39 percent increase over the five-year period. Receipts for these companies increased to $186.3 billion in 1997, up a whopping 142 percent over 1992.

In 1997, as in 1992, California, Texas, and Florida formed a "Golden Trio" of states for Hispanic-owned businesses. Twenty-eight percent of the firms, with receipts of almost $52 billion or 27.7 percent of the total, were in California. Texas was second with 20 percent of U.S. Hispanic firms and receipts of $39 billion or 21.2 percent. Florida was third in number of firms, with $35 billion in receipts.

HISPANIC ENTREPRENEURS

The latest data on Hispanic-owned businesses released by the U.S. Census Bureau in July 2001 shows that Hispanic entrepreneurship is strong across the nation. Compared with 1992, the same states are in the top-ten for Hispanic businesses, but Illinois and Arizona edged out New Mexico for sixth place. All 50 states had Hispanic-owned firms in 1997, another indication of the depth of the penetration of the Hispanic culture and Hispanic households in the United States. Figure 9.4 shows the 20 states with the largest number of Hispanic-owned firms in 1997.

FIGURE 9.4

Twenty States with the Largest Number of Hispanic-owned Firms, 1997

Rank	Firms (number)	Sales in millions US$	Paid employees (number)
1. California	336,405	51,682	392,434
2. Texas	240,396	39,482	289,142
3. Florida	193,902	35,351	192,761
4. New York	104,189	10,311	56,464
5. New Jersey	36,116	5,107	28,134
6. Illinois	31,010	4,815	71,692
7. Arizona	28,894	4,227	42,791
8. New Mexico	28,285	3,668	39,951
9. Colorado	20,859	3,068	27,620
10. Virginia	13,703	1,809	19,375
11. Massachusetts	12,725	1,623	11,146
12. Maryland	11,158	1,567	13,688
13. Washington	10,009	1,808	19,375
14. Michigan	9,997	1,623	13,763
15. Pennsylvania	7,893	1,273	10,090
16. North Carolina	7,270	1,080	8,305
17. Louisiana	6,645	1,283	9,356
18. Connecticut	6,594	1,163	9,670
19. Nevada	6,565	1,221	11,487
20. Ohio	6,448	1,513	11,353

Source: U.S. Bureau of the Census, Economic Census, 1997; released July 2001. Number of employees may be lower than number of firms because only paid employees are included, not owners or unpaid family members who work in the firm.

Not surprisingly, the Metropolitan areas strongest in Hispanic-own businesses are in the states with the largest Hispanic populations. Note, however, that except for Miami, New York, and Chicago cities in California and Texas completely dominate this list (Figure 9.5).

FIGURE 9.5

Ten Metropolitan Areas with Largest Number of Hispanic-owned Firms, 1997

Metro area	Firms (number)	Receipts in millions US$
Los Angeles-Long Beach, CA PMSA	136,678	16,246
Miami, FL PMSA	120,605	26,730
New York, NY PMSA	84,880	8,054
Houston, TX PMSA	41,769	12,415
San Antonio, TX PMSA	34,834	7,697
Riverside-San Bernadino, CA PMSA	32,198	54,085
San Diego, CA PMSA	28,087	5,217
Chicago, IL PMSA	27,482	4,554
Dallas, TX PMSA	25,573	2,753
Orange County, CA PMSA	24,184	8,663

Source: U.S. Bureau of the Census, Economic Census, 1997; released July 2001

As previously mentioned, Mexicans are the biggest sub-group among American Latinos. Business ownership also reflects this dominance, with 39 percent of all U.S. Hispanic-owned firms in 1997 owned by Latinos of Mexican origin.

FIGURE 9.6

Hispanic-owned Firms by Ethnicity, 1997

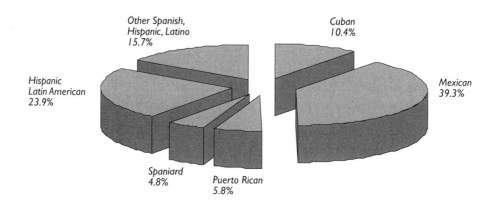

Source: U.S. Bureau of the Census, Economic Census, 1997; released July 2001

SERVICES STILL DOMINATE HISPANIC-OWNED BUSINESSES

Historically, Hispanics have owned service-related businesses and this patterns still holds in the new millennium. However, more—and larger—Hispanic-owned businesses have emerged in the financial, manufacturing, and wholesale industries.

FIGURE 9.7

Types of Firms Owned by Hispanics

This table provides more detail on the types of firms owned.
These numbers include businesses with and without paid employees.

Industry group	Number of Hispanic-owned firms	Share of total Hispanic firms
Services	500,449	41.7%
Retail trade	155,061	12.9
Construction	152,573	12.7
Transportation, communications, and utilities	84,554	7.0
Finance, insurance, and real estate	56,629	4.7
Agricultural services, forestry, and fishing	40,040	3.3
Wholesale trade	31,480	2.6
Manufacturing	25,552	2.2
Mining	1,909	0.2
Other	151,599	12.6
Total	1,199,896	100%*

*May not add due to rounding

Source: U.S. Bureau of the Census, Economic Census, 1997; released July 2001

CORPORATE INFLUENCE

Beyond owning their own businesses, Hispanics also have increasing influence in corporations and in their boardrooms.

Among Fortune 1000 companies in 2000, Hispanics held 152 board seats, up from just 83 seats in 1993, according to a survey by the Hispanic Association on Corporate Responsibility (HACR). About 12 percent of Fortune 1000 companies have at least one Hispanic director, but Hispanics hold only about 1.4 percent of board seats overall in these companies. Fifteen percent of the Hispanic directors were female and they represented 17 percent of Hispanics who serve on multiple boards. HACR finds that, in general, the larger the corporation and the larger its board of directors, the more likely the company has at least one Hispanic on its board. Moreover, 15 Hispanics lead Fortune 100 companies in their capacities as president, CEO, or vice chairman.

THE POLITICAL SCENE

The voting age population of Hispanics in November 2000 was 16 percent higher than it was in November 1996. By the next national election in 2004 the voting age population of Hispanics will have increased by another 2.3 million people, and there are many state and local elections before 2004 that will hinge on the votes of Hispanics. Hispanics are getting the message that their vote matters. In 1994, 31 percent of eligible Hispanics were registered to vote. By 1998, that share had increased to 34 percent.

In the 12 months between October 1999 and September 2000, more than 900,000 Hispanics registered to vote, a 14 percent increase over 1998, bringing the total number of registered Hispanics to 7.4 million. A poll by the Association of Hispanic Advertising Agencies (ahaa) found that 92 percent of Hispanics intended to vote in the 2000 Presidential contest.

According to Hispanic Trends, a polling firm, a higher percentage of registered Hispanics voted than did non-Hispanics, with 71 percent of eligible Hispanics voting in 2000, compared with a national average of 51 percent of all registered voters. This fact should be no surprise. Political campaigns, elections, and participation is part of the Hispanic culture and the "right to be heard" is a highly appreciated right.

In addition, Hispanic Trends estimated that the two major presidential candidates, Al Gore and George W. Bush together spent about $5 million to campaign in Spanish. "This was without precedent," said Sergio Bendixen, president of Hispanic Trends in an interview in January 2001.

However, studies by the Tomás Rivera Policy Institute show that an increase in Hispanic registered voters is not reflected equally in actual voting. Total Hispanic voter participation remains low.

The 2000 election was the first time in which political commentators seriously analyzed and re-analyzed the Hispanic vote and its effect on both

Democrats and Republicans. In 2001, among roughly 5,000 elected Hispanic officials whose party was known, 1,474 were Democrats and 126 were Republicans. However, there were also 2,283 elected officials whose parties were not listed and 1,309 who were elected to non-partisan offices such as school boards.

The National Association of Latino Elected Officials (NALEO), which collects data on Hispanics who are elected to office in the United States, cautions that its most recent data should not be used to make comparisons with prior years, so I have resisted that temptation. However, the table below does show NALEO's numbers for 2001, which include a total of 5,205 elected officials by level of government. The good news is that the number of representatives in state legislatures is growing and it is from this group that candidates for the U.S. House of Representatives often emerge. This suggests that we will see a growing number of Latino elected officials in coming years.

FIGURE 9.8

Hispanics in Government

*In 2001, more than 5,200 Hispanics held elected office in the United States.**

Level of office	Number
U.S. Representatives	19
State officials	7
State Senators	51
State Representatives	146
County officials	403
Municipal officials	1,443
Judicial/Law Enforcement	454
Education/School board	2,557
Special District officials	125
Total	5,205

Includes Local School Council members in Chicago

Source: NALEO Educational Fund, 2001 National Directory of Latino Elected Officials

Foreign-born Hispanic voters who tend to get their information from Spanish-language television vote differently than those who have access to English-language media.

Just as in the consumer marketplace, there are differences in Hispanic political attitudes in various parts of the United States depending on their degree of acculturation. For example, foreign-born Hispanic voters who tend to get their information from Spanish-language television vote differently than those who have access to English-language media. Moreover, different cultural issues can affect voter turnout and vote. In Florida in 2000, it is believed that Cubans turned out to vote against Al Gore to protest the Clinton administration's handling of the Elián González case of the shipwrecked boy who was returned to his Cuban father. Some analysts say this extraordinary growth in Cubans voting Republican rather than Democratic is what confused pollsters about the outcome of the Florida election.

Hispanic voter influence should continue to grow. However, some analysts worry that a higher cost in government naturalization fees may discourage some immigrants from becoming citizens. In that case, the growth in Hispanic voting power could slow down. As one might guess, this issue is at the top of Hispanic politicians' and lobby groups' agendas.

SUMMARY

In sum, the 2000 U.S. Census data confirmed what Hispanic-marketing experts already knew. The U.S. Hispanic market continues to contribute to the U.S. market, not only in size, but also in dramatically increasing income and business ownership. Slowly, but steadily, educational attainment has improved, voter participation is significantly higher and more powerful, and larger numbers of Hispanics are joining the middle class and learning about wealth creation.

Regionalization is still driven by country of origin. Mexicans, Cubans, Puerto Ricans and others tend to concentrate and start businesses in the states where they have historically settled. However, the shift to new areas is now evident as Hispanics can be found in every state of the Union. Moreover, they are becoming the "majority minority" in several states where a decade ago Latinos were a definite minority. With more and more Hispanics joining the middle class, more businesses have targeted Hispanics, learning to capitalize on the opportunity presented by "instant new consumers."

Certainly, not all is rosy. The Hispanic community continues to face problems such as a growing number of teen mothers, high school dropout rates, and problems related to undocumented immigrants. Especially hard hit by the impact of the events of September 11, 2001 and the economic recession that was already in full swing by that time were Hispanics in the labor force, many of whom worked in the travel, tourism, and food service industries. Fortunately, corporate America is more aware of how it can help solve some of these problems while leveraging the marketing benefits of "share of heart." With increased training for works and greater contributions to scholarship funds, they are creating a healthy, wealthy, and well-adapted or acculturated Hispanic market.

TARGETING
THE HEARTS
AND MINDS OF
U.S. LATINOS

Chapter 10

Segmenting Latinos for Profits

Data alone, without strategy and insights, cannot tell you which Hispanic market customers are the most profitable for your specific business—a crucial piece of information. *Profitability,* and more specifically, segment profitability, should always be the starting point of a business marketing and communications plan, Hispanic or non-Hispanic. In other words, it is imperative to know as closely as possible who your most profitable customers are.

LOOKING FOR PROFITS *IN-CULTURE*

Determining your most profitable Hispanic market segment is sometimes quite a challenge, but, in most cases, possible. To find the most profitable market segment:

- First, look for or generate Hispanic market know-how.
- Second, find reliable Hispanic market data.
- Third, find Hispanic consumer insights.
- Fourth, create and execute an integrated *in-culture* marketing plan, as described in Section 5.

In addition, of course, you will need a healthy marketing budget. In two decades of Hispanic marketing, I have seen business efforts wasted because one of these key components was missing, even when the money was there. The best marketer can easily miss a key point if hands-on Hispanic marketing experience is missing. For example, assuming that Hispanics cannot afford to purchase a brand new car is incorrect. Why? First, because there are a growing number of Hispanics joining the middle class and second because many in the lower income brackets spend their dollars differently than the general market.

For example, in many cases, particularly among the non-acculturated, household expenditures are lower than the non-Hispanic household except for the telephone, the "basket" of foods, and children's clothing. Rent and mortgages are lower. Income taxes, when family earners do not work on a cash basis, tend to be lower as well. In sum, the spending approach is different.

Lastly, Hispanic immigrants moving up the economic ladder are ambitious and have tremendous drive. They want to realize the American dream and are willing to sacrifice a lot to save a last penny toward a financial goal such as purchasing a new car or buying a home. To help achieve the dream, the whole family chips in. The disposable household income allocated to purchase the new car or home parallels that of a general market household with a much higher total income. Certainly this description does not include the growing number of higher-income Latinos that spend their dollars and indulge in support services like any average household in the general market.

Foreign-borns tend to have lower household incomes than U.S.-borns. A simple rule of thumb to ascertain household income for foreign-borns is the number of years of residence in the United States. The more years of residence, the greater the chances of a dual income household or even three family earners, and hence, higher incomes. Finally, income also varies by country of origin.

Therefore, when deciding which is your more profitable Latino segment, the true target needs to be identified *in-culture* using different parameters than you would for the general market.

STEP BY STEP

First, identify your most profitable Hispanic customers. Fortunately, many industries have access today to volumetric data in their internal databases (banks, telephone companies, e-commerce companies, airlines, and so on.) In addition, data providers have improved their methodology for gathering Hispanic market data. For example, ACNielsen's Homescan Hispanic panel provides volumetric data for over 800 categories, including sales and retail data reported by language segments, tracked on a quarterly basis, and compared with non-Hispanic household data. Due to the relevance of this data, an entire section of this book is dedicated to the Hispanic Homescan Panel data and examples of applications are given for several categories.

Secondary market data are available for most product and service categories. These can be used to segment clients and prospects into Hispanic "platinums," "golds," "silvers," "coppers," or any other way you may want to group your "preferred" to "less preferred" Latino customers. If no data are available, it is highly recommended that a good quantitative study be conducted with a "robust" sample size to gather approximated volumetric data. However, you always need to remember that the way Latinos spend their dollars, what motivates them, and the cost to reach them all differ from the general market.

Second, focus beyond profit margins. The costs of selling and servicing per customer are key. Additional costs incurred in servicing *in-culture* include those to fully implement a bilingual, bicultural infrastructure, providing translations, telemarketing with *in-culture* expertise, and many others. However, there are cost savings components to be considered that can offset the added costs. For example, lower-profit Hispanic segments can be acquired at a lower cost per person via lower-cost venues and media. This reality can shift your analysis of your "most profitable customers" in your Hispanic market segmentation plan.

Third, add the heart and soul of the consumer. Once you identify your "preferred" Hispanic customers from secondary market data or your own quantitative study, you need psychographic and acculturation components to develop an *in-culture* integrated Hispanic marketing communication strategy, followed by a marketing plan. A detailed case study of this process appears in Section 5.

Several segmentation schemes are described in the following chapters.

1. Segmentation by place of birth and generation

2. Segmentation by language

3. Segmentation by country of origin

4. Segmentation by age.

In sum, you need to know your Latino customer well. This section of the book provides you with several ways to look at the Latino market, get to know your Hispanic customers, and identify the most profitable segments. Given the complexity of the U.S. Hispanic market today, one single approach may not satisfy your specific Hispanic-market intelligence gathering and business-planning needs. Hence, several segmentation tools are provided to help you find the right one for your specific business needs—marketing, advertising planning, and budgeting.

Chapter 11

Segmenting by Place of Birth and Generation

A s a science, marketing presumes that consumers have a basic knowledge, awareness, and experience with products, services, and brands. That presumption is not necessarily valid when you are marketing to consumers who are born and raised in a different country and with a limited knowledge of the U.S. market and retail systems. Because the U.S. Hispanic market has grown exponentially due to foreign immigration, the foreign versus native U.S.-born variable consideration is a must. Plus, as previously mentioned, the U.S. economy will continue to attract new immigrants. The continued growth of the foreign-born and the U.S.-born Latino population segments require a practical tool to manage the diversity within.

Language and Place of Birth

*Over 10 percent of U.S. adults, or **21.4 million adults speak Spanish.***

*Of all Hispanics, **12.8 million are foreign-born.***

*Of all foreign-born Hispanics, **48 percent arrived in the U.S. since 1990.***

Source: U.S. Census Bureau

THE "NATIVE" HISPANIC CONSUMER

The growth rate of the "native" or U.S.-born Hispanic segment will continue to accelerate, even in a hypothetical "zero" Hispanic migration scenario. This is due to several factors. First, Latinos, as part of their cultural beliefs and values system, tend to have on average more children than the average non-Hispanic family. Second, many of the offspring of the foreign-born Latinos are now in child bearing age, contributing to the dramatic growth of the new Hispanic citizens. Even though more-acculturated Hispanics tend to have smaller families, their numbers are still too insignificant to impact the total Hispanic market family size. Third, the Latino population is younger overall, and the greater number of births than deaths in this population contributes to overall population growth.

THE FOREIGN-BORN HISPANIC

At the dawn of the new century, Hispanic immigration continues in an upward trend, contributing to the growth of the foreign-born Hispanic segment, across all socio-economic groups. As it has historically, the U.S. economy continues to absorb foreign-born professional, unskilled and semi-skilled laborers across the country. In addition, business ties with Mexico and other Latin American countries are booming. They are fueled by the synergy of the prosperous U.S. economy of the last decade, the growth of the U.S. Hispanic market, the North America Free Trade Agreement, and international global trade in general. These new business opportunities are attracting professionals in great numbers from Mexico, Central America, and South America.

LENGTH OF RESIDENCE IN U.S. MAKES A DIFFERENCE

Place of birth and length of residence in the U.S. are each factors that will continue to have a major impact on Hispanic marketing programs. Foreign-born Latinos tend to have a different mindset than those who are U.S.-born, especially if immigration took place after the formative years. For example, recently arrived immigrants may have gaps in their information about marketing such as lack of brand or category awareness, which in addition to limited English language proficiency may limit their access to advertising and promotions.

FIGURE 11.1

Income 1999

Latino Mean Household Income as of 1999

Foreign-born	$35,170
U.S.-born	$43,303

Source: U.S. Census Bureau

Household incomes tend to correlate and improve dramatically with years of residence in the U.S. On average, however, the mean household income of foreign-born Latinos continues to lag significantly behind that of their U.S.-born counterparts, as shown in Figure 11.1. However, this income gap is significantly smaller when income data of recently arrived Hispanics—those with

Ties that Bind

Foreign-born Hispanics maintain the deepest ties:

They call their native country an average of 3.3 times per month.

*They visited their home country an average of
5 times between 1995 and 2001.*

They had an average of four visitors from their country of origin between 1995 and 2001.

34 percent want to return to their home country.

53 percent have sent money home to relatives.

They send money on average 9 times per year.

They send an average of $1,256 annually.

Source: Hispanic Opinion Tracker HOT™ Study, 2001, *People en Español*

less than 5 years of residence in the U.S.—is disaggregated and analyzed separately from the rest of the foreign-born group.

"Very recent arrivals" have much lower household incomes than Latinos who have resided more than 5 years in the U.S. Therefore, I strongly recommend that whenever the income variable comes into play, Hispanic household data for the "newly arrived" be analyzed separately.

MANAGING FOREIGN-BORNS

My fellow market researcher, Carlos Arce, devised a practical tool to study foreign-born Latinos. His segmentation model is based on country of birth, age upon arrival, length of residency in the U.S., and generation number.[1]

Based on the length of time a Hispanic consumer has spent in the U.S., Dr. Arce grouped foreign-born Hispanics into three sub-segments: "Newcomers," "Transitionals," and "Transplants." He grouped U.S.-born or native Hispanics, into two sub-segments, "First Born" and "Deep Roots." (Figure 11.4)

Marketers can easily create this segmentation for their own products and services, with very little budget. It can provide managers with marketing insights not only into the differences of the foreign-born and the native (U.S.) born Hispanic consumer mindset, but also their relationship with your brand, category, or service because each segment tends to respond differently to specific brands and categories. Any basic market research study that gathers data on these four fields, (1) country of birth, (2) age upon arrival, (3) length of residency, and (4) generational background, if U.S.-born, can create these segments. The segment profiles will speak for themselves and will clearly show how each segment relates to your brand, product or service. In other words, you can make informed decisions with minimal investment.

FIGURE 11.2

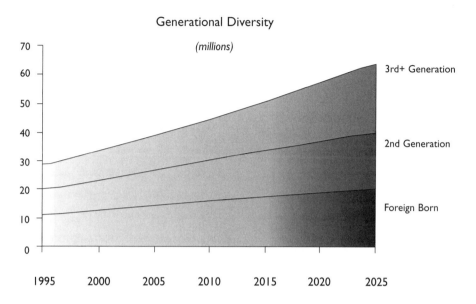

Generational Diversity

(millions)

Source: Isabel Valdés, The Urban Institute, Washington, DC, 1998

FIGURE 11.3

Foreign-Born and U.S.-Born Hispanics

Foreign-born
(First Generation)

- Recent arrivals
- Long-term residents
- Brand heritage/lack of
- Advertising and marketing information hungry
- Mostly Spanish dominant, Spanish preferred

Native/U.S.-born
(Second, Third and more Generations)

- Brand, category "mature"
- Marketing savvy
- Mostly bilingual or English preferred

The following segmentation based on place of birth, years of residence, and generation is a powerful and simple marketing tool that helps manage acculturation issues.

GENERATIONAL SEGMENTS

FIGURE 11.4

Foreign- and Native-born Hispanics

Segment	% of the Hispanic Market (Adults)	Place of Birth	Definition
Newcomers	14%	Foreign	Less than 25% of life has been lived in the U.S.
Transitionals	21	Foreign	Between 25% and 50% of life has been lived in the U.S.
Transplants	22	Foreign	More than 50% of life has been lived in the U.S.
First Born	23	U.S.	At least one parent is foreign born
Deep Roots	20	U.S.	Both parents were born in U.S.

Source: C. Arce, Ph.D., paper presented at The National Hispanic Corporate Council Institute Seminars, NHCCI, 1998, and Hispanic Opinion Tracker HOT™ Study, 2001, *People en Español*

Not every budget allows multi-segment strategies, nor does every product or service benefit from a generational view. However, it does make a big, positive bottom-line difference when marketing strategies take into consideration the existence of these segments and marketing efforts are executed accordingly.

The segment profiles will speak for themselves and describe well how each segment relates to brands, products or services. In other words, you can make informed decisions with minimal or no additional investment.

FIGURE 11.5

Dollars and Segments, Hispanics Over Age 18

Median household income in $ U.S.

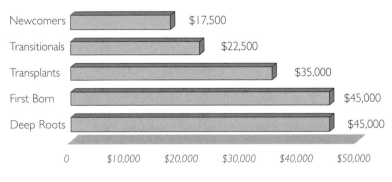

Source: Hispanic Opinion Tracker HOT™ Study, 2001, *People en Español*

SPANISH SPEAKS TO THEIR HEARTS

Foreign-born Hispanics over age 18 prefer Spanish. This figure shows the percentage who prefer to speak mostly Spanish or both Spanish and English equally. Based upon the accumulation of respondents who agreed with each of the following statements: "I speak Spanish exclusively," "I speak more Spanish than English," and "I speak Spanish and English equally."

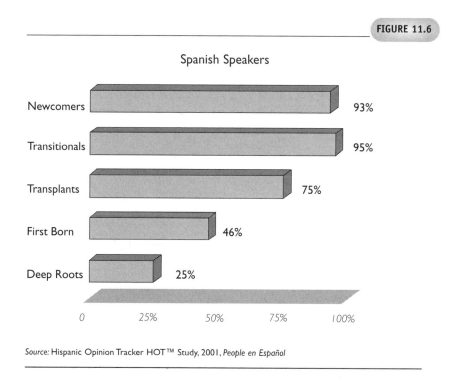

FIGURE 11.6

Spanish Speakers

- Newcomers — 93%
- Transitionals — 95%
- Transplants — 75%
- First Born — 46%
- Deep Roots — 25%

0   25%   50%   75%   100%

Source: Hispanic Opinion Tracker HOT™ Study, 2001, *People en Español*

Segmenting by Language

In the early 1980s when mass marketing to Hispanics was taking off, it was very confusing and hard to analyze the data gathered from Hispanic consumer studies. Responses varied to extremes within categories. Drastic differences in shopping behavior, media use, or psychographic profiles were the norm. It took considerable multi-variate statistical analysis to make sense of the data and to explain why such major variations were present.

To simplify this process, in the mid-1980s, I developed and tested a language-proficiency-based segmentation model together with Jannet Torres, MBA, a market research colleague at Hispanic Market Connections, Inc. It became evident that language-proficiency-based questions cluster Hispanic consumers into clear and distinct marketing segments, simplifying significantly the data analysis process and providing highly valuable strategic marketing insights. After several tests, we reduced the number of questions and developed the basic questionnaire, widely used today in Hispanic marketing.

Language segments facilitate marketing to different Hispanic consumer segments. Most of the time, they can also be used to explain the "whys" of the consumer behavior observed within each Hispanic segment. For example, psychosocial and socio-demographic differences emerge when comparing the foreign-born, recently arrived who speak only Spanish, and long-term residents who prefer Spanish. These segments bring to the surface the variances observed in consumer responses and they can be used to help hypothesize or explain the differences observed in shopping habits, brand loyalty, media usage patterns, and many more relevant marketing issues.

Language Proficiency-based Segments

Language-based segments group consumers into distinct "marketing" groups or cohorts. These are based on *self-reported* levels of proficiency in English and Spanish. The five segments are:

- *Spanish-only or Monolingual.* The consumer depends on Spanish to communicate; has limited or no command of English; is foreign-born, usually adults who are recent arrivals; and in many cases, but not always, of lower socio-economic extraction.

- *Spanish-preferred.* Spanish-language skills are considerably better than English-language skills. The consumer knows enough English to get around; however, feels more comfortable communicating in Spanish. The majority in this segment are foreign-born, and have resided for several years in the U.S. Their socio-economic status improves considerably in proportion to the number of years living in the United States.

- *Bilingual.* Able to communicate freely in either Spanish or English. Consumers in this segment can be either foreign-born or U.S.-born. Most grew up exposed to both cultures, either at home or in their neighborhoods. Socio-economic status improves dramatically.

- *English-preferred.* English-language skills of these consumers are considerably better than Spanish-language skills. They know just enough Spanish to get around, but prefer and are more comfortable communicating in English. Most in this segment are U.S.-born or went to grade school in the United States and have been exposed to both Hispanic and Anglo-American cultures.

- *English-only.* This monolingual consumer communicates only in English; has little or no command of Spanish; tends to have higher socio-economic status and greater exposure to Anglo-American culture, lifestyle, and values.

Source: Isabel Valdés, National Hispanic Database, 1982–1987. ©M. Isabel Valdés, *Hispanic Market Handbook*, 1995, Gale Research

FIGURE 12.1

Language Segmentation—An Example

Los Angeles (4 counties), Adults 18 and older

Spanish-only is dominant in this geographic area at 34 percent, but Spanish-language reach increases to 55 percent when you combine Spanish-only and Spanish-preferred, and 88 percent when bilingual households are added.

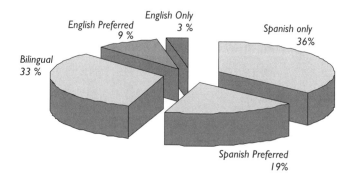

Source: ACNielsen Homescan Hispanic panel, 2000, Language Segmentation Study, Los Angeles (4 counties), August 2000

Bilingual consumers tend to have generally retained fewer habits and lifestyle elements, such as cooking styles and leisure activities, from their countries of origin than Spanish-preferred consumers, and they have accepted more American ways. English-only consumers are the most highly acculturated group; many of their preferences—in some cases, all—are most like the general market.

Language segments work because language proficiency—how much and how well a Latino consumer knows English and or Spanish—is a key indicator of the acculturation level, or how much the consumer has adopted the habits and culture of the U.S. general market. Thus, language-proficiency-based segmentation is an extremely practical and easy-to-use tool in Hispanic marketing today.

Less acculturated consumers seek a different product and service set, and they respond to different emotional cues than do more acculturated consumers. Thus, with language segmentation, a marketer can develop targeted *in-culture* strategies for specific segments or select one or two "high potential" market segments, but with a great deal of supporting intelligence. The same model can be applied to any immigrant population, substituting French, Chinese, or any specific language. Therefore, marketers who manage multicultural consumers can standardize their marketing-intelligence databases.

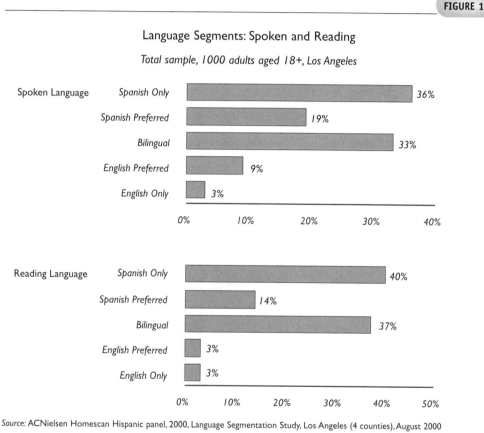

FIGURE 12.2

Language Segments: Spoken and Reading

Total sample, 1000 adults aged 18+, Los Angeles

Source: ACNielsen Homescan Hispanic panel, 2000, Language Segmentation Study, Los Angeles (4 counties), August 2000

Over the years, several language-based segmentations have emerged and are in use today. However, these segmentations may be based on factors other than proficiency in English or Spanish, such as what language Hispanic consumers speak at home or work, or what media they consume.

Why the fuss? This small difference can make a big difference in your marketing intelligence and strategy. For example, I was once contacted for a survey by telephone and asked, "Do you read any newspapers or magazines in Spanish?" At that time—the early 1980s—there was no mature Spanish language newspaper in the San Francisco Bay area, and no U.S.-produced magazines in Spanish. Hence, my reply was "No." Next the interviewer read the familiar "thank you for your participation," and hung up. Had she asked instead, "Do you read in Spanish?" my reply and that of many other Latinos interviewed would have been "Yes." This study could have shown there was a segment of Hispanic readers not being served and a business opportunity. However, by not asking the question properly, the answers led to an erroneous conclusion: "Hispanics don't read in Spanish." This small difference contributed to the pervasive belief that "Hispanics don't read," which is false, judging by the success and growth of the Spanish-language print industry.

THE "PRACTICAL" VERSION

Language segments may be used individually or grouped, combining segments of similar acculturation levels. For example, in the ACNielsen Homescan Hispanic panel, the two least acculturated language segments combine into one, "Spanish-only/Spanish-preferred." Bilinguals are a second segment, and the two most acculturated language segments are combined into a third, "English-only/English-preferred." The three resulting language segments still show distinct habits and preferences. This insight is invaluable when developing and executing targeted *in-culture* marketing plans. Moreover, each segment is larger. This provides a more robust sample for smaller product categories and simplifies the tracking analysis.

Analyzing language preferences is an excellent tool for judging the degree of acculturation. Acculturation is the direct result of interaction with American cultural beliefs, values, practices, and behaviors. Figure 12.4 below shows clearly how the demographics of Hispanics in Los Angeles merge with those of Anglos as Hispanic households become more acculturated. In Section 3 of this book, you will see why the degree of acculturation matters to manufacturers, retailers, and service providers as we compare the buying behavior of acculturated and non-acculturated households and see how it shifts as acculturation increases.

In Figure 12.4 below, I use the term *Spanish-dominant* to include Spanish-only and Spanish-preferred households and *English-dominant* to include English-only and English-preferred.

Acculturation is the direct result of interaction with American cultural beliefs, values, practices, and behaviors.

Again, it must be stated that language proficiency is a self-rated measure. Therefore, participants may either understate or overstate their ability to speak Spanish or English. Thus it is important to validate and cross reference self-rated language use variables with other related variables. For example, if a consumer states that he speaks Spanish very well and speaks almost no English, but also states that he was born outside the United States, and then states that he reads only English, he needs to be re-contacted and re-evaluated. In most cases, language proficiency as stated should correlate highly with place of birth, age at arrival, and media preference when cross-analyzed.

FIGURE 12.4

ACNielsen's Los Angeles Homescan Hispanic Panel Profile

This table shows the household changes that occur in language segments with acculturation. Households become smaller, with a smaller percentage having children. Because more acculturated Hispanics tend to marry later, the average age of the head of household goes up. The educational attainment goes up, as does average income.

Household Characteristics	Spanish-dominant	Bilingual	English-dominant
Average household size (persons)	4.5	3.8	3.1
Percent with children	66.4%	58.8%	39.2%
Average age of household head (years)	30.6	35.7	39.3
Completed high school or more	48%	79%	85%
Average income	$20,200	$32,200	$52,400
Percent foreign-born	Nearly 100%	66%	20%
Average years lived in U.S.	12.7	19.2	25.9

Source: ACNielsen Homescan Hispanic panel, 2000, Language Segmentation Study, Los Angeles (4 counties), August 2000

Combined Language Segments

- **Spanish-dominant** As expected, virtually all of the Spanish-only and Spanish-preferred respondents prefer to communicate in Spanish, when given a choice. These two language segments are often collapsed into one Spanish-dominant segment to simplify market targeting.

- **Bilingual** In contrast, half of the bilinguals report no particular preference for either language; of the other half, two in five prefer to communicate in English, and three in five prefer to do so in Spanish.

- **English-dominant** Among English-preferred and English-only segments, English is the prevalent choice. However, one-fourth of the English-preferred claimed no preference for either language. Presently, these two language sub-segments are often collapsed into one English-dominant segment because most cities have a small number of Hispanic adults in these subgroups.

Chapter 13

Segmenting by Country of Origin

Marketers are always looking for the competitive edge, for a way to slice and dice their target market to "talk to them" as closely as possible. Country of birth or origin can provide a different angle to the Hispanic strategy, opening creative doors and opportunities. Reviewing your Hispanic business plan and marketing strategy through the lens of country of origin can help you uncover unique benefits or barriers. For example, Hispanics from specific countries of origin tend to cluster in different regions of the U.S. (e.g. Mexicans in the West and Southwest). Therefore, it would be wise to take the country of origin into consideration before executing a communications campaign. Whenever possible, take advantage of and capitalize on country-specific benefits of your brand, product, category, or service in the different regions where Latinos from these countries concentrate. Country-specific segmentation can help you:

- Fine tune your business plan and other financial estimates. Some subgroups consume or purchase more or less of certain products;

- "Guesstimate" brand heritage and brand development related issues. Many U.S. brands are marketed in some countries and not in others, hence the need for a different marketing approach,

- Ascertain category differences. For example, cooks from some countries prepare dishes with ingredients that are not as well-known by cooks from other Latin American countries.

- Bullet-proof acceptability. Make sure your national or regional target marketing efforts are culturally attuned to the specific countries represented.

- Use country-specific "cultural cues." They are key to touching emotional buttons.

FIGURE 13.1

Country of Origin

Hispanic (50 U.S. states)	35,305,818 (100%)
Mexican	20,640,711 (58%)
Puerto Rican (Continental)	3,406,178 (10%)
Cuban	1,241,685 (4%)
Other Hispanics	10,017,244 (28%)
Puerto Rico (Island)	3,800,000
Total Hispanic Population with Puerto Rico	39,105,818

MEXICAN LATINOS

Mexican Latinos are the largest sub-segment in the U.S. Hispanic market and they lead in growth of the market. Of the three largest groups (Mexican, Puerto Rican and Cuban), the Mexican-American population grew the fastest between 1990 and 2000.

As a segment, Mexicans have had somewhat declining income in the past couple of years, as shown in Figure 13.2. As mentioned previously, this is a phenomenon created by the large number of newly arrived immigrant Mexicans who have lower incomes, creating a "pull-down" effect.

FIGURE 13.2

Mean Hispanic Household Income by National Origin

National Origin	1979	1989	1999	% change 1979-99
Mexican	$37,891	$38,741	$36,923	-3%
Puerto Rican	29,221	35,285	34,777	19
Cuban	47,543	53,317	52,203	10
Other Hispanic	41,672	43,932	42,438	2

Source: *Hispanic Business* Magazine, December 2001, based on U.S. Census 2000 data

However, when segmented by country of birth and length of residence, the picture changes. The Tomás Rivera Institute study compared average incomes of Mexicans by those born in Mexico and those born in the U.S. For Mexicans born in the U.S., average income in 1998 was $50,423, compared with $38,172 for those born in Mexico who had immigrated.

A similar phenomenon can be observed with the other segments by country of origin. For example, U.S.-born people of Cuban origin had an income of $62,480 versus $49,460 for Cuban-born Hispanics. For U.S.-born Puerto Ricans, income was $39,600, compared with $30,649 for those who were Island-born.

Other demographic differences that can be taken into account by country of origin include educational attainment or average years of education by gender. For example, the Tomás Rivera Policy Institute study reports that Mexicans aged 25 to 64 in 1998 were unlikely to have completed high school. Puerto Ricans averaged more years in school, but most still had not completed high school. Cubans, on the other hand, averaged yet more years, with most completing high school. The Tomás Rivera Policy Institute website, www.trpi.org, contains many more such comparisons. I highly recommend it.

Cultural nuances and language are different in some regions. Understanding these country of origin differences helps in fine-tuning advertising messages to the local Hispanic cultural majority.

DIFFERENT GEOGRAPHIC REGIONS, DIFFERENT HISPANIC CULTURAL BACKGROUNDS

As previously mentioned, it is useful in marketing and advertising to review the top Hispanic metros by country of origin since cultural nuances and language are different in some regions. Understanding these differences also helps to fine-tune advertising messages to the local Hispanic cultural majority. It is often possible to have a national "umbrella" media campaign with homogenized talk-to-all Spanish. However, local efforts in print, outdoor, radio, or TV can be easily adapted to reflect unique regional country-of-origin accents, visuals, and music. The following tables, courtesy of *Hispanic Market Weekly,* list the top Hispanic metros by country of origin.

FIGURE 13.4

Metros by Country of Origin

Twenty-four percent of all Mexicans living in the United States live in the Los Angeles metro.

Top 12 Mexican Metros

	Metro	Hispanic all	Mexican all	Share of U.S. Mexicans
1	Los Angeles- Riverside-Orange County	6,598,488	4,962,046	24.0%
2	Chicago-Gary-Kenosha, IL-IN-WI CMSA	1,498,507	1,121,089	5.4
3	Houston-Galveston-Brazoria, TX CMSA	1,348,588	985,197	4.8
4	San Francisco-Oakland-San Jose, CA	1,383,661	981,311	4.8
5	Dallas-Fort Worth, TX CMSA	1,120,350	889,879	4.3
6	Phoenix-Mesa, AZ MSA	817,012	667,747	3.2
7	San Diego, CA MSA	750,965	628,460	3.0
8	San Antonio, TX MSA	816,037	572,323	2.8
9	El Paso, TX MSA	531,654	447,065	2.2
10	McAllen-Edinburg-Mission, TX MSA	503,100	433,198	2.1
11	Fresno, CA MSA	406,151	349,109	1.7
12	New York- Northern New Jersey-Long Island	3,852,138	343,137	1.7

Top 10 U.S. Puerto Rican Metros

	Metro	Hispanic	Puerto Rican	Share of U.S. Puerto Ricans
1	New York-Northern New Jersey-Long Island, NY-NJ-CT-PA CMSA	3,852,138	1,325,778	38.9
2	Philadelphia- Wilmington-Atlantic City, PA-NJ-DE-MD CMSA	348,135	206,802	6.1
3	Chicago-Gary-Kenosha, IL-IN-WI CMSA	1,498,507	164,509	4.8
4	Aguadilla, PR MSA	144,596	142,474	–
5	Orlando, FL MSA	271,627	139,898	4.1
6	Boston-Worcester-Lawrence, MA-NH-ME-CT CMSA	358,231	137,373	4.0
7	Miami-Fort Lauderdale, FL CMSA	1,563,389	135,265	4.0
8	Hartford, CT MSA	113,540	82,992	2.4
9	Tampa-St. Petersburg-Clearwater, FL MSA	248,642	75,621	2.2
10	Los Angeles-Riverside-Orange County, CA CMSA	6,598,488	66,340	1.9

continues . . .

Metros by Country of Origin (Continued)

Top Puerto Rico (Island) Metros

Metro	Hispanic	Puerto Rican
1 San Juan Caguas, Arecibo, PR CMSA	2,416,024	2,297,244
2 Ponce, PR MSA	358,246	352,938
3 Mayaguez, PR MSA	251,032	245,941

Top 15 Cuban Metros

Metro	Hispanic	Cuban	Share of Cubans
1 Miami-Fort Lauderdale, FL CMSA	1,563,389	701,512	56.5
2 New York-Northern New Jersey-Long Island, NY-NJ-CT-PA CMSA	3,852,138	134,973	10.9
3 Los Angeles-Riverside-Orange County, CA CMSA	6,598,488	53,839	4.3
4 Tampa-St. Petersburg-Clearwater, FL MSA	248,642	41,602	3.4
5 West Palm Beach-Boca Raton, FL MSA	140,675	25,386	2.0
6 Orlando, FL MSA	271,627	18,797	1.5
7 San Juan-Caguas-Arecibo, PR CMSA	2,416,024	17,833	—
8 Chicago-Gary-Kenosha, IL-IN-WI-CMSA	1,498,507	17,251	1.4
9 Washington-Baltimore, DC-MD-VA-WV CMSA	484,902	11,835	1.0
10 Las Vegas, NV-AZ MSA	322,038	11,121	0.9
11 Houston-Galveston-Brazoria, TX CMSA	1,348,588	10,170	0.8
12 Atlanta, GA MSA	268,851	9,206	0.7
13 San Francisco-Oakland-San Jose, CA CMSA	1,383,661	8,980	0.7
14 Philadelphia-Wilmington-Atlantic City, PA-NJ-DE-MD CMSA	348,135	8,641	0.7
15 Boston-Worcester-Lawrence, MA-NH-ME-CT CMSA	358,231	8,404	0.7

continues . . .

Metros by Country of Origin (Continued)

The just over 6 million Hispanics classified as "Others" include Dominicans, South and Central Americans, and about 100,000 Spaniards. The "Other" segment nearly doubled in size during the 1990s.

Top 15 "Other Hispanic" Metros

	Metro	Hispanic	Other	% of U.S.
1	New York- Northern New Jersey- Long Island, NY-NJ-CT- PA CMSA	3,852,138	2,048,250	20.4%
2	Los Angeles-Riverside-Orange County, CA CMSA	6,598,488	1,516,263	15.1
3	Miami-Fort Lauderdale, FL CMSA	1,563,389	669,066	6.7
4	San Francisco-Oakland-San Jose, CA CMSA	1,383,661	359,210	3.6
5	Washington-Baltimore, DC-MD-VA-WV CMSA	484,902	355,841	3.6
6	Houston-Galveston-Brazoria, TX CMSA	1,348,588	337,509	3.4
7	San Antonio, TX MSA	816,037	231,195	2.3
8	Dallas-Fort Worth, TX CMSA	1,120,350	207,208	2.1
9	Chicago-Gary-Kenosha, IL-IN-WI CMSA	1,498,507	195,658	2.0
10	Boston-Worcester-Lawrence, MA-NH-ME-CT CMSA	358,231	189,555	1.9
11	Albuquerque, NM MSA	296,373	184,870	1.8
12	Denver-Boulder-Greeley, CO CMSA	476,627	154,526	1.5
13	Phoenix-Mesa, AZ MSA	817,012	133,807	1.3
14	San Diego, CA MSA	750,965	103,685	1.0
15	San Juan-Caguas-Arecibo, PR CMSA	2,416,024	92,779	–

Source: U.S. Bureau of the Census; Profiles of General Demographic Characteristics," Census 2000, June 2001, Hispanic Market Weekly, June 11, 2001

Chapter 14

In-Culture Age Segments

Until recently, the U.S. Hispanic market did not have enough consumers in some age groups to create a complete age-based market segmentation. However, growth during the past decade allows for key age cohort subgroupings as a practical marketing tool.

Why *in-culture?* Because the ages selected to create the segments are based on the natural breaks of the U.S. Hispanic population and the marketing opportunities these represent. They are not necessarily the age breaks used for the general market. Furthermore, segment construction is based, whenever possible, on *in-culture* principles, that is to say, following the Latino cultural mindset.

FIGURE 14.1

Segment Summary Table

In-Culture Age Segments, Census 2000

5 Main Segments by Age *in thousands* Segment Size (n)	(%) Hispanic Population	9 Sub-Segments (Age)	Size *in thousands*	% of total Hispanic Population
Los Bebés/Los Niños Ages 0–9 n=6,408	18.1%	Los Bebés (0–5) Los Niños (6–9)	3,191 3,217	9.1% 9.1%
Generation Ñ Ages 10–19 n=6,117	17.4%	Tweens (10–14) Teens (15–19)	3,059 3,058	8.6% 8.8%
Latinos/Latinas Ages 20–39 n=11,175	31.7%	Twenty Something (20–29) Thirty Something (30–39)	5,434 5,741	15.4% 16.3%
Latin Boomers Ages 40–59 n=8,307	23.5%	Young Boomers (40–49) Mature Boomers (50–59)	5,045 3,262	14.3% 9.2%
Los Grandes Ages 60+ n=3,299	9.3%	Seniors (60+)	3,299	9.3%
Total	100%		35,306 million*	100%

Does not include Puerto Rico's 3.8 million Hispanics nor Census undercount.

© 2002 M. Isabel Valdés. *Source:* Created by Isabel Valdés, based on data analysis from TGE Demographics

As shown in Figures 14.1, 14.2, and 14.3 there are two segmentation schemes available by *in-culture* age segments. The first includes the five main segments (Figure 14.1). The nine sub-segments are also shown. These sub-segments take into consideration the developmental and lifestage variation within the main age groups, except for "Los Grandes" whose population size is presently too small in the Hispanic market to subdivide. Segment names used reflect both the age lifestage and the *in-culture* aspect.

FIGURE 14.2

In-Culture Latino Segments

five main age segments

Los Bebés/Los Niños (0–9)	18%
Gen Ñ (Tweens/Teens) (10–19)	17%
Latinas/Latinos (20–39)	32%
Boomers (40–59)	24%
Los Grandes (60+)	9%

FIGURE 14.3

In-Culture Latino Segments

Nine age sub-segments

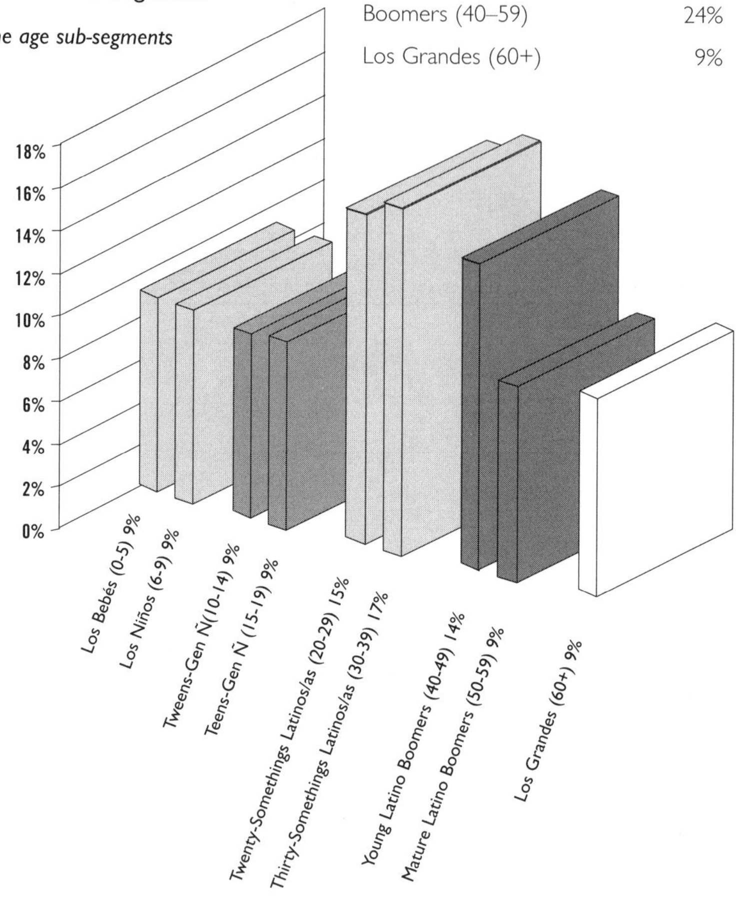

Los Bebés (0-5) 9%
Los Niños (6-9) 9%
Tweens-Gen Ñ (10-14) 9%
Teens-Gen Ñ (15-19) 9%
Twenty-Somethings Latinos/as (20-29) 15%
Thirty-Somethings Latinos/as (30-39) 17%
Young Latino Boomers (40-49) 14%
Mature Latino Boomers (50-59) 9%
Los Grandes (60+) 9%

© 2000 M. Isabel Valdés

THE YOUNGEST LATINO CITIZENS

LOS BEBÉS

Age: 0 to 5   ***Segment size 3.2 million***

The youngest of the Census 2000 Latino age segments—close to 3.2 million Latino babies and toddlers (aged 0 to 5)—will live in a different world than their older siblings. Most of them will be raised in acculturated households with computers and at least one family member will navigate the web not only in Spanish but also in English.

Los Bebés 2000—Health Facts

- Births annually: 734,661
- Fertility rate 2.9 births per woman *vs.* 2.0 for whites,and 2.1 for African-American women
- Birth rate: 101.1 births per 1,000 women aged 15–44
- Percent of births to teenagers: 16.9
- Percent of births to unmarried mothers: 41.6
- Percent mothers receiving first-trimester pre-natal care: 74.3
- Percent low birth weight: 6.4
- Percent births by cesarean section: 20.6

Sources: *Vital Health Statistics Reports,* Vol. 48, No. 3, 1998, Health Department data, and Statistical Abstract of the United States, 2001

The vast majority of the Bebés 2000 are native born, (96 percent were born in the U.S.) and 64 percent were born to foreign-born parents who migrated to the U.S. Given the growing recognition and value of multiculturalism in a global economy and the growing maturity of Spanish-language education and media, it is highly possible that these Bebés 2000 will grow to be bilingual, fluent in English and Spanish, and bicultural.

Selected Myths and Realities—Cultural Impact

by Dr. Aliza Lifschitz

Dr. Aliza is a pediatrician with Spanish-language television and radio programs that answer questions and counsel young mothers. Her shows are broadcast by Univision and the Radio Unica network. Following are selected traditional myths that her listeners have asked her about.

Myths during pregnancy

More births take place during the full moon.

If the woman's womb is pointed, it's a boy, if it's round, it's a girl.

If the baby moves a lot it's a boy, if it's calmer, it's a girl.

You have to eat for two.

Firstborns always arrive late.

A scare can induce birth immediately.

If the mother has a scare, the baby will be born with birthmark or the birth will be induced immediately.

If you dance during pregnancy, you will give birth ahead of schedule.

If you experience a lot of stomach acidity during pregnancy, the baby will be born with a lot of hair.

It's bad luck to buy things for the baby before it's born.

Myths based on folklore

Sexual intercourse is advised after the first trimester, so that the child will grow properly; if he is lacking that source of energy, he will be weak and sickly, but

When the womb is already rounded, sexual intercourse is forbidden because the child will emerge soiled upon delivery, as though he had been bathed in cornstarch, or he will become stuck to the womb and the birth will be long and painful.

If a pregnant woman sleeps during the day, her child will be born with protruding eyelids.

If a pregnant woman chews gum, the baby's palate will harden and his gums will become thick. This will not allow the baby to breast-feed from his mother and he will die of starvation.

If a pregnant woman eats tamales that have stuck to the pan, the child will stick to her womb and not be able to come out at the time of delivery.

FIGURE 14.4

Los Bebés (Aged 0 to 5)

in thousands
Los Bebés represent 9 percent of all U.S. Hispanics.

Total Bebés 0–5	Total Foreign Born 0–5	Total U.S. Born 0–5	U.S.-BORN GENERATION			
			Second	Third	Fourth or greater	Total
100%	4%	96%	1,942	522	519	3,055
3,191	135	3,055	64%	17%	19%	100%

© 2000 M. Isabel Valdés

MARKETING TO LOS BEBÉS

Judging from the growing marketing activity targeting new Hispanic moms, and the proliferation of pre-school cartoons in Spanish, corporate America has discovered at last the value of the youngest Latino citizens. Not only are traditional advertisers developing programs to appeal to these moms, more players are entering the market, including consumer products, toys, healthcare and pharmaceuticals, the financial sectors, magazines and the on-line world.

Talking to the expecting or new mom is a perfect "POE," or Point of Entry venue, coveted by savvy marketers. Finding the new Latina mom is now easier than ever before. Hospitals in high-density, new-immigrant Hispanic areas are glad to distribute to Hispanic moms samples and educational materials in Spanish, or bilingual, since it helps them inform and communicate with these patients. Plus, there are several pre-natal magazines, dedicated on-line websites, sections in TV, radio programs and newspaper articles. These dedicated media talk to the specific needs and wants of the Latina mom, and they do it *in-culture!* For example, the latest magazine to join is *Espera,* a pre-natal Spanish-language magazine designed to communicate to the non-acculturated Latina mom-to-be. Included among many others as advertisers in the first issue of *Espera,* with over 350,000 copies sent to obstetricians and gynecologists, are Johnson & Johnson, Huggies, Nestlé, Playtex, and Mederma. Another such publication is *Lamaze Para Padres* that has more than tripled its original circulation, to over 750,000. A popular magazine read by Latina moms at the clinic or hospitals, *Primeros Doce Meses,* is an annual by American Baby Group with half a million in circulation. As mentioned above, clinics, hospitals and primary-school PTAs are excellent places to distribute samples for new or repeat Latina moms.

Online, several dedicated sites talk to the Hispanic new mom, such as,

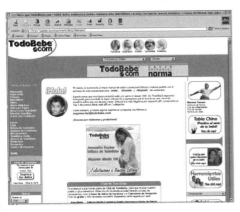

www.Todobebe.com. In addition, many portals and Latino-specific websites like www.Soloella.com talk to the new moms. (See website resource section in this book for a list of sites.) As internet use grows among Latina moms, marketers and advertisers are increasingly including dedicated websites as a part of the communication strategy. For example, see www.nacersano.org, a Spanish-language website developed by JMCP's March of Dimes/Folic Acid education campaign. (See case study below.)

LATIN NAG FACTOR

Market researchers who study children know that the "nag factor" starts at about age 2. Hispanic families add to the "nag factor" a "compensatory" behavior—an over developed need to provide their children with what they themselves did not have growing up, resulting in an even more powerful "Latin nag." In consequence, children's TV programs en Español are increasing the number of advertisements targeting parents. Nickelodeon en Español, *Plaza Sesamo* and many others count on the "influencing" impact of the young "Latin naggers" to sell their products.

And, to take advantage of the growing market of Latino children, the number of programs targeted to Latin children is increasing. For example, Nickelodeon offers *Taina*, the story of a young Puerto Rican dancer in New York City, Galavision launched *Mi Casita* in 2001 to its morning *Galamiquitos.* *Dora the Explorer* an animated bilingual, interactive cartoon about an intrepid 7-year-old, problem-solving Latina, was the number 1 show for pre-schoolers on all of broadcast and cable in mid-2001, according to Nielsen Media Research, Inc.

March of Dimes

For more detail on this case and creative materials, go to
www.incultureapproach.com

Campaign: **Folic Acid Awareness**

BACKGROUND

The March of Dimes is a not-for-profit organization whose mission is to improve the health of babies by preventing birth defects and infant mortality. As part of its overall campaign to reach all women of childbearing age with an educational message about the role of B-vitamin folic acid in preventing birth defects of the brain and spine, the March of Dimes identified Hispanic females as a key target. Hispanic women are at increased risk of giving birth to a baby with this type of defect while at the same time they are much less likely to be aware that folic acid can help reduce the risk.

There was also little awareness of March of Dimes among Hispanic women. The March of Dimes wanted to generate awareness of the benefits of folic acid among Hispanic women of childbearing age and get them to consider taking a folic acid vitamin as part of a healthy diet.

MARKETING CHALLENGE

The campaign had to overcome several barriers. Hispanic women tend to believe that their diets are sufficient to get the vitamins they need until they get pregnant, at which time they will take whatever is recommended by their doctor. There is a belief that destiny plays an important role in the outcome of pregnancies and that there is not much they can do to avoid birth defects. Multivitamins have the perceived disadvantage of causing weight gain.

The challenge was how to reach sexually active Hispanic women under age 18 who are not considering pregnancy as well as women over 18 who are contemplating pregnancy, with a strong prevention message about birth defects and the benefits of folic acid. Separately, the goal was to increase calls to the March of Dimes Resource Center, which provides vital information on prenatal health, and create traffic to the new website.

MEDIA STRATEGIES

The target audience was divided between pregnancy contemplators and non-contemplators each with a different advertising approach. The contemplators were reached with a TV and radio message that counteracts the Latina's sense of fatalism that there is little they can do to affect the outcome of their pregnancy.

The non-contemplators were reached with very tailored, youth-oriented posters, postcards and brochures that do not focus on babies but rather on the importance of taking care of their body and health while underlining the many benefits of folic acid to prevent various diseases.

A Spanish-language website, nacersano.org, was created to provide in-depth information on pregnancy and health issues with special attention given to Hispanic-specific health issues.

All advertising materials feature the Resource Center telephone number and the website address.

The 30-second TV commercial, called *Carritos,* features a moving caravan of babies in shopping carts with signs that read "My mommy took folic acid." The announcer says that when you become pregnant, it's not like going shopping. You cannot pick the ideal baby, but you can prevent his or her having serious birth defects of the brain and spine. This *in-culture* message empowers the mother with a clear action!

PROMOTIONAL STRATEGIES

The media outreach campaign included placement of public service announcements on national TV, spot TV in key markets, radio, and print vehicles. In addition, press releases were disseminated in English and Spanish announcing the launch of the folic acid health education and birth defect prevention campaign.

RESULTS

The campaign was launched in January 2001. At six months tracking, the March Of Dimes (MOD) media exposure was very strong with more airings of the *Carritos* TV PSA than MOD had in a year for its general market campaign.

Calls (in Spanish) into the MOD Resource Center increased from 600 to 2,900 after the campaign and hits on the website also increased dramatically.

AGENCY: JMCP Publicidad, www.jmcp.com

THE MODERN BEBÉ HOUSEHOLDS

At the dawn of the new century, more Latina moms are joining the labor force than ever before and more Hispanics were joining the middle class and becoming modern. Therefore, more Bebés will be going to pre-schools and raised in households pressed for time. Presently about 36 percent of Latino babies and toddlers are enrolled in pre-school programs, compared with 55 percent of children in the general market.

FIGURE 14.5

Early Learners

by Race/Ethnicity, 2000

Enrollment of three- and four-year-olds in pre-primary education programs

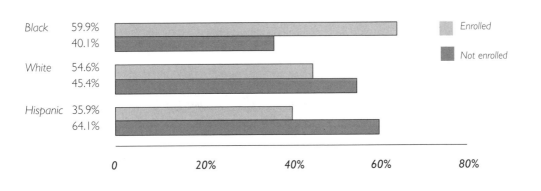

Black	59.9%	
	40.1%	
White	54.6%	
	45.4%	
Hispanic	35.9%	
	64.1%	

Enrolled
Not enrolled

0   20%   40%   60%   80%

Source: U.S. Census Bureau

This difference in enrollment in pre-school is due in part to the strong cultural pull of familismo resulting in a very strong desire to "keep babies at home for as long as possible." Hispanic families tend to delay pre-school entry independently of socio-economic status, both in the U.S. and in Latin America.

Low-income Hispanic families were at the lowest historic levels in 2000, only 21 percent, according to the Census Bureau. However, in view of the emerging economic recession and the 9/11 terrorist bombing in 2001, it is possible that the future of these families and these young lives may experience a set back in their hard-fought battle with low income. As this book goes to press, economic recovery has begun, but it is still unknown what the impact of the recession will have been on the Hispanic market and on foreign-born Latino families in particular.

There are great marketing opportunities for corporate America to build "share of heart" with their brands and products and to help future generations of Latinos to become successful and productive American citizens. To get the ball rolling, leaders in the Hispanic-advertising world have created an education campaign to encourage education among Hispanics. FuturaMente focuses on 3-to-4 year-olds, stressing the importance of early education. The campaign, funded and created by members of the Association of Hispanic Advertising Agencies (ahaa), broadcasts its message in English- and Spanish-language television, radio, print, online and outdoor media. It is a challenge to change deeply rooted cultural values such as *familismo,* but not impossible.

Los Niños

Aged: 6 to 9   **Segment size: 3.2 million**

Between 2001 and 2010, the percentage of Hispanic children, aged 5 to 9, will increase by 21 percent, while the share of white non-Hispanic and non-Hispanic black children will continue to decline steadily. (See Figure 14.6) This demographic shift will continue to fuel the growing diversity in America's grade schools. The pressure to deliver good quality education added to the increasing numbers of students from different cultural backgrounds in already crowded classrooms will push schools to find solutions. *American Demographics* (September 2000) predicts many schools will "mass customize" education, delivering educational materials to meet the specific needs and interests of each student using new computer-based technologies.

Fortunately, many Latino children are becoming computer literate and at a fast pace. As access to a computer at school or at home continues to grow, Los Niños press their parents to get a home computer and then often the children teach their parents how to go online.

From original strategy, Lapiz devised an original spot with unique Hispanic insights and captured passion via "GRRR" mnemonic.

RESULTS

At a time when the category decreased in volume by 8 percent, the campaign grew volume for the brand 9 percent and "re-ignited the passion for Frosted Flakes." It helped drive up the Kellogg's overall ready-to-eat cold cereal business nearly 3 share points.

AGENCY: Lapiz-Integrated Hispanic Marketing a Division of Leo Burnett USA, www.lapiz-advertising.com

---

Another venue is corporate contributions for scholarship funds—and promoting these to the Hispanic community.

Retailers and manufacturers aware of the pull Latino children have on parents' purchase behavior are increasingly partnering to attract this young lucrative segment with programs that give something to all. For example, Kraft used an innovative approach to introduce its new pizza and build "share of heart." Managers of Tombstone Pizza, Kraft's new Mexican Style pizza, partnered with Spanish-language radio KHCK-FM in Dallas, the Six Flags Theme Park, and Albertson's grocery stores. Luis Sosa, a "10-year-old veteran" at the radio station invited young listeners to participate and win. For each purchase of two Tombstone Mexican Style pizzas, KHCK listeners received a free all-day pass to Six Flags. The instant redemption offers were redeemed during KHCK-FM's van visits at 12 different Albertson's locations from 4 to 5 p.m. each weekday. The promotion's success was overwhelming. "To make it effective, we need to sell 4,000 pizzas. We ended up selling over 10,000!" said Mark Vosberg, Dallas Kraft Planning Manager.[3] The product and promotion's media and family fun mix had great appeal to kids as well as the elements to talk to their parents' hearts and wallets.

A successful campaign by Anheuser-Busch demonstrates how manufacturers of sensitive products, in this case beer, can win "share of heart" with Hispanic families. Certainly the beer manufacturer does not want to promote its alcoholic beverages to minors, nor does the company want to miss out on the opportunity to build "share of heart" with targeted Hispanic families. So, Anheuser-Busch teamed up with Major League Baseball teams, including the Los Angeles Dodgers, Florida Marlins, Houston Astros, and New York Yankees, all key Hispanic markets. They created the *Homerunazo* scholarship campaign. Budweiser donated $100 to the Hispanic scholarship fund for every home run hit by participating teams during the 2001 season. By being a good neighbor and giving back to the community, the brand, Budweiser, builds share of heart without selling its product.

NEW *IN-CULTURE* GOODS FOR LOS NIÑOS

Manufacturers continue to target Los Niños with new *in-culture* toys. In mid-2001 Hasbro, Inc. introduced a Hispanic G.I. Joe, Roy P. Benavidez. According to the Associated Press (August 2001), this soldier was an "Army sergeant who won the Medal of Honor" for saving eight Special Forces soldiers during a jungle battle 33 years ago in Vietnam. As far as I know, this is the first time that Hispanic children have been shown, in a fun and playful way, their predecessors' participation in America's battles. It gives them the same information that non-Hispanic children in America have about the way their ancestors contributed to the greatness of their home country.

Mattel also introduced Quinceañera Barbie (Happy Fifteenth Birthday, Barbie) to commemorate the Latina tradition. Dressed in formal gown, the Latina-looking doll comes with a gift box containing the gift (a doll) that the celebrating Quinceañera presents to her younger sister. These *in-culture* toys use culture in a smart way. They build ties with the brand and with the Latin community, communicating implicitly: "We see you, we like you, we want your business."

The food and beverage industry has also tackled this lucrative segment. Following the success story of Häagen Dazs Dulce de Leche ice cream, M&M/Mars launched Dulce de Leche-Caramel candies, its first-ever product designed specifically to target U.S. Hispanic youth. Featuring its product, Sour Skittles, M&M/Mars also sponsored "The Barrio Games" in Los Angeles and Chicago to reach young urban Latinos, a great approach to building share of heart and promoting the new candies. The campaign was created and managed by Zubi Advertising.

"THE BEST OF BOTH WORLDS"

GENERATION Ñ

Aged: 10 to 19   ***Segment Size: 6.1 million***

Generation Ñ is probably the most written about and coveted Hispanic market segment today. At more than 6 million in size, this group is living fully "the best of both worlds." Media, entertainment channels, music producers, manufacturers of apparel foods, beverages, and even cars are targeting Latino tweens and teens, and through them, their parents.

A study by Teenage Research Unlimited in June 2001, said "Latino youths shop more and outspend their counterparts in the non-Latino world—despite coming from lower-income families. The average Hispanic teen spends $320 a month, 4 percent more than the average non-Hispanic teen. Favorite shopping outlets are malls (84 percent), supermarkets (80 percent) and discount chains (78 percent).[4]"

With an estimated $19 billion in spending power, Gen Ñ is not only changing the content of Hispanic TV, radio, and print media, but also general market media. In 2001, two English-language networks announced they would switch to Spanish soon. That is because one-half of the U.S. Latino population is under age 26 compared with age 39 for non-Hispanic whites.[5]

Generation Ñ includes the group aged 10 to 19, transitioning tweens, teens and young adults. More than their predecessors, they are generally bilingual and open to adapting to the American way of life. At the same time, they are proud of their Latino heritage and do not want to lose their Hispanic identity.

FIGURE 14.8

Generation Ñ (Aged 10 to 19)

in thousands

At 6.1 million, Gen Ñ represents 17 percent of the total U.S. Hispanic population.

Total Gen Ñ 10–19	Total Foreign Born 10–19	Total US Born 10–19	U.S.-BORN GENERATION			
			Second	Third	Fourth–Greater	Total
100%	20%	80%				
6,117	1,223	4,894	2,934	841	1,127	4,902
			60%	17%	23%	100%

© 2000 M. Isabel Valdés

This segment is presently leading the growth in the under age 18 category in the United States. While the non-Hispanic youth growth rate continues to decline, the Latino segment has grown exponentially. One in five teens in the United States is of Hispanic descent. Between 2005 and 2020 the Latino teen population is expected to grow 35.6 percent, compared with a decline of 2.6 percent among non-Hispanic whites.

FIGURE 14.9

Total U.S. Youth under Age 18, 2005–2020, projections

	in thousands			
	2005	2010	2020	change 2005–2020
White (non-Hispanic)	43,873	42,474	42,752	-2.6%
Hispanic	13,325	14,894	18,069	35.6
African American	10,292	10,195	10,835	5.3
Asian	3,449	3,887	4,763	38.1
Total	70,939	71,450	76,419	7.7

Source: U.S. Census Bureau, 2000 Middle Series

CROSS-OVER WINNERS

The success of Latin-style food, music, dance, and artists has paved the way for a Latin culture cross-over with mainstream culture. Finally! Nothing will do more for the healthy assimilation and acculturation of Latino youth into American society than to be appreciated by their non-Latino peers. In many cases, Latino youth are becoming trendsetters—as African Americans have done in the past decades. For example, growing numbers of non-Hispanic white, African-American and Asian youth are becoming fans of Latino artists, Latin music and rhythms, and enjoying Latin-style foods, and this has finally gotten the point across to Latino youth. They have nothing to envy. They have the best of both worlds!

Teenage Research Unlimited reported that in 2000 Hispanic teens spent an average of $144 per week, compared with $110 by all U.S. teens. Hispanic teens are less likely to have savings accounts than are their peers in the general market. Only 51 percent of Hispanic teens have a savings account compared with 68 percent of all teens. In general, this higher spending can be attributed to the fact that older Hispanic teens are likely to hold a job, have larger allowances from their families, and are less likely to be putting money into a savings account.

The mainstreaming of Hispanic entertainers such as Ricky Martin, Jennifer Lopez, Shakira, Marc Anthony and many others has provoked interest in Latino culture among non-Latino youth nationwide and made learning Spanish more attractive.

The U.S. Census Bureau confirms this growing national interest in the Spanish language. The percentage of U.S. public high school students taking Spanish courses more than doubled between 1982 and 1994, from 12 percent to 27 percent. In less than a decade, the number of registrations in Spanish courses at U.S. colleges and universities climbed by nearly 50 percent, from 411,000 in the fall of 1986 to 606,000 in the fall of 1995.

THE LANGUAGE AND MEDIA PUZZLE OF GEN Ñ

Language preferences for English or Spanish by Gen Ñs are a challenge to understand. A large percentage of Hispanic teens, especially foreign-born teens, speak Spanish at home, speak some form of "Spanglish" and Spanish with their Latino friends, and speak English with their non-Latino peers. Depending on the area where these teens go to school, their chances to speak and write using either good English or good Spanish are greatly limited, particularly in lower income areas. According to a July 2001 study by Harvard University's Civil Rights Project, "The abolition of bilingual education programs has led the students that have English as a second language to an environment where almost nobody speaks English." The study conducted nationwide states "racial segregation in U.S. schools has increased over the past decades and Hispanics are the group most affected by the rise." The most segregated states for Latino youth are New York, Texas, California, New Jersey, Illinois, and Florida."[6] Despite this, Hispanics continue to join the ranks of college students in growing numbers.

The most segregated states for Latino youth are New York, Texas, California, New Jersey, Illinois, and Florida.
—Harvard University Civil Rights Project

FIGURE 14.10

Total Enrollment in Higher Education

in thousands

Higher education has swelled in size and Hispanics have contributed to the growth.

	1988	1998	% change
Hispanic	680	1,260	85.3
Asian American/Pacific Islander	497	902	81.5
African American	1,130	1,585	40.3
White, non-Hispanic	10,289	10,196	-0.9

Source: American Council on Education. Minorities in Higher Education, 2000, *Hispanic Business,* December 2001. Used by permission.

Although many Latino teens speak English all or most of the time, many also may watch Spanish-language TV with their parents and relatives.

THE MEDIA PUZZLE

Media use by Latino youth is a puzzle as well. On the one hand, their exposure to mainstream media is much greater than previous generations of Latino youth since more than three-quarters were born and raised in the U.S. On the other hand, Spanish-language media have matured dramatically during the past decade making their programming more appealing to young viewers. These young Latinos take for granted, that they will find entertainment and other information in Spanish and English in all of their local area media, including newspapers, radio, TV, magazines and online sites. For example, a few years back *La Opinión,* the largest circulation Spanish-language newspaper in the U.S., launched a dedicated youth entertainment section, in both its print and on-line versions, that attracts large numbers of Gen Ñ readers. Spanish-language television and radio captures large shares of Latino youth, who are particularly drawn to their musical, entertainment, sitcom, and sports programs. More and new media formats are emerging to capture Hispanic youth. *Urban Latino TV,* a news-magazine-style show premiered in early 2002 on New York's local cable channel, Metro TV. Another example is Maya and Viva TV, formerly TV Ñ, that tested its one-of-a-kind English TV show that targets young Latinos.

Lastly, although many Latino teens speak English all or most of the time, many also may watch Spanish-language TV with their parents and relatives. The elders may watch *novelas* (soap operas), news and programs *en familia*—with the entire family—and so these teens grow up exposed to Spanish language. Hence, they tend to respond well to advertisements in Spanish. This positive response to Spanish-language advertisements has to do with two variables. First is the use of Spanish, "the language of the heart and emotions" of the Latino consumer. Second is the *in-culture* attunement of campaigns and ads specifically designed to talk to the mind set of this cultural segment.

EVERYDAY PROMOS FOR GEN Ñ

Marketing to the Emerging Majorities,[7] a monthly newsletter published by EPM Communications, Inc. summarizes Hispanic, African-American, and Asian research studies and provides up-to-date target, promotion, and marketing information. The newsletter reports a growing number of companies targeting Hispanic teens. For example, Frito-Lay, following the lead from its sister company in Mexico, is busy developing products that appeal to Hispanic teens' taste buds. Based on their qualitative research, they are introducing products such as Frito's Flaming Hot Corn Chips, a spicier version of Frito's Corn Chips, designed to satisfy the palate of Hispanic teens.

Soccer, baseball and basketball are good examples of activities where Latino teens and their parents can be found. Coca-Cola, for example, is taking advantage of this excellent "eye-level" marketing venue. They have extended their Latin American Copa Coca-Cola, a soccer competition for high-school students, to include U.S. high schools with significant Hispanic populations.

Fox Sportsworld Español, with its aggressive and all-inclusive sports programming, enjoys a large following of young and older Latinos. By representing sports teams ranging from the well known to the unknown from all countries in Latin America, they are able to talk to sports fans of all ages and interests.

PepsiCo

For more detail on this case and creative materials, go to
www.incultureapproach.com

Pepsi and Doritos

Campaign: *El Reventón De Sabór* (Mega-Party of Fun and Flavor)

BACKGROUND

Pepsi and Doritos (Frito-Lay) are the two global brands in PepsiCo's beverage and salty snack product portfolio. While both brands are a natural fit, PepsiCo had never developed joint advertising for the two brands. The *El Reventón de Sabor* (Mega-Party of Fun and Flavor) campaign that resulted from the pairing of Pepsi and Doritos was targeted to Hispanic consumers under age 24.

Regarding category use for both brands, the Hispanic market indexes at 50 percent below the general market in total salty snack consumption (Source: USDA Consumption Data). Conversely, the Hispanic market indexes at 80 percent above the general market in total carbonated soft drink (CSD) consumption (Source: advertiser data).

Overall, soft drinks are purchased and consumed more frequently than salty snacks. The marketing challenge was to link consumption of salty snacks to soft drinks to elevate consumption of the highly profitable salty snack category. On the other hand, as the soft drink that is usually consumed with a salty snack is a Coke, another challenge was to convert that behavior to a Pepsi.

In addition to driving joint consumption, Frito-Lay wanted to develop a campaign that would reverse the equity and awareness declines that the Doritos brand was experiencing among Hispanics. As well, Pepsi sought to build brand loyalty among Hispanics, specifically Mexican Hispanics, who migrate to the U.S. from their country of origin with a strong preference for Coke because of the brand's dominant position in international markets.

By developing a culturally-relevant message that was fun and engaging to Hispanic consumers, the *El Reventón de Sabor* campaign sought to drive joint Pepsi/Doritos consumption while increasing the profits of urban stores in 10 Hispanic markets, the campaign's channel and geographic focus.

CAMPAIGN OBJECTIVES

1. To establish momentum in both the Frito-Lay and Pepsi organizations to develop an inner city class of trade.
2. To contribute to 15 percent sales growth in urban stores in 10 key Hispanic markets.

3. To increase joint purchase intent/interest of Pepsi and Doritos by 5 points.

4. To increase unaided brand awareness for Doritos to 1996 levels of 87 percent. (Pretest results had shown that brand equity had fallen to 66 percent.)

5. To stem Doritos brand equity declines. (Doritos brand equity fell 23 percent between 1996 and 2001.)

TARGET AUDIENCE

The primary target audience for the *El Reventón de Sabor* campaign was Urban Influentials aged 18 to 34. From fashion to music to brand usage, this target sets the trends for the broader U.S. market. As well, this target was selected because both the carbonated soft drink (CSD) category for Pepsi and the salty snack category for Doritos (Frito-Lay) skew young. In addition, while the campaign sought to drive joint consumption among all Hispanics, the target audience skewed young to maintain and invigorate the youth and vitality of both brands.

The secondary target for the campaign was Hispanic Moms with Kids (Gatekeeper). The secondary target was of great importance because, while usage for Pepsi and Doritos skews young, Hispanic women are involved in 79 percent of all grocery purchase decisions (Source: SRC).

CREATIVE STRATEGY

The creative strategy for the campaign was: Pepsi and Doritos taste great on their own, but they're even better together. This strategy led to the creation of the branded expression *El Reventón de Sabor*—the "Mega-Party of Fun and Flavor"—when Pepsi and Doritos come together.

Two insights led to the development of this branded expression. First, "Reventón" is urban slang for party among Hispanic youth, speaking to the importance of social gatherings among all Hispanics.

Second, "*sabor*" is a term with profound meaning in the Spanish language. In addition to meaning "flavor" (a critical brand attribute for both Pepsi and Doritos), it also speaks to the flavor of life, especially as evoked among the richness and vibrancy of the Hispanic culture.

The first step in bringing this expression to life among our consumers was to select two Latino music artists that both represent the essence of the two brands and resonate with both the creative target (Hispanics aged 18 to 24) and the broader Hispanic audience. The individuals selected were Chayanne of Puerto Rico and Lucero of Mexico, two artists who represent two worlds of the U.S. Hispanic population (Caribbean Hispanics and Mexican Hispanics). Upon selection of Chayanne and Lucero, a proprietary piece of music was developed that played to the strengths of the two artists and that was indicative of the Latin music trends that have crossed over into the greater U.S. population. Through the two Latin music artists and the proprietary piece of music, the strategy was to create a magical moment that would communicate the fun and flavor that happens when Pepsi and Doritos come together—*El Reventón de Sabor.*

MEDIA STRATEGIES

The primary media for the campaign were Spanish-language television and radio, both of which index at 139 (Source: Nielsen) for Hispanics versus the general market. Based on historically successful launches and the campaign objectives, an aggressive communication goal of 80 percent 3+ effective reach was established. Total TRPs were weighted 64 percent against television and 36 percent against radio. The majority of TRPs were weighted against television to drive immediate reach for the joint consumption message while radio increased the frequency of message during the critical first four weeks of the campaign. The media strategy included a 17-week, product integration sponsorship on *Sábado Gigante,* (*Giant Saturday*) a program noted for being the longest-running variety show in the history of television. The *Sábado Gigante* sponsorship featured the host, Don Francisco, holding Pepsi and Doritos while the studio audience sang and danced to the *El Reventón de Sabor* music. The media strategy also called for the use of three creative units—:60, :30 and :15. The :60 unit was used to launch the campaign and for high-profile music and entertainment specials included in the media schedule. The :15 unit was run within the same commercial pod as the :60 or :30 units as a fun way to reinforce the message that, every time you put Pepsi and Doritos together, you start up *El Reventón de Sabor.*

PROMOTIONAL STRATEGIES

In addition to traditional media, the campaign utilized grass roots marketing tactics, specifically radio merchandising (i.e., radio remotes, van hits). The goal of these initiatives was to bring *El Reventón de Sabor* to our consumers, creating a fully-integrated, screen-to-street brand experience. At these events, consumers sampled Doritos and Pepsi and were given a collectable poster featuring Chayanne and Lucero, the two Latino music celebrities featured in the advertising. The poster was given to consumers with proof of Pepsi/Doritos joint purchase.

In addition, point-of-purchase materials featuring Chayanne and Lucero were developed to drive joint Pepsi/Doritos consumption in the critical inner city channel (*bodegas,* small independent grocery). These materials featured the headline, *Ponlos Juntos* (Put Them Together).

EVIDENCE OF RESULTS

Through the *El Reventón de Sabor* campaign, Frito-Lay and Pepsi created the first ever, fully-integrated, cross-divisional, cross-brand, multimedia program seeking to effect consumer behavior. As evidenced by the results, it succeeded in achieving each of the program's stated objectives.

- Succeeded in developing an inner city class of trade in 10 key Hispanic markets with a joint Pepsi/Frito-Lay sales organization to support it. In 12 months, the program went from 0 to 6,000 stores (Source: advertiser data).
- Achieved 25 percent sales growth for Frito-Lay and 31 percent sales growth for Pepsi in urban stores in 10 Hispanic markets, versus sales goal of 15 percent (Source: advertiser data).
- Increased joint purchase intent/interest of Pepsi and Doritos by 10 points, versus goal of 5 points (Source: Hispanic Equitrak study).
- Increased Doritos unaided brand awareness by 35 percent, returning the brand to the 1996 bench mark level of 87 percent brand awareness (Source: Hispanic A&U Study).
- Increased Doritos brand equity score by 46 percent (Source: Hispanic Equitrak study).

In addition to the results above, the television advertising succeeded in achieving 80 percent claimed ad awareness (Source: advertiser data), evidence of the impact of the program and of the memorable expression *El Reventón de Sabor* created to brand the joint-consumption occasion for Pepsi and Doritos.

SUMMARY

In the face of fierce competition, especially in the CSD category, PepsiCo sought to leverage the strengths of its two global brands for the first time in 36 years in a concentrated effort to drive joint consumption in the Hispanic Market. Through two of the Latino world's brightest stars and a proprietary piece of music, PepsiCo communicated the fun and flavor that happens when Pepsi and Doritos come together—*El Reventón de Sabor.* The result has been a significant contribution to sales increases in PepsiCo's key urban markets and dramatic gains in equity and awareness for the Doritos brand.

AGENCY: Dieste, Harmel & Partners, www.dieste.com

ONLINE TEEN PROMOS

Hispanic teens are navigating the web like their non-Hispanic counterparts, both in English and in Spanish. Advertisers are targeting them on their favorite websites. For example, Procter & Gamble developed an interactive on-line game for its Head and Shoulders product, providing teens, in a fun and light way, with all of the information they need about dandruff and how to win the battle.

Terra.com: Marketing Strategy Leverages Online/Offline Audiences

Global company, Terra Lycos, is a popular internet network and the largest internet-access provider in the Americas. Its family of 16 country-specific Terra sites in the Americas reaches 70 percent of the Latin American internet audience.

In 2001, Terra.com implemented an innovative and comprehensive marketing plan which integrated "above the line" (traditional mass media), "below the line" (field marketing, grassroots efforts, and special events), and "online" activities (sub channels and specials). Via this strategy, Terra.com offers its Hispanic audiences in the U.S. many different activities over the internet. An example is TerraGol.com, the first ever national soccer championship of beach soccer, offered throughout the five major U.S. Hispanic markets. Tens of thousands of spectators attend and hundred of teams compete in the matches held on the sand. For those who do not live in areas where matches were held, Terra.com offers the *La Copa Virtual* the first ever soccer tournament on-line.

Ice Cream Patrol

The first bilingual kids programming on a Spanish-language portal serves to unite kids with their parents. Studies show that Latino children lose their Spanish fluency as they grow older. The Ice Cream Patrol is a fun and interactive way to keep Spanish in the home and on the internet, while teaching kids important values.

Terra Compras-Pan Regional Latin America

Terra Compras offers several shopping options for U.S.Hispanics, one of which is *Regalos Sin Fronteras* (Gifts without Borders). This service allows Hispanics living within the U.S. to send gifts to friends and family via Terra Networks offices in Latin America. This service eliminates international shipping charges and the difficulty of local customs delays and expenses. Gifts arrive more quickly and the local Terra offices provide customer service. *Regalos Sin Fronteras* offers U.S. Hispanics the ability to be part of each special holiday back home. Terra.com is reportedly the only portal offering this service under this business model where goods are already in country and where the service is available in all markets of the region.

Canal Teen

This website (www.Terra.com/teen/) for adolescents brings them topics close to their hearts, like fashion, entertainment, first kiss, education, and gossip about celebrities. Canal Teen offers teens personal support in an entertaining and interactive medium, while offering a window to reflect and express themselves. The channel includes Chica Teen, a model-search contest, and Mode-look, an opportunity to win a professional photo portfolio.

EMERGING MEDIA FOR GEN Ñ

As previously mentioned, mass media in all shapes and forms are targeting this profitable Hispanic segment. English-language TV seems to have cracked the nut with the Latino-produced *The Brothers Garcia,* an English-language show with occasional Spanish.

Univision launched its second Spanish language network in 2002 and plans to focus more on youth-oriented programming—a smart move to ensure loyalty to Spanish-language media in the short term and long run as well. Meanwhile, Univision is developing programs for its teen audience with shows like *Amigas y Rivales (Friends and Rivals),* a new teen *novela.* It is also bringing back *Control,* a teen news and entertainment magazine, and a beach and bikinis music show called *Caliente.* Another new program, a weekly comedy hour called *Los Metiches (The Busybodies),* will roast U.S. celebrities and others, including well-known Latin personalities. Beefing up its sports programming in its new network is also expected to bring back the coveted youth segment. Soccer's World Cup will be broadcast on both networks.

On the cable front, Univision added to its Galavision cable network, "Telefutura" in January 2002. It targets young bilingual Hispanics. In October 2001, Telemundo network relaunched its Gems television cable network as Mun2 or MunDos ("worlds" in Spanish), also targeting the younger Latino segments.

Walt Disney Company's ESPN is offering a Spanish-language sports block on

Sunday nights, following the format of Fox Sports Español.[6] Maya Communications aired a new Latino teen program "in English with Spanish flavor" in mid 2001, with sponsorships by USAirways, Verizon, and others.

Young Latinos also turn to radio in surprising numbers, and radio operators are noticing! Three radio stations in Dallas, Texas, reformatted their programs to appeal to this segment, whose tastes include pop, ballads, salsa, rock en español, hip hop, and others.

Although there are analysts who believe that U.S. Hispanic teens are assimilating so well into U.S. culture that English-language media are all that is needed to reach them, others see Hispanic tweens and teens becoming increasingly interested in Spanish-language media. Olivia Llamas, project director for Yankelovich Hispanic Monitor, says their research shows that more than half of U.S. Hispanic teens identify themselves as "Hispanic Only" while only 6 percent consider themselves more American than Hispanic.[7]

GEN Ñ IN THE LABOR FORCE

School is not the only focus of this age group. Among men aged 16 to 19, just over half are in the labor force; among women in that age group, 41 percent are active in the labor force. Unemployment is also highest among this group of 16-to-19-year-olds—nearly 16 percent for men and 18 percent for women.

MARKETING TO GEN Ñ

From a marketing perspective, Generation Ñ has the importance of American baby boomers when they were in their "Woodstock" years. These young consumers are adopting brands and making them their own. Marketers who fail to attract this generation today may have lost them for their adult spending years. Aware of Gen Ñ's economic clout through influencing their parents, and the long term benefit to their brands, many corporations target Gen Ñ, in Spanish, English, or in both languages, since these teens tend to move quickly between languages.

However, the psychological differences within this age segment are too broad for easy definition. Their interests, likes, dislikes, and aspirations require a subdivision of the group. Therefore, Gen Ñ is subdivided into two groups, usually Tweens and Teens.

TWEENS

Aged: 10 to 14   *Segment Size: 3.1 million*

Aged 10 to 14, Latino tweens are at the center of the swelling growth of Hispanic youth, significantly outpacing the growth rate of all other Hispanic and
non-Hispanic age groups, except Asian youth.

FIGURE 14. 11

U.S. Children Aged 10 to 14, Projected Growth, 2001 to 2010

in thousands

| | Population | | Change | |
	2001	2010	Number	Percent
Hispanic	3,036	3,914	878	28.9%
White non-Hispanic	13,117	11,940	-1,177	-9%
Black non-Hispanic	3,071	2,757	-314	-10.2%
Asian	903	1,187	284	31.4%

Source: Adapted from American Demographics, September 2000, based on U.S. Census Bureau data

FIGURE 14.12

Generation Ñ "Tweens" (Aged 10 to 14)

in thousands

Like the younger Latinos (Los Bebés and Los Niños), 84 percent were born in the
U.S., and most (64 percent) born to foreign-born parents. They represent 16 percent
of the total U.S. Hispanic population.

Total Tweens 10–14	Total Foreign Born 10–14	Total US Born 10–14	U.S.-BORN GENERATION			
			Second	Third	Fourth–Greater	Total
100%	16%	84%				
3,059	501	2,558	1,651	379	529	2,558
			65%	15%	20%	100%

© 2000 M. Isabel Valdés

Although this generation of Hispanic teens is growing closer experientially
and psychographically to general market teens, it will take more than one generation to stave off the strong familismo bonds and family interactions. For
example, Latino tweens tend to be more dependent on their parents than their

Anglo counterparts. This phenomenon helps explain, in part, the strong adherence to traditional Hispanic value orientation observed in older acculturated Latinos and Latinas.

"Chicoismo" as mentioned earlier, is a powerful Hispanic cultural value that centers the child at the core of the family's dynamic. In fact, many Hispanic immigrant parents say the main reason behind their immigration to the U.S. is to provide their children with opportunities for a better life (see Latina/Latino Segments and Latin Boomer Segments later in this Section). The parents therefore tend to expect more attention, social time, and support from their children. In other words, these family centered cultural values are a two-way street that opens marketing opportunities to both children and parents.

HISPANIC TEENS

Aged: 15 to 19   ***Segment Size: 3.1 million***

The older group of Generation Ñ, Latino teens aged 15 to 19, will continue the dramatic growth experienced during the past decade. Mostly bilingual and bicultural, they may look like other teens to the outside world, and in many ways, they are like general market teens. However, culturally speaking, these teens are highly bicultural as mentioned above, and they move swiftly between two cultures. Most are proud to be Latinos, ready to "show-off" their Hispanic roots. Many have embraced the best-of-both-worlds attitude like no other Hispanic consumer segment before them. Today's teens are leading the dramatic growth of U.S.-born Latino consumers. Of all Hispanic teens, 77 per-

FIGURE 14.13

Generation Ñ Teens (Aged 15 to 19)

in thousands

Teens aged 15 to 19 make up 7 percent of the total U.S. Hispanic population.

Total Tweens 10–14	Total Foreign Born 10–14	Total US Born 10–14	U.S.-BORN GENERATION			
			Second	Third	Fourth–Greater	Total
100%	23%	77%	1,283	463	598	2,344
3,058	714	2,344	55%	20%	25%	100%

© 2000 M. Isabel Valdés

cent are native-born. Just over one-half are born to recent immigrant parents (55 percent) while a large segment have U.S.-born, third and fourth generation parents, 20 percent and 25 percent, respectively.

There is a tremendous variation in terms of value orientation, language preference and socio-economic status within Generation Ñ segment—between teens born to long-term, deep-rooted Hispanic parents of several generations and teens born to recently immigrated parents. Most teens born to deep-rooted parents have the advantage of parents who know English well and have a complete picture of U.S. society, can guide them in their homework, help them in college preparation, and so forth. In contrast, teens born to first generation immigrant parents who are themselves adjusting and learning the ropes, in many cases with little or no command of English, face unique challenges and disadvantages. This results in additional frustrations and stress to the typical teenagers' life, and higher dropout rates.

HispanTelligence estimates that Hispanics aged 16 to 24 have purchasing power of more than $25 million.

Many organizations are working to encourage Latino students to stay in school. The mission of the Hispanic Scholarship Foundation (HSF) is to double the current rate of Hispanics earning a college degree, from 9 percent to 18 percent by 2006. Sara Martinez Tucker, president and CEO of the Hispanic Scholarship Fund, is the leading authority fighting to improve the college attendance rate. "Of the 2 million Latinos who graduated from high school in 1996, 1.3 million will drop out from the educational system. Of the 700,000 who will start college, 400,000 will start at a community college. Less than 35,000 will get their associates degree, and then, less than 9,000 of those will transfer to the four-year institution. They will join the 300,000 who started there, but ultimately only 68,000 will get their college degree."[8]

Two national foundations, the Lilly Endowment, Inc. and the Bill and Melinda Gates Foundation contributed $50 million each to the HSF. In addition, corporations like Philip Morris, PepsiCo, Frito-Lay, Anheuser-Busch, Coca-Cola, AOL Time Warner, Univision, Disney, and many others contribute with scholarship funds and support educational programs for Latinos. The marketing return on investment is enormous. For example, I have observed from many market research studies that brand recall tends to be significantly higher when promotions contain an educational component.

MARKETING TO LATINO TEENS

Latino youth are increasingly targeted by English-language media; however, many seem to relate to traditional Hispanic programming and enjoy it more than English-language programming.

HispanTelligence, the research division of Hispanic Business, Inc., (www.HispanicBusiness.com) estimates that Hispanics aged 16 to 24 have purchasing power of more than $25 million. "An investor dreams of finding a trend like this," said a San Francisco-based merchant banker.

Marketers have learned that general market translation or adaptation does not work when targeting Hispanics, and teens are particularly sensitive to this issue. "Latino Teens are really bicultural," says Giuseppi D'Alesandro, senior marketing manager of PepsiCo. Latino youth are increasingly targeted by English-language media; however, many seem to relate to traditional Hispanic programming and enjoy it more than English-language programming. For example, in the first half of 2001, Univision carried 23 of the 25 Spanish-language teen programs, the majority of which were soaps, or novelas. Why is that? Because many watch with their parents. Following traditional family values, Latino families tend to be closely-knit and spend a lot more time together than non-Hispanic families.

Understanding Hispanic culture and reflecting their values and beliefs in ads for Hispanic teens can make or break the ad. This Latino teen culture is a hybrid between the general market teen and the Latino *"barrio* teen" culture that can also vary by U.S. region. It's not just about being bi-cultural. As with their younger siblings, they entered primary school later in life and many reside at their parents' home longer than their Anglo counterparts, as is traditional in Hispanic culture. They feel the pull of *familismo,* the strong Hispanic family orientation, sometimes at odds with the lifestyles and values of their non-Hispanic peers. Often this dichotomy leads them to a conflict of allegiances. Because second, third, and fourth or

"Twenty- and Thirty-Somethings"

Latinas and Latinos

Aged: 20 to 39   *Segment Size: 11.2 million*

This group of young Hispanic adults, aged 20 to 39, is in its main household formation years. About 14 percent of Hispanics are in their 20s, and another 16 percent in their 30s. They are responsible in part for the growing Latino baby boom, as they begin to have families and settle down. By the time they reach age 39, about one-half will be married and 12.6 percent divorced. Thirty-seven percent are either single or not "legally" married. ("Common law" marriage is more common among low income Hispanics, and in the rural areas in Latin America.) Someone in this age group heads 4.5 percent of Hispanic households.

FIGURE 14.14

Latinos/Latinas (Aged 20 to 39)

in thousands

Nearly one-third of U.S. Hispanics are aged 20 to 39. Nearly half are foreign-born.

Total Latinos/as 20–39	Total Foreign Born 20–39	Total US Born 20–39	U.S. BORN GENERATION			
			Second	Third	Fourth–Greater	Total
100%	47%	53%	2,866	1,242	1,781	5,887
11,175	5,287	5,887	49%	21%	30%	100%

© 2000 M. Isabel Valdés

Slightly over one-half (53 percent) of this group were born in the U.S. The rest are first-generation immigrants (47 percent). Members of this Latino age segment tend to be bilingual and bicultural. They are the fastest growing group among first-time employed persons. They are hard workers and intent on providing for their families by taking advantage of all the United States has to offer while at the same time retaining their strong family and cultural ties. Many work two jobs.

LA "OLA LATINA"

La Ola Latina, the positive Latin wave that emerged in the past decade, caught many Latinos and Latinas by surprise. For many, it has been a great labor bounty as insurance, financial, and many service corporations, social organizations, and even government agencies continue aggressively to recruit bilingual professional and para-professional Hispanic men and women. Radio and TV programming, in both Spanish and English, cable, magazines, on-line businesses, and websites compete for their attention.

On the high-tech front, many Latinos and Latinas have leapfrogged into the cyberworld, have started new companies, and have learned to take advantage of financial products and services. For the Christmas holiday in 2001, our family received an unusual gift from a Hispanic advertising agency—delicious frozen tamales. These were ordered online from a Latina business owner, www.sylviascanasta.com.

Many younger Latinas and Latinos have banking relationships, use credit cards, and value the stability of the banking system in the United States. They are more likely than previous generations to save their money and buy a home using a mortgage, travel by plane, and purchase new cars. Median income for households in this age group ranges from about $24,000 for those under age 25 to $34,000 for those in their late thirties.

EDUCATIONAL ATTAINMENT

FIGURE 14.15

Educational Attainment of Latinos Aged 25 and Older, 1999

No College	70.3%
Some College	18.7
College Graduate	8.2
Graduate Degree	2.8

Source: Tomás Rivera Policy Institute, "Latinos Have the Power," 2000

Most men in this age group are in the labor force, ranging from 89 percent among those aged 20 to 24 to 94 percent of those aged 30 to 34. About 65 percent of Latinas are in the labor force. Before September 11, 2001, young Latinas and Latinos were experiencing much lower unemployment rates than in previous years, lower than 7 percent for men aged 20 to 24, and less than 4 percent for the older groups. Among Latina women, unemployment rates were slightly higher—just under 9 percent for those aged 20 to 24 and about 6 percent for the older group. Labor force participation rates for Hispanics are expected to remain relatively stable for this decade, according to projections from Bureau of Labor Statistics. By mid-2002, the circumstantial evidence suggests the economic slowdown of 2001 and early 2002 had a detrimental impact on the employment rates of young Latinas and Latinos.

Before 9/11, young Latinas and Latinos were experiencing much lower unemployment rates than in previous years.

YOUNG ENTREPRENEURS

One way that Latinas are taking their labor force participation into their own hands is by starting their own businesses. Latinas have the fastest growing small-business-ownership rate in the United States. From construction businesses to beauty salons, restaurants, and child care centers, Latinas are pursuing entrepreneurial careers. However, corporate America has still not discovered the Hispanic "business-to-business" sector. "B2B" is still in its infancy, yet a growing opportunity is there.

Concerned with the need to have more Latinas in management and involved in making executive-level decisions, many corporations are sponsoring community based organizations that train and prepare the professional Hispanic women to become business, government, and community leaders of the New Millennium. For example, the National Hispana Leadership Institute (NHLI) in Washington, D.C., has already trained many women leaders. Created in 1987 with the funding support of Coors Brewing Company, NHLI has graduated many Latinas who today fill corporate and government positions across America. Corporations that want to attract top-level Latinas would be smart to help fund these types of organizations. It builds "share of heart" and at the same time opens the doors to recruit top performers.

Other organizations that fulfill the same role include Hispanic trade organizations and the National Society of Hispanic MBAs.

Home Ownership Rates

National Average	66%
Non-Hispanic White	73
African-American	47
Latino	46

Source: Tomás Rivera Policy Institute, "Latinos Have the Power," 2000

NOT ALL ACCULTURATE QUICKLY

The acculturation process can take several generations and, even then, some aspects of the "newly acculturated mindset" continue to be traditional.

As discussed in detail in my previous book, the acculturation process can take several generations and, even then, some aspects of the "newly acculturated mindset" continue to be traditional. In September 2001, I conducted focus groups with immigrant Latinas in their twenties and thirties in Los Angeles and Miami for this book. Although this was a small sample from which to extrapolate, I was surprised to observe that many of these women are retaining "traditional" behaviors and not shaking off some of their parents' behaviors that are today old-fashioned. For example, some of these women were reluctant to have checking accounts or credit cards, or to pay bills by mail, still hiding their hard-earned money under the bed. Unfortunately, this behavior makes Hispanics and their households targets for crooks who prey on them. Their lack of familiarity is surprising to me since so much effort has been directed at them from many financial institutions. This shows how resilient certain beliefs and behaviors are, and how hard it is for some Latinos to acculturate. However, based on data I have reviewed for the past ten years, this type of traditional behavior tends to rise with the growing number of recent immigrants, but then declines steadily after ten to twenty years of residence in the United States.

YOUNGER VERSUS OLDER LATINOS AND LATINAS

Despite the 19-year age span within this segment aged 20 to 39, these Hispanic consumers have many things in common. For example, parents in the younger group, aged 20 to 29, are forming their families with a first child, while couples in the older group, aged 30 to 39, are also having children. Some Latina moms continue having children well over age 40. These later-in-life births are not a new trend among Hispanic women. On the contrary, they follow a social tradition prevalent in many Latin America countries. For example, it is common to find Latin American families where the first grandchild of the family is the same age as the youngest child of the grandparents. In sum, the childbearing years of the traditional Hispanic woman are longer than those of the white non-Hispanic woman in the United States. This has far-reaching marketing implications since companies selling diapers and baby food, for example, need to address a wider range of ages and issues than they do in the general market. For other products or service categories however, such as car insurance, cosmetics, apparel, etc., the broad age range does make a difference. Marketers should split the age segment following the specific needs of the category of business.

TWENTY-SOMETHING LATINAS/OS

Aged: 20 to 29   Segment size: 5.4 million

For the first time, twenty-somethings and thirty-somethings within the U.S. Hispanic market are enjoying dedicated new media. With more than 11 million strong, more disposable income than preceding generations and greater assimilation to American mainstream culture, American businesses have created special media vehicles to talk to them directly. Magazines like *Latina Magazine, People en Español,* and *Latina Style* spearheaded the trend. Today many TV, radio, and print media are available to target American Latinas and Latinos.

FIGURE 14.18

Latinos/Latinas "Young" (Aged 20 to 29)

in thousands

Young Latinos and Latinas represent 15 percent of the total U.S. Hispanic population.

Total Young Latinos/as 20–29	Total Foreign Born 20–29	Total US Born 20–29	U.S.-BORN GENERATION			
			Second	Third	Fourth-Greater	Total
100%	38%	62%				
5,434	2,067	3,367	1,748	659	961	3,367
			52%	20%	28%	100%

© 2000 M. Isabel Valdés

LATINA MINDSET

New studies confirm what many businesses in the personal care and apparel business already knew. Most Hispanic women are very fashion conscious and like keeping up with the latest styles. A study by Cotton, Inc.,[9] found that 68 percent of those Latina women surveyed said they buy new and different items rather than replacing the staples in their wardrobes. In addition, 49 percent said they tend to buy the latest styles at the beginning of the season, rather than waiting for the prices to drop. The same study says Latinas and African-American women were more likely to have spent more than $100 on apparel in the month before the survey than their non-Hispanic and Asian-American counterparts. The same over-indexing pattern takes place in cosmetics, fragrances, creams, hair-care products, and any item that has to do with personal appearance.

People en Español created a tracking study to follow the Latino-Latina segment called Hispanic Opinion Tracker, the HOT™ Study. The study shows that like many Latina women around the world, and most American Latinas make every effort to "look gorgeous" by spending considerable amounts of money on cosmetics and related items.

FIGURE 14.19

Latinas Are Getting Gorgeous

Percent using cosmetics and beauty services

Among Hispanic women:

- 93 percent wear lipstick
- 56 percent wear lipstick daily, *vs.* 38 percent of non-Latinas
- 91 percent of Hispanics wear fragrance
- Almost half (48 percent) use fragrance daily
- Almost 65 percent own at least three fragrances,
     vs. 48 percent of non-Hispanics
- Latinas are twice as likely (36 percent) as non-Latinas (18 percent)
     to visit a nail salon at least once a month
- They are 29 percent more inclined to use sunscreen makeup
     (18 percent) than non-Latinas (14 percent)

Source: Hispanic Opinion Tracker HOT™ Cosmetic Module, *People en Español*, 2001

THIRTY-SOMETHING LATINAS/OS

TABLE 14.20

Latinos/Latinas "Thirty-Something" (Aged 30 to 39)

in thousands

Latinos and Latinas in their thirties make up 16 percent of the U.S. Hispanic population. They are 20 percent more likely to be foreign-born than their Twenty-Something counterparts.

Total "30-Something" Latinos/as 30–39	Total Foreign Born 30–39	Total US Born 30–39	U.S.-BORN GENERATION			
			Second	Third	Fourth–Greater	Total
100%	56%	44%	1,118	583	820	2,521
5,741	3,220	2,521	44%	23%	33%	100%

© 2000 M. Isabel Valdés

IN SEARCH OF IDENTITY

Like so many immigrants, Latinas are in search of their own identity. They would like to have a comfortable picture of themselves. The focus groups I

conducted recently with Latinas in Los Angeles and Miami echoed the issues raised in the book *The Maria Paradox,*[11] on the struggle to live and succeed in two cultures, in two worlds.

Deborah Rosado Shaw, a Latina mother of three and successful businesswoman, wrote a book sharing her experiences, growing up poor in the *barrio* in New York City and then making it big. Her book, *Dream Big!*[12] has touched the psychology of many Latinas in search of role models. The many letters she received from readers attest to the search of these women and how ready they are to grow and play a role in American society. She contributed the following comments from her readers.

From an aspiring entrepreneur, age 56: "My daughter and I are working on starting a new business. There are times I am so tired, I just can't see, and there seems to be no time for my friends and family. . . . I like your idea of finding mentors. I will take what you said and apply it to my life. It's certainly my time to live."

A 23-year-old executive assistant from Florida: "Since I started reading *Dream Big!* I have not put it down. I have found focus, registered for school and changed my major to business administration. I owe that all to you. Thank you for the inspiration."

A customer service trainer in Georgia wrote: "I read the entire book on my flight back from New York to Georgia. I used several passages from the book when I was teaching Customer Service seminars. . . . [and] shared other women's triumphs over tragedy and bad luck."

MARKETING WIN-WIN-WIN[13]

These comments show a reality many Latinas face today while trying to live, raise a family, and succeed in a different culture. And it is a fact that many suffer from depression. In many cases, depression is a novel experience. Spearheading the new wave of pharma-marketing to Latinos, Pfizer Pharmaceuticals has targeted Latinas directly with an *in-culture* multi-level educational campaign for Zoloft, its antidepressant drug.

As many Latinas need information and role models, and businesses are trying to connect with their target audience and "win," marketers can find many opportunities here to connect and build their businesses and their "share of heart." This we refer to as "win-win-win" strategies. For example, Harris Bank partnered with a call-in problem-solving show, *Carina Su Mejor Amiga* (*Carina, Your Best Friend*), anchored by a clinical social worker. The show addresses many concerns and issues shared by Latina women today. This is another example of an *in-culture,* integrated campaign, where the ad agency, Sanchez and Associates, Harris Bank's agency of record for the Hispanic market, goes well beyond the typical advertising campaign by capitalizing on Latinas' need for support, role models—and a friend. Harris Bank builds "share of heart" and opens its doors for business in a very friendly manner, and Latinas both learn about a bank with a heart and how to deal with their emotional issues—a win-win-win strategy.

In the packaged goods category, Procter & Gamble pioneered a win-win-win, integrated Hispanic marketing model by developing a multi-media educational marketing venue, *Avanzando con tu Familia.* Before retiring from a 30-year career at P&G, Neil Comber—probably the first U.S. Hispanic marketer—devised and executed this original *in-culture* marketing tool. In one Spanish-language magazine that meets the mindset of Hispanic moms, it brings together retailers, advertising, promotions, product information, scholarships and more. Thanks to P&G, the *Avanzando con tu Familia* case study is presented below.

Procter & Gamble

For more detail on this case and creative materials, go to www.incultureapproach.com

Campaign: Avanzando con tu familia (Getting Ahead with your Family)

BACKGROUND

In 1999, Procter & Gamble reviewed its approach to Hispanic marketing and con-cluded it needed a major revamping in effort, resources and the programs them-selves. The *Avanzando con tu Familia* program, (Getting ahead with your Family) was the first outcome of this new approach, and has become its signature His-panic effort. It is a comprehensive multibrand program designed to reach out to the consumer on many different levels.

Marketing is undergoing the most radical change since television or radio were invented. This seismic change comes from the electronic revolution in media and personal computing. As a consequence today's consumers have much more information, which in turn has made them less passive/more activist and most importantly, put them more in control.

P&G believes that to be heard in today's world marketers need to deliver real, added value. Simply delivering a media plan with crisp product messages in :30 TV or radio ads, or slick ad pages in magazines will not suffice. Consumers are looking for brands and companies to deliver solutions to problems or, better yet, relationships to satisfy needs on an ongoing basis.

Hispanic consumers are no different in their expectations. They are not sim-ply Latin Americans living in the U.S. Their whole environment changes when they come to the U.S. They are influenced by many more worlds than in Latin America. They have many more choices, and they have more control of their lives, too.

Realizing all of this, P&G stepped back from its Hispanic marketing efforts in 1999 to re-evaluate its approach. This was driven in large part by the fact that although P&G continued to be one of the biggest Hispanic marketers, individual brand efforts had begun slipping, with a consequent slip in market shares. A.G. Lafley, now President and CEO, had returned to the U.S. and led the charge. Early on, it was determined that a successful renewed effort would need a dedicated organization with a separate budget from the general market. Given the quantity and caliber of people available in Puerto Rico and the need to move quickly,

Puerto Rico was designated the lead for the effort. The Puerto Rican team's understanding of the culture and language would be invaluable, along with support from Cincinnati headquarters. Dieste Harmel & Partners was added to the roster of Hispanic agencies to help with the strategic, conceptual, and creative development of the *Avanzando* program.

THE OBJECTIVES

- To build a deeper relationship/connection of the brands and company with the Hispanic consumer.
- To generate commitment and support from the food/drug/mass retailers to these consumers.
- To leverage P&G scale through a cohesive multibrand program.

RESEARCH

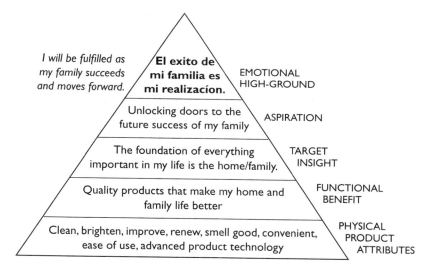

In-depth interviews in home and focus group settings revealed the wholehearted focus of Latina mothers on their children. This is probably an outgrowth of the very strong Latin American family centricity and the American immigrant dream of building a better life not so much for themselves as for future generations.

Additionally, research revealed that consumers had very strong attitudes about P&G brands like Tide, Pampers, Pantene, Bounty and Crest. Latinas were effusive about how these brands cared about them because they delivered such great performance, making their lives easier. Based on these insights it became clear there was an opportunity for P&G and its brands to help Latina consumers make their lives even better by delivering on a higher order of need, as depicted in the hierarchy below. The hierarchy culminates in *El exito de mi familia es mi realizacíon* (The success of my family is my fulfillment). This became the driving concept around the *Avanzando* program.

After brainstorming, it was decided to focus on four pillars, namely education, health, home, and traditions, as being the ones central to helping Latinas get their family ahead.

TARGET AUDIENCE

The primary target audience selected was Spanish-dominant Latinas aged 18 to 49, with households of 3+ persons. The secondary audience was bilingual Latinas, aged 18 to 49, with 3+ person households. The reason for the primary selection was that these are the women who are least reached by general market information, and yet are most likely to have the kind of aspirations for their families that were uncovered.

Further demographics indicated that these target consumers were likely born in Latin America, married young, and probably followed their husbands to the U.S. Pyschographically they want the American dream, primarily for their family ("my children are my life"), while maintaining and wanting to pass on their Latin-American heritage ("the traditions of my home country are important to me").

MEDIA STRATEGIES

A magazine focused on the mother, but with something for all the family, became the central piece to reach the target audience. It was concentrated in New York, Chicago, South Florida, key parts of Texas, and Southern California. Door-to-door delivery to 4 million homes (around 50 percent of Hispanic homes) allowed unprecedented direct-to-consumer reach.

The magazine format was designed to reach the consumer at different levels of her hierarchy of needs starting at the bottom. It delivered incentives to purchase the brands through coupons and samples; made the connection to the brands and product benefits in an uncluttered environment; and provided information the consumer was seeking for the care and development of her family. From the core of the door-to-door effort though, many other elements were developed to further reach out.

EXECUTIONAL EXAMPLE

The third edition (Wave III) ran in Fall 2000 and focused on education. It covered topics from how parents can get involved in their children's school, to opening the doors to college, and what to know before buying a computer. This magazine was supplemented with TV spot promos announcing the magazine and consumer offer. In addition, a radio effort reiterated some of the tips from the magazine.

The education theme was extended into the consumer promotion and the trade incentive. Specifically, in-store demonstrators handed out $50 off coupons for Gateway computers when consumers purchased three participating P&G brands. Additionally consumers who mentioned Avanzando got $300 worth of free software. Retailers were offered computers in exchange for agreeing to merchandise the offer and P&G brands. In turn, they were encouraged to give the computers back to the community. Kmart, for example, fully endorsed this idea and donated its 200 earned computers to the educational arm of LULAC, a Hispanic civil rights organization. Finally, on the eve of national elections a live webcast was held for the community to discuss key educational issues affecting the Latino community with representatives of the presidential candidates.

RESULTS

In the first two years, there were four waves of the program. With each wave, sales results increasingly improved as each time more retailers participated with a greater number of stores. In the latest waves, more than 2000 stores supported the program. This became the biggest contributor to P&G sales among Hispanic consumers, generating in excess of $40 million in incremental sales.

Beyond the raw sales data, however, *Avanzando* delivered significant other benefits. It became the bellwether project internally and externally evidencing P&G's commitment to this market and consumer. It won awards both internally and externally. Importantly, in many cases it was the key to opening retailers' doors to doing joint Hispanic marketing efforts with P&G. And finally, research indicated very positive perception of *Avanzando* by the community with almost 90 percent approval.

AGENCY: Dieste Harmel & Partners, www.dieste.com

LATIN BOOMERS

Aged: 40 to 50   *Segment size: 8.3 million*

Now in their 40s and 50s, Latino "boomers" were born between the mid 1940s and the mid 1960s. Their biggest difference from other boomers is that many of them were born outside the United States. The younger boomers (aged 40 to 49) represent 14 percent of total Latinos, and the older group (aged 50 to 59) about 9 percent of the Latino population.

Many of these Hispanic consumers are among the 27 percent of the Hispanic population who entered this country before 1980. They have lived in the United States about one-half of their adult lives, and they are likely to have obtained citizenship.

FIGURE 14.21

Latino Boomers, "Young" and "Mature" (Aged 40 to 59)

in thousands

The Latino boomers represent 24 percent of the total U.S. Hispanic population.

Total Latin Boomers 40–59	Total Foreign Born 40–59	Total US Born 40–59	U.S.-BORN GENERATION			
			Second	Third	Fourth–Greater	Total
100%	59%	41%				
8,307	4,941	3,366	1,187	1,091	1,088	3,366
			35%	32%	33%	100%

©2000 M. Isabel Valdés

THE SANDWICH GENERATION

Like their Anglo counterparts, Latin boomers are the sandwiched generation, often responsible for parents and other family members while they still have children living at home. Unlike their Anglo counterparts, however, they also are caught between two cultures. Their host country's culture and their children motivate them to acculturate, as do continuing opportunities to get ahead. However, changes in value systems and lifestyle do not happen easily, particularly as we get older. Therefore, a large segment of Latin boomers is very traditional, enjoys the "very close knit" family ties, prepares meals made from scratch, believes more in curative than preventive medicine, and tend to distrust financial institutions, large organizations, or government agencies.

To take advantage of all that the U.S. has to offer, many Latina boomers work outside the home to help pay for the college education of their children, send money back home, and save for retirement. However, they are least likely to have been able to take advantage of higher education opportunities themselves. Their English-language proficiency lags behind and they may toil in low paying service jobs, with long hours, to give their family the good things in life. Overall, they are more concerned with financial matters than previous generations.

The more acculturated Latin boomers have credit cards, many own two or more new cars which are an important status symbol, and an increasing number are taking out mortgages. Among this age group, there is almost universal ownership of durable goods such as cameras, television sets, microwave ovens, and DVD players. Computer ownership is one of the top priorities of these families as is their childrens' financial education, math ability, and other skills. For example, a VISA 2001 study conducted with Hispanic parents shows a very strong interest and focus on skills beyond the traditional subjects. The vast majority (94 percent) believes "it is very important for students to learn practical  money skills before graduating from high school" and that schools should be required to teach those skills. However, on a more practical note, 93 percent said they learned about managing money from their own life experiences, and only 13 percent think that money management is learned in school.

FIGURE 14.22

Important School Issues for Hispanic Parents

	Percent who agree
Enforcing discipline in the classroom and on school property	97%
Ensuring students learn practical money skills before graduation	94
Improving technology in the classroom	94
Improving school facilities	91
Reducing class size	82

Source: VISA's Annual Back-to-School Survey, VISA U.S.A.

FIGURE 14.23

Latin Boomers "Young" (Aged 40 to 49)

In thousands

The younger segment of boomers represent 14 percent of U.S. Hispanics.

Total Young Boomers 40–49	Total Foreign Born 40–49	Total US Born 40–49	GENERATION			
			Second	Third	Fourth–Greater	Total
100%	59%	41%				
5,045	2,952	2,092	778	647	688	2,092
			37%	31%	32%	100%

©2000 M. Isabel Valdés.

The group aged 45 to 54, whether foreign or native born is most likely of all age groups to be middle class.

LATINO MIDDLE CLASS

Unlike previous generations of 40-to-60-year-old Latinos, the boomers, "young" and "mature" have increasingly improved their incomes. Many of them are becoming active members of the growing Latino middle class, specifically those born in the U.S. Their income has risen consistently an many have seen their dreams come true. An age-standardized study by Tomás Rivera Institute, released in 2001, estimates that almost 2.7 million Hispanic households had incomes of $40,000 or more. This represents about 40 percent of Latino households, compared with 60 percent of Anglo households that were considered middle class by the same measurement. The group aged 45 to 54, whether foreign or native born is most likely of all age groups to be middle class. Education of native-born Hispanics is helping to raise the number of middle-class households, whereas increased immigration by foreign-born Hispanics is making it more difficult to increase the overall share of Hispanic households that could be considered middle class.

BANK ONE'S APPROACH

A special section in *Hispanic Business* in December 2001 examined Hispanic middle class growth. The magazine

FIGURE 14.24

Latin Boomers "Mature" (Aged 50 to 59)

In thousands

The older segment of boomers represent 9 percent of all U.S. Hispanics.

Total Mature Boomers 50–59	Total Foreign Born 50–59	Total US Born 50–59	GENERATION			
			Second	Third	Fourth–Greater	Total
100%	61%	39%	409	444	420	1,274
3,262	1,989	1,274	32%	35%	33%	100%

©2000 M. Isabel Valdés

reported that one reason Hispanic households attain middle-class status is that adult and teenage members of the household often pool their incomes.

Baby-boom Latinos are buying into one of the main factors in the American dream. Of households with incomes of $40,000 or more, 79 percent own or are buying a home. Even among those with household incomes of less than $40,000, 30 percent own or are buying a home, according to *Hispanic Business* data published in December 2001.

Stephen Trejo, an associate professor at the University of Texas at Austin and an expert on labor economics, concluded that the geographic concentration of Hispanics is an aid to increasing the number of middle class households. Large numbers of middle-and-upper class households clustered in a region can help each other, he notes. These are "magnet" areas for marketing financial, insurance, and upper-end products and services. While at Cultural Access Group (CAG), I had the pleasure to devise a strategy for Bank One, targeting these consumers. This is how the "magnet" areas were identified and the recommendations that followed the study.

First Chicago Bank's merger with Bank One was completed with a name change in September 1999. In order to transfer brand equity from First Chicago and build awareness for the Bank One brand in Chicago, Bank One identified specific business opportunities to target Hispanic consumers. In 1999, Chicago was the fourth largest Hispanic market and home to 1.1 million Hispanics who constituted 14.3 percent of the population of Chicago. The Hispanic population grew 33 percent from 1990 to 1998, significantly faster than the total Chicago market. Accelerated growth was expected.

Baby-boom Latinos are buying into one of the main factors in the American dream: of households with incomes of $40,000 or more, 79 percent own or are buying a home.

Analysis showed that Chicago Hispanics were younger than the market in general with 65 percent of Hispanics under age 35, versus 50 percent of the total market.

Chicago's Hispanics were found to be more affluent than Hispanics in other Bank One markets. They are, however, less affluent than the general market. One-quarter have incomes of less than $25,000 compared with 18 percent of the general market.

Bank One identified an opportunity to target affluent Hispanics in Chicago. CAG's Zip Value Clusters™ were used in conjunction with GeoScape International to generate maps of population clusters in Chicago residential areas. Zip

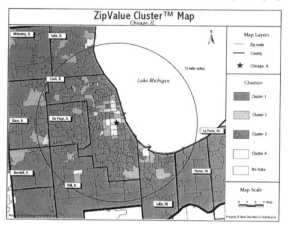

Value Cluster data were compared with customer data from the bank to help define the targeted customers. Of four clusters in Chicago, one was identified as having the highest upside potential for Bank One. This cluster contained 84,053 households spread over 255 zip codes. Estimated average income in this cluster was $76,719 and the customers in the cluster represented 21 percent of Chicago households, but 41 percent of Chicago's upside banking potential.

Another cluster was identified as having a less-acculturated segment with 181,433 households concentrated in 17 zip codes. Estimated average income in this cluster was $40,948 and analysis showed that households in this cluster were likely unbanked or underbanked.

Cultural Access Group (CAG) recommended that Bank One use a media campaign to increase awareness and branding of the bank, retain current customers of First Chicago during the conversion, maintain market share, and build its database for future marketing. The media campaign used English- and Spanish-language television, English and Spanish outdoor, English and Spanish newsletters, bilingual direct mail, inbound bilingual telemarketing, and outbound telemarketing, which responded to the potential customer's language of preference.

LOS GRANDES

Aged: 60+ Segment size: 3.3 million

The population of the U.S. is aging fast and becoming more multicultural and ethnically diverse. The number of Americans older than age 65 will double over the next 30 years to close to 70 million, or 20 percent of the population by 2030.

Los Grandes, the senior members of the Hispanic market, aged 60 and over in this segmentation, represent about 9.5 percent of all Hispanics. They must learn the ropes of both being seniors and being in a very different culture. Their social activities tend to center around the family, and many take care of their grandchildren and other family members. It is estimated that about 11 percent live with their extended families. Often they become surrogate parents while their sons and daughters are studying or at work. These "triple-decker" households often live with three generations under one roof.

I call them the "triple-decker" households for marketing purposes. Many communication strategies can target one or more of these "triple-deckers" to get to the purchase decision-makers.

FIGURE 14.30

Three Generations Under One Roof

Hispanics vs. non-Hispanics

Hispanic	11%
White	6
Black	7
Asian	9

Source: Based on AARP's 2001 "In the Middle" report, Washington, DC

FIGURE 14.31

Los Grandes Segment (Aged 60+)

In thousands
Los Grandes are 9 percent of the total U.S. Hispanic population.

Total Los Grandes 60+	Total Foreign Born 60+	Total US Born 60+	U.S.-BORN GENERATION			
			Second	Third	Fourth–Greater	Total
100%	64%	36%	525	260	404	1,189
3,299	2,110	1,189	44%	22%	34%	100%

©2000: M. Isabel Valdés

About 1 million Hispanic households or nearly 11 percent of total Hispanic households are headed by someone aged 65 or older.

Overall the minority senior population is growing faster than the non-minority population and Hispanics are the fastest growing minority segment in this age group. By 2030, one quarter of the population will be composed of what are now minority groups. The challenge and opportunity created by the multicultural senior population will be huge, impacting healthcare, consumer products, and all kinds of service industries.

Presently, about 1 million Hispanic households or nearly 11 percent of total Hispanic households are headed by someone aged 65 or older. This share is projected to increase dramatically as the percentage of Hispanics in this age group increases during the coming decades.

FIGURE 14.32

Projected Growth in Los Grandes Segment

in thousands*

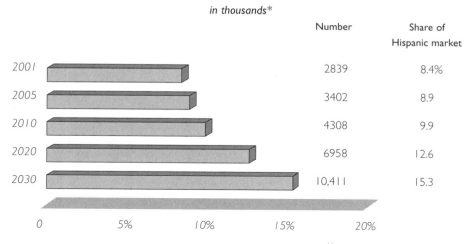

	Number	Share of Hispanic market
2001	2839	8.4%
2005	3402	8.9
2010	4308	9.9
2020	6958	12.6
2030	10,411	15.3

*Does not include population of Puerto Rico

Source: U.S. Census Bureau (NP-D1-A) Projections of the population by age, sex, race, and Hispanic origin for the United States: 1999 to 2100 (Middle series)

The vast majority of Latino seniors have married at one point in their lives. Among the group aged 65 and older, only 5.7 percent report having never married. By this age, about 62 percent are still married, 11 percent are divorced, and nearly 22 percent are widowed.

Spanish is the only language for the majority, particularly among women. As expected, this has a major impact on these

Latino seniors' socio-economics are the most disadvantaged

- Household income tends to be the lowest of all Hispanic age segments. The median personal income of Latinos aged 65+ is $6,411 while that of non-Hispanic whites is $10,764.

- 21 percent of Latinos aged 65+ live below the poverty level, compared with 10 percent of non-Hispanics

- Fewer Latino seniors have completed high school; only 29.4 percent have a high school diploma, compared with 67 percent of the rest of the population in this age category.

- Latinos aged 65+ are less likely to receive social security benefits than their non-Hispanic counterparts.

consumers' quality of life, access to information, and so forth. A Southern California study by Latino Health Access with Latinas over age 65 found that 9 out of 10 participants were monolingual Spanish-speakers. This limits senior communications and social interactions outside their family and peer groups. The study concluded, "Language barriers may be presumed to restrict access to healthcare and public services, let alone comprehension of prescription drug inserts or completing applications for various public services."[14] The same report quotes the National Academy on Aging's data, stating "incomes were lower among older, single Latina women than any other group."

The vast majority of Hispanics in this age group adhere to traditional Hispanic culture values and do not want to lose the "old ways" of the Hispanic family. Some, particularly the foreign-born who migrated for political and economic reasons, are coping with issues of nostalgia and acculturation. Aging in a different culture is not an easy process for many. For example, many wonder and worry who will take care of them as they age, especially if they do not have a personal pension or a personal network, and no family lives near by. Only about 21 percent of Hispanic men and 23 percent of Hispanic women aged 65 and older had a pension in 1998, according to the Bureau of the Census. Unfortunately, Hispanics lose both affluence and education as the group gets older. A 2001 study by The Media Audit with almost 10,000 Hispanics shows that only 4.6 percent of Latinos older than age 50 have annual incomes of $50,000 or more. In contrast, 14.3 percent among non-Hispanic white, and 7.3 percent among African-Americans have incomes of more than $50,000.[15]

Los Grandes Health Snapshot

- The Cancer Registry reports that 60 percent of women diagnosed with cervical cancer have never had a pap smear. Latinas, especially older women, tend not to have pap smears.

- Cardiovascular disease, high cholesterol, and other conditions have higher prevalence among Hispanic seniors.

- Diabetes is significantly higher among senior Latinos.

- The mortality rate of Latinos over age 65 is nearly twice as high as the overall rate in California.

- Retired Hispanics have less health insurance than non-Hispanic retirees.

- Latinos tend to rely on pharmacists for medical advice and avoid seeking medical care due to lack of insurance, along with language, and cultural barriers.

- Non-traditional medicines (herbal, homeopathic, healers) are popular among Latino seniors.

Healthwise, Hispanic seniors tend to present a sad picture. Unfortunately, preventive healthcare is not presently a part of our culture, as fatalism ("It is the will of God") tends to be the norm. Many of the present health conditions could be improved drastically with health-care education and preventive check-ups. Corporate America could extend its programs to the Los Grandes segment as a part of their community marketing initiatives. As with the younger age segments, this is an opportunity to build "share of heart" with the Hispanic community.

Seniors are presently the most disadvantaged segment of the Hispanic market. In 2000, anthropologist Dr. Judith Fridenberg published *Growing Old in the Barrio,* an ethnographic picture of aging in Spanish Harlem that illustrates the urban New York City *barrio.* Under her direction, the Smithsonian brought to life the "Latino Virtual Gallery" (http://latino.si.edu) that includes a program with photographs, video clips, and oral histories of Latino seniors. This first-of-its-kind web-based program is a real-life immersion of what daily life is like for an elderly person whose income barely covers basic needs.

It is always important to underline, though, that not all Hispanic seniors are poor nor Spanish-monolingual. However, the lower-income group tends to be over-represented in large urban areas and any program for targeting Los Grandes needs to consider their socio-economic realities.

LOS GRANDES' MINDSET

Over half, 64 percent of Los Grandes, are foreign-born and most migrated to the United States as adults. The presence of older Hispanics varies considerably by market. For example, Cubans in Miami are over-represented in this age group, whereas in Los Angeles Cubans are under-represented.

As in the general market, the Latino senior market segment is divided into two distinct age sub-groups that are important to consider because they have quite different needs and realities. The "Young Senior" segment is aged 60 to 69, and the "Senior Senior" group is aged 70 and older. Because women tend to live longer than their male counterparts, the share of Latina seniors in this segment increases with age.

FIGURE 14.27

Los Grandes by Age (60+)

In thousands

Young seniors are about 5 percent of the total U.S. Hispanic population. An additional 1.3 percent are in their 70s and only about one of one hundred Latinos is aged 80 or older.

Age	Total	Males	Females
Young Seniors			
60-64	1,031	478	553
65-69	788	349	439
Sub-total for age 60-69	1,819 (100%)	827 (45%)	992 (55%)
Senior Seniors			
70-74	606	250	356
75-79	442	168	274
80+	432	147	285
Sub-total for age70-80+	1,480 (100%)	565 (38%)	915 (62%)
Total of Los Grandes	3,299 (100%)	1,392 (42%)	1,907 (58%)

© 2000 M. Isabel Valdés

Like most seniors today, Latino seniors are caught between generations, and, as previously mentioned, they have to live between different cultures and sometimes conflicting cultural values. They are caught between their personal aging and health needs, the needs of their children and grandchildren, and occasionally even the needs of their own aging parents—"Triple-Decker," or "Sandwiched Generation" households. According to AARP, an organization that studies the U.S. senior market on an ongoing basis, far more Latinos tend to feel sandwiched between generations compared with other cultural groups.

For example, cultural differences between seniors and their more Americanized family members in daily or weekly interaction with *el abuelito* (grandpa) or *la abuelita* (grandma) can be a challenge. The younger generation's perspective and world views sometimes disagree with the senior's "non-acculturated" perspective. This often creates emotional gaps. On the other hand, the more acculturated family members can provide seniors the help, degree of "comfort," and support they need. As a matter of fact, the family, when available, can be a great help in communicating with or marketing to Latino seniors.

FIGURE 14.29

Hispanics and non-Hispanics Who Feel "Sandwiched"

All	18%
Hispanic	32
White	16
Black	19
Asian	28

Source: AARP "In the Middle: A Report on Multicultural Boomers Coping with Family and Aging Study," 2001

MARKETING TO "LOS GRANDES"

The need for Latino senior marketing is finally being recognized. For example, AARP has been the leader in targeting the Los Grandes with its 2001 launch of a national branding and membership campaign and a complete re-engineering of their services and products to meet the needs of Latino seniors. Another example is a special program announced by Pfizer to reduce the cost of drugs for low-income people. This brings Pfizer to the forefront of Latino "share of heart" while building brand recognition. It not only captures seniors' attention with a positive spin but the attention of their families, building loyalty within the entire Hispanic community. We all notice when a company does something special to help those in need.

The suggestions that follow can help make sure your Latino senior marketing program is on target.

Targeting "Los Grandes" Senior Seniors *In-Culture*

Communication challenges that affect seniors need to be considered when targeting Latinos *in-culture*.

- As most are foreign-born, assume many Latino seniors will have little or no knowledge of the basics of your program, service, or product. These need to be explained in clear, basic terms.

- Assume most have vision problems, hence print must be large and clear.

- Use simple sentences; repeat key points of the message in user-friendly formats.

- Good and basic Spanish is essential. Bilingual communication is recommended to reach seniors and their caretakers.

- Low literacy is an issue with "Los Grandes." Therefore, consider visual communications with verbal explanations (photographs, videos, radio, and toll-free numbers manned by Spanish-speaking operators). Distrust of government organizations and small legal print is common.

- Include the family, the adult children, and grandchildren whenever possible, either in the promotions (e.g. "Ask your family") or in the actual programs, if applicable. Communications messages should show the grandparent at the table with the grandchild, or going to the clinic or theater with another family member.

- Repeat and communicate slowly in a pace that feels relaxed and joyful

- Show uplifting, smiling faces in visual materials, ads, and commercials.

- When developing Hispanic senior communications strategies or campaigns, include caretakers in the research. They will act as gatekeepers.

- Always show respect. Use the more formal, traditional communications approach.

- Test for linguistic barriers. Depending on country of origin, some words will not be known to all. Make it as easy as possible.

- Don't expect seniors to look for your telephone number. Provide it.

- Traditional Hispanic social customs, familismo, and religious traditions and values must be considered and used whenever possible.

- Senior Latino children are many times the "official" shoppers, caretakers or

continues . . .

"managers" of their parents. Hence, the strategic analysis has to determine if the primary target is the senior, the caretaker-children, or both.

• To reach seniors and their caretakers, campaigns need to integrate mass media with community organizations. They need to support print and new electronic media as well. Latino seniors, some more than others, are highly skeptical and often reluctant to try new services or to go to unknown places, or use unknown brands or products. They will prefer to wait and see how others like a new product or service before trying it themselves. Therefore, additional time needs to be included in the marketing process to allow the social-network, word-of-mouth communications system to work.

GETTING OLDER—YOUNGER

A small segment of Latino Grandes follows a similar pattern as the general population "age compression phenomenon," that is, older consumers who behave, feel, and live as younger people more so than any older age consumer before them. This small Latino segment will most probably grow significantly as the Latina/Latino segments reach middle age. Presently little is known beyond the author's qualitative measurement. However, based on the present financial and educational gains of younger Hispanics, it can be guessed that the older-younger señors and señoras are more acculturated, professional, and have more education, higher incomes, and are bilingual or mono-lingual, English.

Notes

1. I am indebted to Hispanic marketing expert Jorge Calvachi, NFO Chicorsino, for this Hispanic culture value name.
2. Term coined by Hispanic advertising guru Norma Orci, La Agencia de Orci and Asociados, to address the level of emotional connection of consumers with a brand, company or category or others.
3. Katz Hispanic Media, *Radio Check* newsletter, July 2001.
4. "Untapped teen segment," *Marketing to the Emerging Majorities,* Vol. XIII, No.7, EPM Communications, Inc.

5. "Better Reception: TV Sets Out To Engage Young Latinos," *Dallas Morning News,* Online June 3, 2001.

6. "Schools More Separate: Consequences of a Decade of Resegregation", quoted by *Hispanic Business*.com, EFE, July 18, 2001

7. Published by EPM Communications, www.epmcom.com

8. *Morning News On-line,* Dallas (TX), June 3, 2001.

9. For more on Hispanic teens and media, see "Habla English," by Rebecca Gardyn, *American Demographics* magazine, April 2001.

10. *Hispanic Outlook,* January 28, 2000.

11. Hispanic Market Radio Check, October 2001.

12. Gil, Rosa Maria and Carmen Vasquez, *The Maria Paradox: How Latinas Can Merge Old World Traditions with New World Self-Esteem.* New York: G.P. Putnam's Sons, 1996.

13. *Fireside,* January 1, 2001.

14. Win-win-win strategy by Emily Gantz McKay, a pioneer in Hispanic community marketing.

15. Aging Latinas study, Latino Health Access, Executive summary, p. 3, 2001.

16. Research Brief from The Media Audit, August 27, 2001.

SECTION 3

HISPANICS AS CUSTOMERS

Chapter 15

Using *In-Culture* Household Intelligence

Thanks to the generosity of ACNielsen, I am able to make available for the first time to the general public selected findings from the ACNielsen Homescan Hispanic panel.™

This panel, which captures the specific purchase behavior of more than 1,500 Hispanic households, is a unique and rich resource of data about what Hispanics buy and where they shop for different kinds of items, especially in comparison with non-Hispanic households and degrees of acculturation within the Hispanic market. First, this section provides information about the methodology of the ACNielsen Homescan Hispanic panel. Next, it provides examples of actual categories of products illustrating the differences between Hispanic and non-Hispanic spending and purchase behavior in five different types of retail channels.

Through these examples it is easy to gauge the powerful strategic value of *in-culture* household panel data for business marketing and media planning.

THE PANEL

The ACNielsen Homescan Hispanic panel was launched in early 1999 in four counties in the Los Angeles market. It captures the purchasing habits of over 1,500 Hispanic Households on an ongoing basis. Its national expansion is currently planned.

Given that Los Angeles' four-county "market" is the largest U.S. Hispanic market (6.6 million Hispanics) and predominantly Mexican (75 percent), by far the largest sub-cultural segment in the Hispanic market, the data from the ACNielsen Homescan Hispanic panel is a reliable predictor of purchase behavior in other Hispanic Mexican markets.

To protect ACNielsen's client proprietary information, examples presented are reported only to the category level, rather than for specific brands. To learn more about ACNielsen's Homescan panel and what their data and research services can do for your company, you can go to their website http://acnielsen.com or call V.P. of marketing, Ken Greenberg at 516-682-6041.

The panel is designed to represent the complete buying-behavior spectrum of Hispanic households, both acculturated and unacculturated. It tracks all purchases by language segments: Spanish-only/Spanish-preferred, bilingual, and English-only/English-preferred. It reports UPC (products with bar codes) purchases from all retail outlets including large supermarkets, small grocery stores, and small bodegas. Even products purchased outside the United States are captured if they have a bar code. The ACNielsen Homescan Hispanic panel also allows comparisons between Hispanic and non-Hispanic households.

The primary shopper and the family members in the recruited households are trained and given a small electronic device, the scanner or *Escanito,* that scans the barcodes of all household purchases brought into the home, by all family members. The scanner stores the information on the nature of the item purchased (brand, flavor, size), the price paid, and also consumer and other information such as who was present on the shopping trip and where the item was purchased. Panelists send this information to ACNielsen weekly by calling a toll-free number and holding the scanner up to a telephone where it transmits to a central computer.

Panel information is provided by store department (such as dry grocery), by category (e.g. household cleaners), by segments (e.g. abrasive cleaners–powdered), and by brand. The measures that are captured, their definition, a potential application, and a specific example of their use are listed below.

MEASURE	DEFINITION	APPLICATION	EXAMPLE
Dollar Volume per 1,000 Households (see below for a definition)	The projected dollar purchases for a product group, category, or brand expressed on a per 1,000 household basis.	This measure shows the true "dollar value" of a household to a manufacturer or retailer.	For every 1,000 Hispanic households, $42,047.59 was spent on baby food during the twelve-month period ending December 23, 2000. This was significantly more than non-Hispanics whose dollar volume per 1,000 households was $12,983.41. **Implication:** On average, marketing baby food to the Hispanic household and home market is likely to yield greater dollar volume.

DOLLAR VOLUME

Dollar volume per 1,000 households is the result of several measures of purchase behavior. It is determined by how many households in the group or segment purchase the product (Penetration), how often they buy (Occasions per buyer), and how much they spend when they buy (Dollars per occasion, buying rate/dollars per buyer). These measures are described below.

MEASURE	DEFINITION	APPLICATION	EXAMPLE
Penetration	*How many* The percent of households that purchased the product group, category, or brand at least once.	This measure shows the potential to sell a product to more consumers in a particular segment based on how many are buying it now.	33.1% of Hispanic households and 16.4% of non-Hispanic households purchased baby food at least once during the twelve month period. **Implication:** Hispanic house-holds are more than twice as likely to buy other baby products as are non-Hispanic households.
Occasions per Buyer	*How often* The average annual number of product group, category, or brand purchase occasions among product group, category, or brand buyers.	This measure shows whether the group in question buys frequently or infrequently—often a good indicator for timing promotions or for planning multiple unit purchase promotions.	Among Hispanic households, the average baby food buyer purchased baby food 6.3 times per 12-month period. Non-Hispanics purchased slightly less often at 6.0 times per 12-month period. **Implication:** Purchase incentives for both groups should be planned at two-month intervals.
Dollars per Occasion	*How much* The average product group, category or brand dollars spent per product group, category, or brand purchase occasion.	This measure is an indication of heavy, moderate, or light purchase rates, and hence heavy, moderate or light usage. It can indicate whether a particular segment is likely to add significantly to sales if you can capture its buyers.	Among Hispanic households, the average baby food buyer spent $20.13 on each baby food shopping occasion. Non-Hispanics spent $13.25 on each baby food shopping occasion. **Implication:** Hispanic house-holds could be more receptive to high multiple unit purchase incentives or specially priced multi-packs that retain them as your customer.
Buying Rate (Dollars per Buyer)	*How much* The average annual dollars spent on each product group, category, or brand among households that purchased.	This measure is a combination of dollars per occasion and occasions per buyer, showing the dollar volume of purchases in a year.	Among Hispanic households, the average baby food buying household spent $127.23 during the 12-month period on baby food. Non-Hispanics spent $79.24 during the 12-month period. **Implication:** Capturing a Hispanic household can lead to 60% more dollar sales in baby food than capturing a non-Hispanic household.

PENETRATION INDEXES

Side-by-side comparison of the data on the Hispanic and non-Hispanic house-holds in conjunction with information on household penetration allows marketers to project the *probable or estimated* number of buyers of a given product or product category in the entire Los Angeles market. With this number and the data on dollars spent per buyer in the panel, it is possible to gauge the total dollars spent by a particular group and/or a specific Hispanic language segment in the entire Los Angeles market. These two measures are described below.

MEASURE	DEFINITION	APPLICATION	EXAMPLE
N = Raw Buyers	The unprojected (raw) number of product group, category, or brand buying households.	Used to project the number of buyers in the entire market area (see below).	175 Hispanic Homescan Panel households purchased baby food during the 12-month period. 176 non-Hispanic Homescan Panel households purchased baby food during the 12-month period.
Projected Buyers (000)	The number of pro-jected households that purchased a given product group, category, or brand at least once.	This measure could show the number of target consumers in a market for media planning purposes.	On an LA market basis, 513,300 Hispanic households purchased baby food during the 12-month period. 620,100 non-Hispanic households purchased baby food during the 12-month period. **Implication:** Despite the dispar-ity in their total number in the population of Los Angeles, there are almost an equal number of Hispanic baby food consumers as non-Hispanic.
Projected Dollars (000)	The projected dollar purchases for a prod-uct group, category, or brand.	This measure indicates the poten-tial dollar volume of a category in the entire market, possi-bly for use in setting priorities for market-ing spending across several markets.	On an LA market basis, Hispanic households spent $65,312,520 on baby food during the 12-month period. Non-Hispanic households spent $49,138,300 on baby food during the same period. **Implication:** If only one special program is affordable, all other things being equal, a Hispanic marketing program in Los Angeles could yield greater ROI than one directed to the general market.

CATEGORY PURCHASES BY SUB-SEGMENTS

By using measures *at the total market level,* you can compare directly the data from the ACNielsen Homescan Hispanic panel for Hispanics and non-Hispanics. Normalizing the projected dollars for non-Hispanics to 100 and indexing the projected dollars for Hispanics to this measure permits a quick and highly accurate comparison of Hispanic and non-Hispanic purchases for categories, segments, and brands. This measure is described more completely below.

MEASURE	DEFINITION	APPLICATION	EXAMPLE
Dollar Index *(vs. non-Hispanics)*	The vertical percent of total projected dollars indexed to non-Hispanics.	In a portfolio of brands, a company with a Hispanic-marketing program might see which categories or brands are underdeveloped and which are over-developed among Hispanics in order to set objectives and priorities for the program.	Hispanics have a dollar index of 359 for baby food. Everything being equal, Hispanics spent 3.59 times as much on baby food as non-Hispanics. **Implication:** Baby food is highly over-developed among Hispanics, due to higher penetration and a higher buying rate. Marketers can gain a great deal by increasing share among current buyers.

STRENGTH OF BRANDS

Two measures demonstrate the *strength of brands* within product categories. Dollar share shows a given brand's share of all category purchases in a given time period. This measure can point out significant differences between the strength of a particular brand among Hispanic and non-Hispanics. Another measure, Loyalty, shows how dispersed category purchases are among brands or how much brand switching occurs. These measures are described below. As previously stated, to protect ACNielsen's clients and subscriber's proprietary data, branded data is masked in the examples below.

MEASURE	DEFINITION	APPLICATION	EXAMPLE
Dollar Share	The percent of dollar sales accounted for by each brand (based on total module).	A manufacturer can see if its brand(s) are as widely used among the Hispanic market as in the general market.	Among Hispanic households, Brand X has a 60.6% dollar share of the baby food—strained category. Among non-Hispanics, it is 21.8%. Implication: Brand X's share of baby food purchases is nearly three times as high among Hispanics as among non-Hispanics. This may be due to a number of factors including successful *in-culture* marketing in the U.S. or familiarity with the brands from country of origin, what I call "brand heritage."
Loyalty (Share of Requirements)	Among brand buyers, the percent of their category dollar volume that was satisfied by the brand. The remaining dollar volume went to competitive brands.	A manufacturer can see if many consumers are loyal to their brand or competitors, or rather, if consumers seem likely to switch based on advertising or price promotions.	Among Hispanic households that purchased Brand X of baby food, it satisfied 62.2% of their total strained baby food dollar volume requirements, compared with 22.4% loyalty for Brand X among non-Hispanics. Brand Y has 46.4% loyalty among Hispanics and 73.3% loyalty among non-Hispanics. **Implication:** Hispanics are more loyal to Brand X than they are to Brand Y, and more loyal to Brand X than are non-Hispanics. Brand Y has an uphill battle to capture new Hispanic buyers from Brand X.

PRICE INFORMATION

The ACNielsen Homescan Hispanic panel also captures price information. Two key measures include price paid and percent of volume purchased with some type of consumer incentive (e.g. reduced shelf price, or coupon). These measures are described below.

MEASURE	DEFINITION	APPLICATION	EXAMPLE
Average Price Paid (Dollars per Unit)	The average price paid, in dollars and cents, per unit purchased.	Marketers and retailers can see how the price paid for a given brand compares with other brands or how the price Hispanic consumers paid compares with the price paid by non-Hispanics.	Among Hispanic households that purchased strained baby food, the average price paid was $.49 per unit purchased. This compares to $.53 per unit paid by non-Hispanics. This price disparity may be size, brand, or channel driven. **Implication:** Hispanics in Los Angeles paid more for a jar of strained baby food than did non-Hispanics.
Percent of Dollar Volume Purchased on Deal	The percent of product group, category, or brand dollar purchases on which the consumer perceived that a deal was present. Deals are defined as features, displays, store coupons, manufacturer coupons, price packs, and bonus packs.	Marketers and retailers can see how many Hispanic consumers are taking advantage of store and consumer promotions as compared with non-Hispanic consumers. Such information may lead them to increase their *in-culture* programs or to re-assess their current programs.	Among Hispanic households, 12.7% of all baby food dollar purchases involved a consumer-perceived deal. For non-Hispanics, it was 23.8%. **Implication:** Hispanics in Los Angeles are either not being offered the same number of deals (due to language/culture related reasons, different media or shopping patterns), or they are not taking advantage of them for a variety of reasons.

POINT OF PURCHASE (CHANNELS)

The ACNielsen Homescan Hispanic panel records where consumers buy each item that they scan. These purchase locations are classified into eight channels or store types:

- Large, $2 million-plus grocery stores
- All other types of food outlets (butcher, bakery, etc.)
- All other grocery outlets (e.g. smaller supermarkets)
- All other outlets (e.g. swap meets, department stores)
- Drugstores
- Discount stores
- Warehouse clubs
- Convenience stores/gas stations (which includes *bodegas*)

By looking at the percentage of each product category that is purchased in each channel by Hispanics and non-Hispanics, significant insights can be gained about differences in where each group shops. Point-of-purchase varies considerably for Hispanics, depending on the specific product or category.

MEASURE	DEFINITION	APPLICATION	EXAMPLE
Percent of Dollar Volume— **Total Grocery**	The percent of product group, category, or brand dollars distributed across the total grocery channel.	How much of a given category was spent by each group in traditional grocery stores?	Among Hispanic households, 81.8% of all baby food dollars were spent in the total grocery channel. For non-Hispanics, it was 75.8%. **Implication:** Hispanics' baby food purchases are more heavily concentrated in traditional grocery stores than are non-Hispanics'.
Percent of Dollar Volume— **$2 million-plus Grocery**	The percent of product group, category, or brand dollars distributed across the $2 million-plus grocery channel.	How much of a given category was spent by each group in larger supermarkets? This channel was traditionally the primary recipient of major marketer's trade programs, particularly food manufacturers'.	Among Hispanic households, 78.3% of all baby food dollars were spent in the $2 million-plus grocery channel. For non-Hispanics, it was 74.6%. **Implication:** Hispanics' baby food purchases are more heavily concentrated in large supermarkets. Due to traffic volumes, promotions delivered to larger stores are likely to be cost efficient for the manufacturer.
Percent of Dollar Volume— **A/O Grocery**	The percent of product group, category, or brand dollars distributed across the All Other grocery channel.	How much of a given category was spent by each group in smaller supermarkets? This channel was traditionally given less attention by major marketers due to its fragmented nature and the presence of wholesalers.	Among Hispanic households, 3.5% of all baby food dollars were spent in the All Other grocery channel. For non-Hispanics, it was only 1.2%. **Implication:** Hispanic consumers also buy more baby food in smaller grocery stores than do non-Hispanics.
Percent of Dollar Volume— **A/O Food**	The percent of product group, category, or brand dollars distributed across the A/O food channel. A/O food channels may include such outlets as bakery, butcher, beverage, fruit stands, coffee, and candy stores.	How much of a given category was spent by each group in other types of food outlets?	Among Hispanic households, 0.9% of all baby food dollars were spent in the A/O Food channel. Virtually no measurable purchases were made in A/O Food outlets by non-Hispanics. **Implication:** While its share of volume is low, the A/O Food channel contributes to baby food purchases among Hispanics.

MEASURE	DEFINITION	APPLICATION	EXAMPLE
Percent of Dollar Volume— **A/O Outlets**	The percent of product group, category, or brand dollars distributed across all other outlets. All Other outlets may include such outlets as department stores, hardware stores, dollar stores and swap meets.	How much of a given category was spent by each group in non-food outlets?	Among Hispanic households, 3.8% of all baby food dollars were spent in All Other outlets. For non-Hispanics, it was 3.4%. **Implication:** Hispanic and non-Hispanic consumers shop these stores equally for baby food.
Percent of Dollar Volume— **Drug**	The percent of product group, category, or brand dollars distributed across the Drug channel.	How much of a given category was spent by each group in drugstores?	Among Hispanic households, 1.3% of all baby food dollars were spent in the Drug channel. For Non- Hispanics, it was 1.1%. **Implication:** Hispanic and non-Hispanic consumers shop these stores equally for baby food.
Percent of Dollar Volume— **Discount**	The percent of product group, category, or brand dollars spent at discount stores.	How much of a given category was spent by each group in discount stores?	Among Hispanic households, 3.8% of all baby food dollars were spent in Discount stores. For non-Hispanics, it was 8.4%. **Implication:** Presently, non-Hispanics buy significantly more of their baby food in discount stores than do Hispanics. This may represent an opportunity for baby food manufacturers, particularly if they are already selling and promoting in this channel, to attract Hispanic families, particularly those less acculturated (in Spanish).
Percent of Dollar Volume— **Warehouse Club**	The percent of product group, category, or brand dollars distributed across the warehouse club channel.	How much of a given category was spent by each group in warehouse clubs?	Among Hispanic households, 4.9% of all baby food dollars were spent in the Warehouse Club channel. For non-Hispanics, it was 11.3%. **Implication:** Non-Hispanics buy significantly more of their baby food in warehouse clubs than do Hispanics. This may represent an opportunity for baby food manufacturers, particularly if they are already selling and promoting in this channel.

MEASURE	DEFINITION	APPLICATION	EXAMPLE
Percent of Dollar Volume— **Convenience/Gas**	The percent of product group, category, or brand dollars distributed across the Convenience/Gas channel. The Convenience/Gas channel includes such outlets as *bodegas* and *autoserv marketas*.	How much of a given category was spent by each group in convenience stores, bodegas and autoserv marketas?	Among Hispanic households, 3.7% of all baby food dollars were spent in the Convenience/Gas channel. For non-Hispanics, it was 0.0%. **Implication:** While their share of volume is relatively low small nearby stores realize a meaningful amount of baby food purchases among Hispanics.

Source: Adapted from ACNielsen Homescan Hispanic panel materials

In sum, analyzing data from the ACNielsen Homescan Hispanic panel can help manufacturers and retailers not only ascertain and measure actual market volumetrics by many indicators, but also identify opportunities to satisfy Hispanic consumer needs more effectively. In addition, marketers, manufacturers, and ad agencies can use trended data to assess the impact of dollars invested in advertising, marketing, and promotion dollars to reach Hispanic households, across Hispanic language segments or degree of acculturation. Lastly, the ACNielsen data provides reliable, longitudinal intelligence and insight to help retailers execute more effective merchandising programs and measure their impact.

Chapter 16

What Latinos Buy

Culture and acculturation have a measurable effect on the choices Hispanics make, the volume they buy, and the places where they shop. The following case studies of six categories, based on actual household data from the Los Angeles market demonstrate two things. First, the need to understand culture and acculturation at the outset of a business and marketing plan. Second, the value of tracking Hispanic volumetric data with a strategic tool such as the ACNielsen Homescan Hispanic panel, which compares non-Hispanic and Hispanic market purchases based on acculturation. Acculturation is measured by comparing the data by the three main language segments: Spanish-dominant, bilingual, and English-dominant.

To simplify the data analysis by language segments in this chapter, I refer to Spanish-only/Spanish-preferred simply as Spanish-dominant and to English-only/English-preferred simply as English-dominant. A word of caution: Hispanic language segments vary in size because of large immigration, and there are therefore far more Spanish-dominant Hispanic households in the United States than English-dominant. It must be kept in mind at all times while interpreting the data that the *value*, size, and volume of the Spanish-dominant household is greater across the board.

SHORTENING PRODUCTS

Overall, we Hispanics consume more shortening products than non-Hispanics. Like the French who rely on "best flavor" every day and prefer to cook their favorite dishes with animal fats such as goose, Latinos in many countries use lard as shortening in cooking and baking. Meals prepared with lard have a distinct flavor that tastes delicious to those who grew up with this cooking style. Lard is an essential ingredient in some recipes such as *empanadas,* where other shortenings do not have the chemical properties needed to produce the same results. In addition, the use of animal fat is particularly pervasive in rural areas where it is readily available. Hence, despite declines taking place annually, many U.S. Hispanic immigrants continue to cook with lard today. However, you must keep in mind that the non-acculturated segments are presently significantly larger than the acculturated, English-dominant.

In addition to lard, Hispanic households tend to use more oil than do non-Hispanic households because frying is a common cooking method. In addition, Hispanic households tend to cook from scratch at home rather than buying prepared meals from the grocery store or eating out at restaurants. Together, these behaviors increase the use of shortening in Hispanic households.

ACCULTURATION AND SHORTENING PRODUCTS

However, acculturation often brings with it a change in meal preparation that affects the choice of shortening products. Why is this change tied to acculturation? For two main reasons: 1) In the U.S., Hispanics are exposed to more health-related information and advertising that leads them to choose products that are advertised as being healthier such as margarine or oil, rather than lard. 2) Hispanics in the U.S. have a growing awareness of alternative products, such as vegetable shortening, via word-of-mouth, advertising, and promotion of packaged products.

This link between acculturation, behavior change, and its consequent new product adoption can be seen clearly in household penetration levels of lard, oil, vegetable oil, vegetable shortening, and butter in the ACNielsen Homescan Hispanic panel and Scantrack data shown below. (Figure 16.1)

Household penetration of both lard and cooking oil, for example, is significantly higher among Hispanic than non-Hispanic households. However, as Hispanic households become more acculturated, fewer buy oil. Household penetration declines from 88 percent among Spanish-dominant consumers, to about 82 percent among bilingual consumers, to just over 65 percent among English-dominant consumers. The latter group of more acculturated Latinos tend to behave more like non-Hispanics and may eat out or purchase ready-to-eat meals at similar rates as the average American household in Los Angeles. Penetration of lard shows a similar pattern, albeit at lower levels, whereas penetration of vegetable shortening, margarine, and butter show the reverse trend. Both trends are due to the same forces that have influenced the general market. More acculturated households may cook less because of busy lifestyles, smaller families, and increased disposable income. Increased proficiency in English results in greater awareness of health issues related to eating lard, and greater use of more healthful cooking methods such as sautéing rather than deep-frying. Butter, which non-Hispanic households learn to avoid because of cholesterol, seems more popular in Hispanic households. Qualitative studies show that butter is a popular "luxury" item in Latin America and also in lower-income Hispanic households in the U.S. Hence, butter consumption increases with acculturation, despite a greater awareness of health issues.

FIGURE 16.1

Impact of Acculturation

Percent household penetration of types of shortening

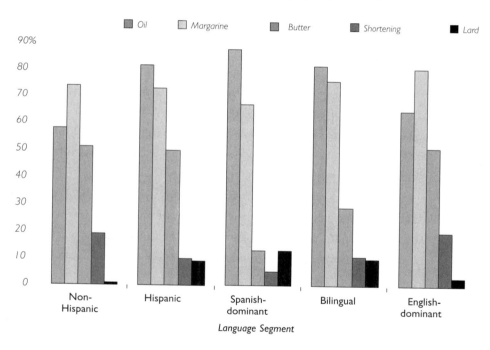

Source: ACNielsen Homescan Hispanic panel

Dollar Amount and Shopping Trips

Household penetration does not tell the entire shortening category story. The number of shopping trips and the amount spent on these items also varies by market groups and with acculturation. Non-Hispanics, for example, make an average of 2.6 shopping trips a year for cooking oil, whereas Hispanics make

5.4 trips. However, frequency declines with acculturation. Spanish-dominant consumers make more trips—6.3 per year, bilinguals 4.7 trips, and English-dominant make fewer—3.6 trips. Non-Hispanics spend an average of $2.85 for oil when they shop for oil. Hispanics spend more, $3.96. With acculturation, however, the spending declines. Spanish-dominant spend $4.27, bilinguals, $3.75 and English-dominant, $2.69. However, you must keep in mind that the non-acculturated language segments are presently significantly larger than the acculturated, English-dominant.

Dollar Index

The result of acculturation and its effect on the purchase of shortening products is best reflected in the Dollar Index—each group's total projected dollars indexed to non-Hispanics. The dollar index for each type of shortening and each language segment is shown at right. The five products are shown on two separate plots due to scale.

For example, overall, Hispanics spend 4.5 times as much as do non-Hispanics for cooking oil, resulting in an Hispanic marketing index of 450 compared with an index of 100 for non-Hispanics. However, the variations by language segment in this category show how dramatic the impact of acculturation can be: 703 index among Spanish-dominant, an index of 371 among bilinguals, and an index of 120 among English-dominant Hispanics.

For vegetable shortening, margarine, and butter, overall, Hispanics spend less than non-Hispanics. Therefore, they have a total market index of 45 versus the index of 100 for non-Hispanics. This composite number hides the continuum of acculturation, with an index of 28 for Spanish-dominant, 39 among bilinguals, and 87 among English-dominant.

Overall Hispanics buy more shortening than non-Hispanics

Regardless of the type of shortening purchased, Hispanics buy it more often and spend more on it. Hispanics spend 2.49 times as much as do non-Hispanics for oil and shortening. Therefore they have an overall or composite index of 249 vs. the index of 100 for non-Hispanics. The index by language segment is 351 among Spanish-dominant, an index of 223 among bilinguals, and an index of only 106 (equal to non-Hispanics) among English-dominant Hispanics. As mentioned earlier, in many categories, this high index and its downward trend

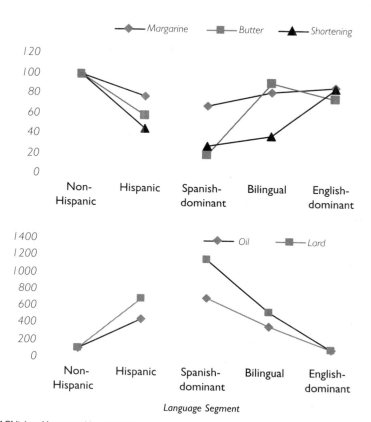

Impact of Acculturation

Dollar Index vs. Non-Hispanic

Source: ACNielsen Homescan Hispanic panel

with acculturation is the result of traditional Hispanic recipes, larger Hispanic families, and a greater prevalence of home cooking among unacculturated Hispanics. Shortening is one product category, however, where Hispanic culture wins over acculturation when flavor and having food that tastes like "home" tends to be the overriding factor. Even fully acculturated Hispanic households use lard occasionally and use butter frequently.

Implications

- Manufacturers of oil have an opportunity to retain American-Latino market share through the acculturation process by extending their brands to the various forms of shortening discussed above. Through targeted advertising, promotions, recipes, and retail distribution planning, a manufacturer of an oil brand can retain Hispanics' business as these consumers transition to shortening, margarine, and butter for cooking.

• Manufacturers of margarine and butter must understand and account for acculturated consumer patterns when marketing to Hispanics. If a consumer is still cooking using more traditional methods, she is unlikely to be receptive to a basic advertising message for margarine. However, if the message uses elements of traditional cooking, shows her how to substitute margarine for lard or oil, and clearly states the benefits to her family's long-term health, the message may be persuasive enough to cause trial.

• Retailers who serve less acculturated Hispanic neighborhoods may want to give oil and lard priority shelf space, whereas those who serve more acculturated neighborhoods may want to emphasize butter and margarine.

INSTANT COFFEE IS HIGHLY POPULAR, WHOLE BEAN AND GROUND COFFEE ARE SLOWLY RISING IN USE

As anyone who has ever tried to skip a morning cup of coffee knows, some habits are hard to break. Most consumers like their coffee served at the same time, in the same form, and with the same flavor. One may be willing to try new foods when traveling, but some familiar habits and foods provide comfort, especially when you are an immigrant far from home.

As expected, consumers in coffee-producing countries like Brazil, Venezuela, Colombia, Mexico, and some Central American countries have greater consumption of fresh-ground coffee than non-producing countries. Moreover, the intelligentsia in all Latin American countries tend to prefer "real" coffee.

However, with those exceptions, instant coffee is probably one of the most popular beverages consumed throughout Latin America. At breakfast, afterwards, a tea-time break, after dinner, and in some cases, throughout the working day, having *una tacita de café instantaneo* is the norm. Any visitor or relative who stops by will be greeted with *"un cafecito?"* This is usually instant coffee!

Nestlé made an early and successful penetration of the Latin American market with its instant coffee. Even today, many households, independent of socio-economic status, consider instant coffee a sign of modernity and practi-cality and its consumption is pervasive throughout these countries.

This pervasive and popular use of instant coffee is also apparent in the U.S., where it is reflected in the mass consumption of instant coffee by non-acculturated U.S. Hispanics. This preference changes directionally with accul-turation. The more years in the United States, the greater the consumption of coffee beans and the lower use of instant coffee.

In sum, many Hispanics immigrate to the United States with a "heritage" of drinking instant coffee. They bring this preference with them along with a search for familiar brands. This explains why instant coffee is overdeveloped among Hispanics in the Los Angeles market, and a $21.6 million business (when both unflavored and flavored products are included), whereas ground coffee is only a $13.6 million category among Hispanics in that market.

In contrast, non-Hispanics presently spend $28.1 million on instant coffee but $67.1 million on ground coffee. This translates to Hispanics spending 3.2 times as much per household on instant coffee, but only 55 percent as much on ground coffee as do non-Hispanics. As acculturation increases, consump-tion of instant coffee declines, and the use of ground coffee increases.

FIGURE 16.4

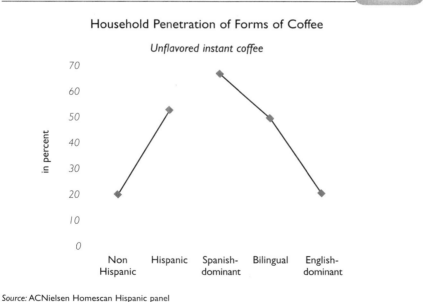

Household Penetration of Forms of Coffee

Unflavored instant coffee

Source: ACNielsen Homescan Hispanic panel

Category penetration of instant coffee is significantly higher among His-panics than non-Hispanics (53.4 percent vs. 20.5 percent). As Hispanics become acculturated, panel data show that fewer buy instant coffee, with household penetration declining from 67.5 percent among Spanish-dominant consumers, to 49.8 percent among bilingual consumers, to 20.9 percent among English-dominant consumers. In contrast, penetration of ground coffee shows the opposite pattern. Both trends are due to the same force that influenced the general market about two decades ago when the availability of simple, less expensive drip coffee appliances led many American families to shift from instant to ground coffee at home.

Frequency of Purchase

The number of shopping trips for coffee is also affected by acculturation. Non-Hispanics make an average of 5.9 shopping trips per year for ground coffee. Hispanics make only 4.5, but the number increases with acculturation. This trend for both ground and instant coffee is shown above. Homescan's Hispanic data has the power to provide this level of detail for over 1200 product categories tracked on a quarterly basis.

FIGURE 16.5

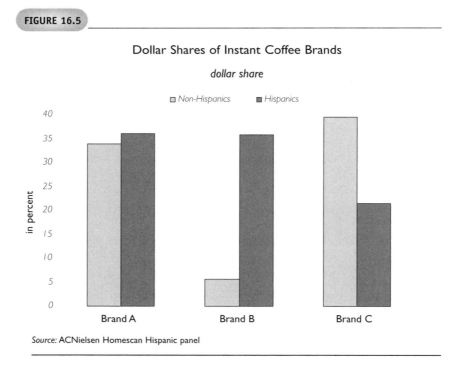

Dollar Shares of Instant Coffee Brands

dollar share

Source: ACNielsen Homescan Hispanic panel

Brand Loyalty

Which brands enjoy the Hispanics' loyalty to instant coffee? Brand A is from a

U.S.-based manufacturer that has actively marketed many of its brands to Hispanics. Therefore, Brand A has a dollar share among Hispanics in the Los Angeles market that is slightly higher than its share among non-Hispanics. Brand B is a global brand that is widely marketed outside the U.S. Because of its familiarity to many Hispanics from their countries of origin, Brand B has a significantly higher market share among Hispanics in the Los Angeles market than it does among non-Hispanics. Finally, Brand C is another U.S.-based brand of instant coffee that has never had any targeted *in-culture* marketing efforts behind it. Therefore, its share in the Los Angeles market among Hispanics is significantly lower than its share among non-Hispanics there.

Implications

- Global brands that are heavily marketed in countries outside the United States often enjoy "brand heritage" and get a lift when foreigners move to the U.S. These companies could lose this competitive advantage when they choose to market the same product under different brand names in the U.S. or foreign countries.

- Manufacturers of coffee have an opportunity to capture newly immigrated Latinos in the instant-coffee segment via *in-culture* marketing efforts.

- In addition, coffee marketers can retain American Latinos through the acculturation process by extending their brand to the various forms of ground coffee (drip, beans). Through *in-culture* advertising, and promotions strategies as well as retail distribution planning, a manufacturer of an instant coffee brand that is well accepted by non-acculturated Hispanics can retain their business as these consumers transition to ground coffee. Alternatively, appropriate *in-culture* marketing programs may cause non-acculturated consumers who are devoted to instant coffee to remain loyal to their current brand, or to switch brands. I can attest to many long-term Hispanic residents who still ask their relatives to bring their favorite brand of instant coffee when visiting from their home country.

HOT BREAKFAST PRODUCTS

Freshly prepared foods are part of the culture of most Hispanics, regardless of their country of origin, and breakfast food is no exception. Americans who are used to gobbling down a bowl of cold cereal or grabbing a toasted waffle to eat in the car have all-but-forgotten the lowly pancake. However, among Hispanic households pancakes are popular, and their popularity is still growing in some Latin countries.

Hot, freshly made pancakes satisfy both physical and emotional needs. Mixing, forming, flipping and serving the hot pancakes makes "Mom" feel like she is doing something special for the meal—an expression of love. Moreover, the family expects this daily personal and caring service. Pancakes are also versatile; they can be served as a side dish or a main course. Finally, pancakes are economical; a large box of pancake mix costs an average of $1.89 and can provide three breakfasts for a family of six. Given these factors, it is no surprise that pancake mix is popular in Mexico, producing another tradition that has traveled with Mexicans to the U.S. and the Los Angeles market. Based on the dollar index, Hispanics spend 2.8 times as much on pancake mix as do non-Hispanics. Like family size, which declines with acculturation, so too does the dollar index.

FIGURE 16.6

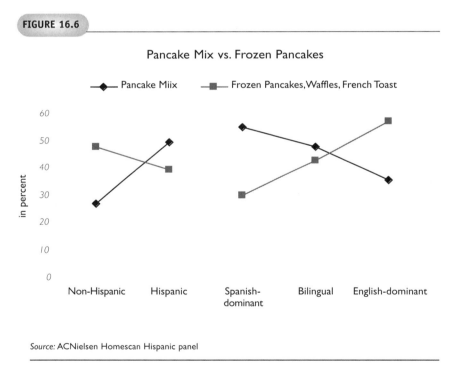

Pancake Mix vs. Frozen Pancakes

Source: ACNielsen Homescan Hispanic panel

Pancake Mix vs. Frozen Pancakes

The hot breakfast category includes other items in addition to pancakes. Convenience has replaced the "from scratch" pancake with frozen waffles and similar foods. Acculturated Hispanic households have learned to use frozen pancakes, waffles, and French toast. It may also be that more-acculturated Hispanics have smaller families and hence fewer children who drive mom's selection of breakfast products. Others who are in more demanding jobs and higher income brackets may have adopted the "eat-on-the-go" breakfast method, dropping the pancake habit. These facts, combined with the higher cost per serving of frozen foods, leads to the hypothesis that the purchase and use of pancake mix might decrease with acculturation.

Spending

As a group, Hispanic consumers spend significantly more on pancake mix purchases than do non-Hispanics ($2.61 vs. $2.43). However, spending declines with acculturation such that English-dominant consumers actually spend less on average per occasion than do non-Hispanics ($2.18 vs. $2.43). Where purchase dynamics—occasions per buyer and dollars per occasion—decline with acculturation, these same measures increase with acculturation for frozen breakfast products.

Hispanics spend 2.8 times as much on pancake mix as do non-Hispanics, but like family size, the dollar index for pancake mix declines with household acculturation.

In-Culture Brand Comparisons

How do the various brands fare given the interaction among coffee, pancakes, and frozen breakfast products? A look at brand shares in all three categories suggests those non-acculturated consumers who like Brand A for pancake mix will probably stick with their brand when it comes to the frozen products. Brand A, which has products in all three categories and is consumed more often or "overdeveloped" among Hispanic consumers in the pancake mix category, is also overdeveloped among Hispanics in the syrup and frozen breakfast categories. Brand B has products in both pancake mix and frozen breakfast and is "underdeveloped" or consumed less often in both.

FIGURE 16.7

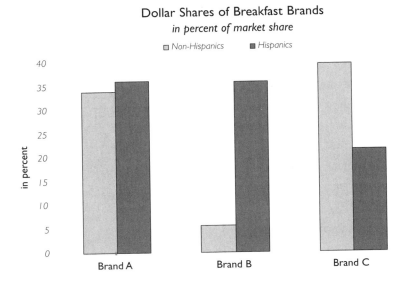

Dollar Shares of Breakfast Brands
in percent of market share

□ *Non-Hispanics*   ■ *Hispanics*

Note: Brand shares are based on small sample sizes. Data should be used with discretion.

Source: ACNielsen Homescan Hispanic panel

Brand A, manufactured by an American company, has been aggressively distributed and marketed in selected countries outside the United States, including Mexico. This support behind pancake mix—the category entry point—enables Brand A to establish a strong position among Hispanics outside the U.S. In addition, Brand A's *in-culture* marketing programs target American Latinos for all its products and allows it to retain Hispanic consumers when they move to the U.S. and keep them as they acculturate, making the transition to frozen food products. Conversely, Brand B has not actively marketed to Hispanics either inside or outside the U.S. so far. Consequently, Brand B's competitive position vs. Brand A's position among Hispanic consumers is weaker than it is in the general market.

Implications

• Brand equity carries across the hot breakfast category and related items such as table syrup. *In-culture* marketing support behind a branded product can extend beyond that particular product to other products in the same brand family.

- A corollary to this conclusion is that *in-culture* product line marketing efforts can be effective, particularly if the products in the line have a cohesive reason for their grouping. In the case of hot breakfast products, marketing support for the product line is particularly effective. It addresses the needs of both unacculturated (pancake mix) and acculturated consumers (frozen breakfast) allowing for seamless transition from one category to the other as consumers became acculturated.

OVER-THE-COUNTER COLD REMEDIES

One product category that clearly shows the impact of larger households is over-the-counter (OTC) cold remedies. Because the category has products specifically for adults and children, it is easy to compare the data for the two age segments between Hispanics and non-Hispanics.

With an average of 3.6 members, Hispanic households in the Los Angeles market are larger then non-Hispanic households, which average 2.3 members. The difference in household size usually can be attributed to the presence of children. Fifty-nine percent of Hispanic households in Los Angeles have one or more children compared with only 32 percent of non-Hispanic households in that market.

Based on the dollar index (total projected dollars spent indexed to non-Hispanics), children's cold remedies are overdeveloped or purchased in greater quantities among Hispanics. This index of 252 indicates that Hispanics spend 2.5 times as much on children's cold remedies as do non-Hispanics. Like family size, which declines with acculturation, so too does the dollar index. Penetration and occasions per buyer, or purchase dynamics, also decline with acculturation, but the dramatic drop in dollars per occasion really drives spending down among English-dominant consumers. (See Figure 16.8)

When data are analyzed for adult cold remedies, a very different picture emerges. The dollar index for all Hispanics buying adult cold remedies is 101, exactly in line with the general market. Even more telling is the fact that this measure increases slightly with acculturation, although it rises to only 117 among English-dominant consumers, still statistically on par with the general market. This shows clearly that the greater purchase of OTC children's medicines is driven by families who need more kids' medicines along with other child-oriented products.

FIGURE 16.8

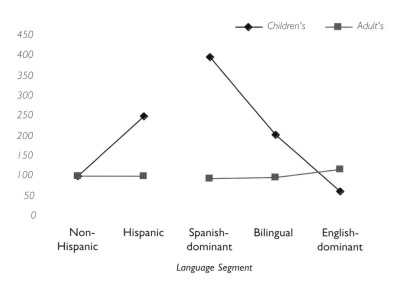

Children's and Adults' Cold Remedies

dollar index vs. non-Hispanics

Source: ACNielsen Homescan Hispanic panel

Cold Remedies and Household Penetration

Penetration and occasions per buyer of adult cold remedies increase with acculturation, exactly the opposite of the trends for children's products. This is due in part to the significantly lower presence of children in the acculturated market segment. However, like children's products, dollars per trip decrease, probably because the number of shopping trips overall increase with acculturation. Therefore, less is spent on any given trip.

Spending

As a group, Hispanic consumers spend significantly more when they buy children's cold remedies than when they buy cold medicine for adults.(Figure 16.9) This relationship holds for Spanish-dominant consumers where the gap is the largest ($9.33 for Hispanics, $7.35 for non-Hispanics). However, spending reverses among English-dominant consumers, who spend $6.58 on adult medicines but only $5.66 on remedies for children.

FIGURE 16.9

Children's and Adults' Cold Remedies

dollars per occasion

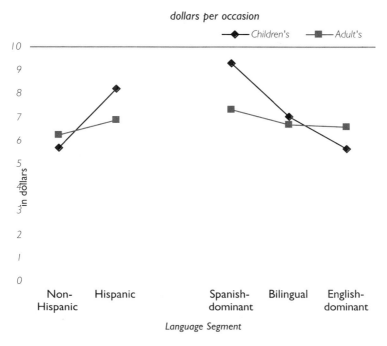

◆ Children's ■ Adult's

Language Segment

Non-Hispanic Hispanic Spanish-dominant Bilingual English-dominant

Source: ACNielsen Homescan Hispanic panel

FIGURE 16.10

Dollar Shares of Children's and Adults' Cold Remedies

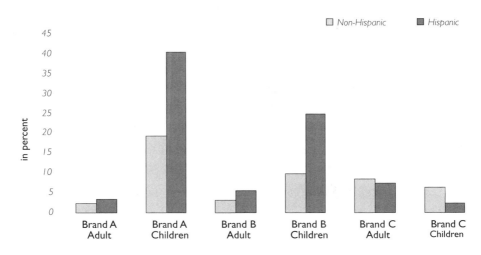

☐ *Non-Hispanic* ■ *Hispanic*

Note: Segment data for children's medicines are based on small sample sizes. Data should be used with discretion.

Source: ACNielsen Homescan Hispanic panel

Brand Shares

A look at brand shares in both the adult and children's segments suggests that equity transfers between age segments. Overdeveloped brands among Hispanic consumers in the adult segment also are overdeveloped among Hispanics in the children's segment. The other brand that has products in both segments is also consumed less, or is underdeveloped, in both.

Implications

For manufacturers of over-the-counter cold medications, Hispanics represent an excellent opportunity to grow volume and share. A manufacturer that already has a brand in the children's category should consider an *in-culture* marketing program targeted—for example, co-promoting both products—to newly arrived Hispanics as the Spanish-dominant segment has more children and spends the most on these remedies. Manufacturers of adult cold medicines also should consider marketing to acculturated Hispanics as they spend more than other market segments in this category.

BOUILLON IS POPULAR, CANNED SOUP IS NOT

Canned soup was one of the first convenience foods for many Americans. Shelf stable, versatile and inexpensive, canned soup represents a convenient way to provide a hot centerpiece to a meal, without a great deal of time and effort.

Like many convenience foods, Americans adopted canned soup quickly after its introduction. Consequently, its awareness and penetration levels are highest in the U.S., with other nations lagging behind. Latin Americans lag behind in part because canned soup is not marketed, nor always readily available in their markets, but also because traditional cooking methods are cherished. Thus, canned soup (a $105 million industry in the Los Angeles market) is underdeveloped among Hispanics ($19 million vs. $86 million among non-Hispanics). All things being equal, Hispanics in Los Angeles spend only 58 percent as much as do non-Hispanics on canned soup. This is a classical case of an "underdeveloped category" that requires *in-culture*, ongoing marketing communications to introduce and support the conversion of Latinas to the category.

Conversely, bouillon is popular among Hispanics, due to its popularity throughout Latin America where it is widely used as a flavorful ingredient in daily cooking. For example, many rice, potato, or meat dishes are always pre-pared with chicken or beef bouillon to add flavor. Although bouillon is only a $13 million business in the Los Angeles market, $10 million worth is sold to Hispanics and only $3 million is sold to non-Hispanics. Hispanics spend 9.7 times as much on bouillon as do non-Hispanics, with Spanish-dominant Hispanics spending an incredible 17.5 times more.

Dry Soup Mixes

Dry soup mixes are a $32 million industry in the Los Angeles market; $20 million among non-Hispanics and $12 million among Hispanics. Because non-Hispanic households far outnumber Hispanic households in the Los Angeles market, this means that Hispanics spend 1.6 times per household as much as non-Hispanics for dry soup mixes. Single-male immigrant households tend to use dry soup mixes when nobody is available to prepare a meal from scratch—the old-fashioned way.

FIGURE 16.11

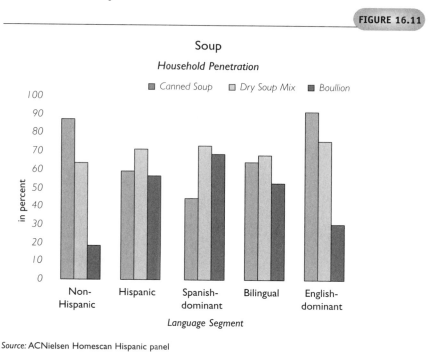

Source: ACNielsen Homescan Hispanic panel

Household Penetration of Forms of Soup

As would be expected, given Latino household purchase patterns of bouillon and dry soup mixes, household penetration of bouillon is significantly higher among Hispanics than non-Hispanics (56.7 percent vs. 18.5 percent). Again, once Hispanics become acculturated, fewer use bouillon, with household penetration declining from 69 percent among Spanish-dominant consumers, to 52.6 percent among bilingual consumers, to 30.3 percent among English-dominant consumers. Conversely, and correlating with acculturation, penetration of canned soup shows the opposite pattern.

Shopping Trips

The Homescan Hispanic panel data shows internal consistency in the stories as observed in the different indices. Household penetration alone only tells part of the story. For example, the number of Hispanic households using bouillon declines with acculturation, and the number using canned soup increases, and the number of shopping trips together with the amount spent on these items in each shopping trip follow this pattern as well. For example, Non-Hispanics make an average of 7.7 shopping trips per year for canned soup. Hispanics make only 5.6. The number of trips increases with acculturation; Spanish-dominant consumers make 3.6 trips per year, bilinguals make 5.9 trips and English-dominant consumers make 7.8 trips.

FIGURE 16.12

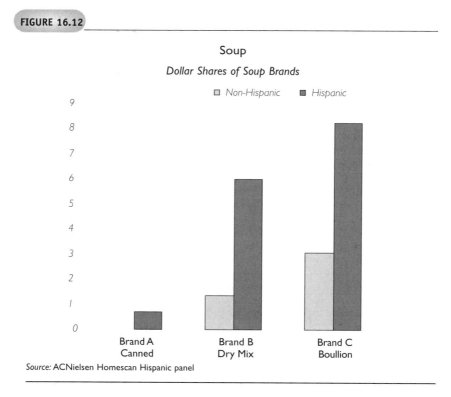

Soup

Dollar Shares of Soup Brands

☐ *Non-Hispanic*   ■ *Hispanic*

Source: ACNielsen Homescan Hispanic panel

Different Canned Soup Styles

Which brands in each segment benefit from an understanding of how Hispanics use soup products? Canned Brand A is a Hispanic brand that contains *menudo* or tripe. A traditional soup and stew ingredient, menudo in canned soup is an *in-culture* product in a convenient form. Therefore, Brand A, as expected, has a significantly higher share among Hispanics than non-Hispanics. Dry Brand B is a global brand with noodles and seasonings in a cup that provides an inexpensive small meal when boiling water is added. This combination of global recognition and economical convenience has led to a strong Hispanic franchise as well. Finally, Brand C is a bouillon product, thus immediately appealing to Hispanic consumers. In addition, a global manufacturer that is well known by Hispanics markets it. (Figure 16.12)

Implications

Soup manufacturers have an opportunity to capture newly immigrated American Latinos in the canned segment via *in-culture* soup varieties and marketing strategies. In addition, soup marketers can increase penetration of American Latino households throughout the acculturation process by extending brands to the various forms of soup (bouillon, dry, canned) that are appealing to their taste buds, or with an *in-culture* strategy that communicates, for example, that canned soup can do the same job as bouillon and "even more." Alternatively, appropriate *in-culture* marketing programs can continue appealing to non-acculturated consumers who are devoted to bouillon, to remain loyal to their current brand, or to switch brands.

CARBONATED SOFT DRINKS

The global marketing efforts of the leading American brands of carbonated soft drinks and their successes date back to World War II. These marketing efforts have contributed to the familiarity and popularity of carbonated drinks among Hispanics in South America and in Europe; they made the brands household names. Foreign-born Hispanics enjoy carbonated beverages as a staple of American life. They consumed these regularly in their native countries and continue to drink them as often or more often in the U.S.

The majority of all Hispanic households in the Los Angeles market purchase regular-calorie carbonated soft drinks. There is only a small decline with acculturation. Ninety-nine percent of households who prefer Spanish or speak only Spanish buy these drinks, compared with 95.3 percent of English-dominant households. Just over 91 percent of non-Hispanic households buy these drinks. It can be observed there are no major differences with carbonated soft drinks as with some other products because Hispanic and non-Hispanic households have had similar amounts of exposure to these products and their advertising, abroad as in the U.S.

However, culture does make a difference by type. Purchase and consumption of regular-calorie carbonated soft drinks is higher among Hispanic households than non-Hispanic households. While the differences are less dramatic than for some other products, the data show that in the Los Angeles market, for example, the average Hispanic household spends 1.7 times as much on carbonated soft drinks as does the average non-Hispanic household. Spending declines as acculturation occurs from Spanish-dominant households with a dollar index of 210, to bilinguals (dollar index of 151) to English-dominant (dollar index of 111).

FIGURE 16.13

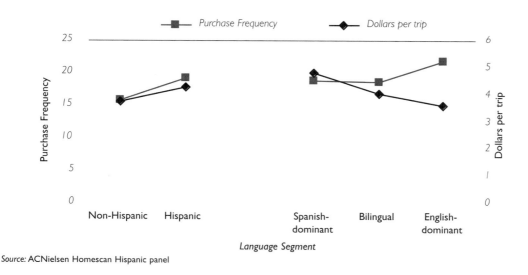

Regular Soda

Purchase Dynamics—number of trips and dollars per trip

Source: ACNielsen Homescan Hispanic panel

Purchase Frequency

On the issue of purchase frequency, non-Hispanic households buy regular calorie carbonated drinks slightly less often, but they may also buy them in higher quantities when they do make a purchase. The purchase frequency of English-dominant Hispanic households (21.8 times) is highest among all Hispanic language segments whereas we usually expect that these households would show a frequency closer to the 15.2 times of non-Hispanic households.

Acculturation shows up most clearly in the trend toward spending on carbonated soft drinks, which is lowest for English-only households among all Hispanic households. English-only households spend about $3.58 per shopping trip for these beverages, compared with $4.78 for Spanish-only households. It is possible that this more "acculturated spending" has to do with a better knowledge of prices and of sales among the English-only group. It is also possible that non-acculturated Hispanics consume more soft drinks out-of-home and hence, are not tracked by the ACNielsen panel.

Acculturation shows up most clearly in the trend toward spending on carbonated soft drinks, which is lowest for English-only households among all Hispanic households.

Fruit Flavors

The beneficiaries of Hispanics' propensity to buy regular calorie carbonated soft drinks fall into two categories: familiar brands and fruit flavors.

Familiar brands include those that were developed in consumers' native countries and are also sold in the U.S. (examples include Jarritos and Señorial) as well as American brands that have been successfully marketed globally for decades. Brand A is the best example of this type of brand. With a dollar share of 29.5 percent among Hispanics in the Los Angeles market compared with a 17.7 percent share among non-Hispanics, Brand A clearly has a strong following among Hispanics. However, this strength erodes with acculturation as many Hispanics discover the variety of alternatives available in the U.S.

The other group of winners is the fruit-flavored brands.

These brands combine the appeal and economy of carbonated soft drinks with the fruit flavors so popular among Latinos who were born and raised in countries where flavorful fruits grow almost by themselves. Orange and grape flavors are particularly popular, with several garnering market shares that are nearly double those in the general market.

To Diet or Not To Diet?

Many Hispanics find it hard to accept the "diet" versions of carbonated beverages. Hispanics are much less likely to buy low-calorie soft drinks, but as acculturation occurs and there is increased consciousness about weight and health issues, consumption of low-calorie carbonated soft drinks increases. This is reflected across the Homescan Hispanic panel data. All purchasing measures for low-calorie, carbonated soft drinks—household penetration, occasions per buyer, and dollars per occasion—are higher for non-Hispanics than for Hispanics. All these increase in direct correlation with acculturation and the same phenomenon is observed with light foods, beers, and any "diet" versions of products. Latinos tend to be much more attached to the traditional flavors than non-Hispanics, and Hispanics are known for having a sweet-tooth.

As Latinos acculturate and learn the benefits of these new "lighter" product varieties, their consumption trends show change in favor of healthier foods and beverages.

Implications

- Leading brands of carbonated beverages have done an excellent job of global marketing, creating a brand loyalty that carries over when Hispanics move from their native lands to the United States. With such high penetration rates in Hispanic (and non-Hispanic) households, it is hard to increase consumption. Therefore, most strategies to win share are based on linking brands to other benefits, or converting households into consuming other new beverage types or varients. As Hispanic households acculturate, they are more accepting of information that links "diet" drinks to weight and a healthier lifestyle. However, marketers must also realize that if Hispanic households move massively to alternative beverages, they will be lost as consumers of regular calorie beverages.

• For non-leading brands, the Hispanic market also represents an opportunity to grow volume and share, since many flavors and brands that are popular in Latin American are missing in the U.S. market. However, the challenge of rising above familiar brands is significant. Fruit drinks such as Orange Crush or Fanta may represent the best opportunity to make gains against the leading brands.

FEMININE PROTECTION

When Latinas migrate they also bring the beliefs and values (of their counties of origin) and many times retain them long after immigrating to the United States. Most Latin American countries are predominantly Catholic. Religious beliefs combined with other cultural influences have led many women to reject using feminine protection products such as tampons that require "touching" intimate parts. These traditional values transcend all aspects of daily life including products that they buy and use. However, as they become more acculturated and more comfortable with the "relaxed" relationship with the body that most American women have, Latinas' product choices slowly change and eventually resemble those of the general market.

One category of packaged products that clearly illustrates this phenomenon is feminine sanitary protection. A $68.3 million category in the Los Angeles market ($49.4 million among the general market and $18.9 million among Hispanics), sanitary protection as a whole is at parity among Hispanic households (103 dollar index). However, it is the trend within the category's two segments—sanitary napkins and tampons—that demonstrates the acculturation dynamic of the transition to product alternatives.

Household penetration of sanitary napkins, while virtually the same across all language segments, is significantly higher among Hispanics than among non-Hispanics (58.8 percent vs. 47.9 percent). Therefore, it is not surprising that household penetration of the alternative—tampons—is significantly lower among Hispanics than among non-Hispanic consumers (13.2 percent vs. 26.8 percent). It is also no surprise that tampon use increases sharply with acculturation to the point that household penetration of tampons among English-dominant Hispanics exceeds that of non-Hispanic (33.2 percent vs. 26.8 percent).

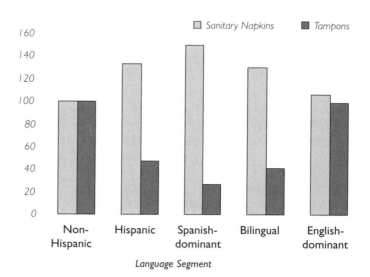

FIGURE 16.14

Spending on Sanitary Products
Dollar index vs. non-Hispanics

Source: ACNielsen Homescan Hispanic panel

Spending on Sanitary Products

This higher incidence of sanitary napkin use among Hispanic women translates to a larger Hispanic dollar index of 133 for sanitary napkins. This means, everything else being equal, Hispanic households spend one-third more on sanitary napkins than non-Hispanic households. However, this ratio declines with acculturation with Spanish-dominant consumers spending 50 percent more, bilinguals spending 30 percent more, and English-dominant consumers spending 6 percent more. As mentioned above, Hispanic consumers switch to tampons as they become more acculturated—essentially equal to spending in the general market.

Because the non-acculturated market segment is presently significantly larger than the acculturated segment, the sanitary napkin takes the lion's share of the category. This will eventually change as Latinas acculturate and age, and with well-developed *in-culture* campaigns that address these taboos with the more traditional segments, including moral concerns in addition to product benefits and advantages.

FIGURE 16.15

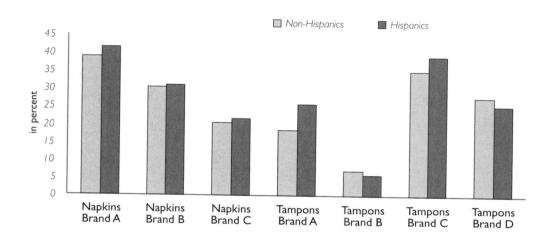

Dollar Shares of Sanitary Products

in dollars spent

Source: ACNielsen Homescan Hispanic panel

Brand Comparison

Which brands are capturing the larger share among Hispanics in one or both segments? Brands A, B, and C have a significant presence in both napkins and tampons. However, while all three brands' napkins are equally well developed among Hispanics and non-Hispanics in the Los Angeles market, only Brand A's and Brand C's tampons capture a slightly higher share among Hispanics than in the general market. Both Brands A and C actively market to Hispanic women. Therefore, they retain consumers attracted at the category entry point—sanitary napkins—as these consumers transition into tampons.

Because the non-acculturated market segment is significantly larger than the acculturated segment, the sanitary napkin takes the lion's share of the category.

Implications

- As with other product and service categories, *in-culture* marketing efforts for feminine protection products that attract Hispanic women when they first enter the U.S. can be successful at retaining them when they acculturate and their preference changes to tampons.

- Next, these marketers can increase their market share and retain Latino women through the acculturation process by using culturally sensitive strategies to extend their brand to tampons. Through *in-culture* advertising and promotions as well as eventually sampling and educational materials, a manufacturer can convert Latinas to tampons.

Alternatively, appropriate *in-culture* marketing programs may cause the non-acculturated consumer who is devoted to napkins to remain loyal to her current brand, or to switch brands, or better yet, to consider both products.

Chapter 17

How Get Your Products in Front of Latinos

THE RETAIL END

As you know, the best marketing strategy will fail if your products don't "meet the eye" of your core target segments at the point of purchase, "POP." It is common for corporate marketing departments to have little knowledge about where and how Hispanics shop and their product mix preferences and differences. They may also not know how to locate products in the floor plan and shelf space in a way that "talks to" the immigrant consumer. Similarly, many supermarket managers and storeowners with shops in high-density and mid-density Hispanic areas position products in the aisles as if they were appealing to the general market. However, Latinos may be shopping quite differently at these stores. They may not find the products they need or the specialty products for which they are willing to pay more.

An expert on this topic, Xavier Saucedo, general manager of Gamesa (a PepsiCo company), has observed in the marketplace that Hispanics tend to look for Mexican-style foods in specific locations within the store. If there is a dedicated ethnic foods section, that is the area to be in and with a display *en Español*. Latinos will look for that special item in these aisles. In addition, many are willing to pay a premium for the coveted brand or product from their home country or for a good "look-alike". The profit margin for these items can be several times that of the same item placed in other aisles of the store. For example, in Mr. Saucedo's experience, only 7 percent of a store's products may be Latino, but these bring 20 percent of the store's profits.

This chapter will cover several Hispanic retailing issues and explore possibilities to test new approaches to execute *in-culture* marketing at the store level, based on a small store audit in Chicago. What is the shopping experience like for Hispanics? What have we learned is expected? How are selected stores responding to these needs, by acculturation level? Strengths and weaknesses in Hispanic retailing are described and provide you with a checklist.

Finally, ACNielsen's Homescan Hispanic panel data and Scantrack Ethnic Service™ data will be used to illustrate shopping patterns of Latinos by type of store and selected departments.

UNDERSTANDING THE MARKETS WITHIN
THE HISPANIC MARKET

As previously discussed, it is a mistake to think of Hispanics as one homogenous group, and this is even more relevant when it comes to foods. The Latino market consists of several segments defined by language preference as well as their degree of acculturation into mainstream culture and their rich cultural backgrounds, unique to their countries of origin. What does this have to do with understanding how to sell to Hispanic consumers? A lot! Mexicans, Cubans, Puerto Ricans, and Central Americans have distinct cuisines and product preferences that are similar within groups and distinct among groups, based on country of origin. They also tend to concentrate in specific geographic areas. As can be expected, channel differences emerge when shopping behavior is analyzed by regions and by acculturation levels.[1]

Using ACNielsen Scantrack Ethnic Service data and Homescan Hispanic panel data, clear differences among Hispanics in six U.S. cities emerge. For example, Figure 17.1 below shows the five food products purchased more often by Hispanics than by consumers as a whole in these markets. Please note that these are not the products that Hispanics purchase most often in general, but in comparison with the total market in these cities.

ACNielsen Scantrack Ethnic Service uses Universal Product Code (UPC) data from products purchased in large grocery stores located in areas within each market where at least 50 percent[2] or more of the population is of Hispanic origin. This

FIGURE 17.1

Products Purchased More Often by Hispanics than Non-Hispanics

Purchases in large grocery stores in six key Hispanic markets

Los Angeles	Miami	New York
Lard	Cooking wine & sherry	Lard
Canned ham	Canned chiles/pimientos	Other refrigerated packaged meat*
Dry beans	Flaked soda crackers	Dry beans
Bouillon	Strained baby food	Rice
Dry Mexican foods	Other crackers*	Frozen grape juice

San Antonio	Houston	Chicago
Lard	Lard	Lard
Canned Mexican foods	Other all-purpose flour*	Glazes
Shelf-stable orange juice	Imported cheese	Refrigerated cranberry juice
Infant formula	Dry stew mixes	Infant formula
Dry beans	Canned Mexican foods	Other refrigerated packaged meat*

Source: ACNielsen Scantrack Ethnic Service Data, 2001

*"Other" refers to brands that are not included in the ACNielsen listings.

data is then compared with that of the total purchases in large grocery stores in each city.

There are similarities, such as the use of lard across markets. Lard is an ingredient popular in Mexican, Central, and South American cuisine, used in such dishes as *tamales, enchiladas, empanadas, pan amasado* (homemade-style bread) and many others. However, there are also important differences observed. The data also show differences within the traditional "Mexican" markets, such as Los Angeles, San Antonio, and Houston. With the exception of lard, canned Mexican foods, and dry beans, there are few similarities. It is interesting to observe though, how different Miami data is from all the others markets and how non-traditional brands ("Other") are popular in several markets. This suggests that Hispanic shoppers are probably purchasing imported or non-mainstream brands.

continues page 189 . . .

Strengths and Weaknesses in Retailing to Hispanics

To learn what works and what doesn't in Hispanic retailing, from the Hispanic point of view, 15 stores were audited in Chicago, Illinois in early September 2001. The stores were selected by level of acculturation of the neighborhoods where they were located, using *in-culture* geo-segmentation tools:

- 5 stores were observed in less acculturated areas,
- 5 in more acculturated areas, and
- 5 in highly acculturated areas.

Although this sample is too small to be representative of the U.S. Hispanic market, Chicago is a typical Hispanic market. The findings of the audit observations are consistent overall with those of the author in other studies, and can serve as guidelines.

RETAILERS TARGETING LESS ACCULTURATED HISPANICS
Tend to be particularly effective in:

- **Welcoming the shopper**
    Outside store signage, primary and secondary, through bilingual and *in-culture* signage that is visible and easy to read
- **Window displays**
    Displaying family-oriented products
    Communicating effectively
    Communicating strong value proposition
    Displaying familiar and trusted brands
- **Entering the store—first impression**
    Displaying a welcoming diverse staff
- **Merchandising**
    Placing the leading Hispanic brands prominently and giving them their fair space in dedicated areas
    Having *in-culture* special displays
    Having end displays of key brands or crossover products that have significance to Hispanic consumers
    Having surprise impulse and *in-culture* items for Hispanics

Tend to be less effective at:

- **Entering the store—first impression**
    Communicating the retailer's primary strategy to shoppers as soon as they enter the store
    Providing "self-serve" product and pricing information
    Having merchandise stand out more than fixtures

- **Store operations**

    Having good clear signage (in either language) to help "self-serve" customers navigate and make quick purchase decisions

    Having wide uncluttered aisles

    Maintaining high housekeeping standards

- **Customer service**

    Going the extra mile, customer service "beyond the service counter"

    Providing fast and efficient checkout

    Having help available when needed

RETAILERS IN MORE ACCULTURATED HISPANIC AREAS

Tend to be particularly effective at:

- **Welcoming the shopper**

    Using bright colors and visuals in parking areas, promoting appearance of an event or a vibrant marketplace. This is more feasible for these retailers because they are located in less congested areas than retailers targeting less-acculturated Hispanics. Typically they own their parking lots in contrast with retailers in less acculturated areas where parking is often on-street.

- **Entering the store—first impression**

    Quickly communicating their primary strategy to shoppers as soon as they enter the store, e.g. wide selection, specialty merchandise, value, low cost, or service

- **Customer service**

    Having available help visible

Can improve on these areas:

- **Window displays**

    Adding family-oriented displays

    Having colorful, engaging, depiction of family lifestyle

- **Merchandising**

    Having Hispanic displays

    Having exciting impulse merchandise and *in-culture* items for Hispanics

RETAILERS IN ACCULTURATED HISPANIC AREAS

Tend to excel at:

- **Entering the store—first impression**

    Quickly communicating their primary strategy to shoppers as soon as they

continues . . .

enter the store, e.g. wide selection, specialty merchandise, value, low
cost, or service
- **Merchandising**
Carrying "hip and trendy" merchandise popular with Latino teens
Designing the store so that the shoppers see merchandise rather than
fixtures
- **Store operations**
Providing good signage and great information to help shoppers make
purchase decisions without asking for help
Having wide aisles and uncluttered stores allowing the whole family to
easily shop together
Maintaining highest standards of housekeeping
- **Customer Service**
Providing visible evidence of customer service throughout the store

Significantly lag behind other retailers in:

- **Welcoming the shopper**
Having bilingual signage
Merchandising the outside of the store as a vibrant marketplace
- **Window displays**
Displaying family oriented products
Having depictions of family lifestyle
Effectively communicating a strong value proposition such as large quanti-
ties for families
Displaying products familiar and trusted by Hispanics
- **Entering the store—first impression**
Displaying a diverse staff, store personnel
- **Merchandising**
Including authentic Hispanic products
Displaying leading brands for Hispanics relative to the customer base
Having end caps displaying key brands or crossover products
Having special Hispanic targeted displays or ethnic product aisles
Having exciting impulse merchandise for the Hispanic shopper
- **Customer service**
Providing "hassle-free" customer service through easy to find
bilingual staff

Source: Thanks to Julian Posada and the J.C. Williams Group, Chicago and Arminda Figueroa, V.P. Santiago & Valdés Solutions

Hispanic retail channel preferences show you how to select venues for your products. Hispanic shoppers tend to have distinct shopping channel preferences compared with the non-Hispanic market and these also vary by Hispanic consumer segments.

THE SMALLER GROCERY AND CONVENIENCE STORE EXPERIENCE

From a retail perspective, Hispanics tend to follow different channel-selection patterns than non-Hispanics. Many tend to prefer smaller grocery stores and convenience stores instead of the large supermarkets. This behavior can be traced to two consumer insights. On the one hand, the European influence in many American Latinos' native countries make a social event of the daily shopping trip to local, family-owned mom-and-pop stores to buy food for that evening's dinner. This is more the pattern in large cities in Latin America. On the other hand, many immigrant Hispanics come from small towns and villages where the weekly farmer's market is the common place to do their shopping, if food is not grown at home. Each of these approaches secures high quality and fresh produce every time. This heritage, combined with lack of familiarity with large American stores and, in some cases, limited transportation options, causes less-acculturated Hispanics in major U.S. cities to spend less money for food at large ($2 million-plus) grocery stores and significantly more in smaller grocery and convenience stores. New immigrants are also more at ease shopping in stores that are around the corner and more like their small shops back home. Being able to quickly locate desired products certainly facilitates the shopping experience, as do shopkeepers who speak Spanish and relate to them as friends, which is many times the case. However, as Latino consumers acculturate and move out of the *barrio,* their shopping patterns begin to more closely resemble those of non-Hispanics. This finding is consistent through all six of the food departments analyzed in this chapter based on the data from the ACNielsen Homescan Hispanic panel in the Los Angeles, four-county area.

As Latino consumers acculturate and move out of the barrio, their shopping patterns begin to more closely resemble those of non-Hispanics.

Small percentages, but big bottom-line differences

According to the Homescan Hispanic panel's findings, non-Hispanics in the Los Angeles market spend 72.5 percent of their dry-grocery dollars in large ($2 million-plus) grocery stores. Hispanics, spend 71.3 percent at these large stores. This may not look like a meaningful bottom line difference. However, this 1.2 percent of Los Angeles Hispanics' dollars translates to 1.2 percent of $1.53 billion[3] spent on dry grocery products in this market in stores outside large grocery chains, or $13.8 million in one department alone (dry grocery).

As might be expected, the percentage of dry-grocery dollars spent in $2 million-plus grocery stores increases with acculturation. Spanish-dominant consumers spend 70 percent of their dry-grocery dollars in large food stores. Bilinguals spend 71 percent, and English-dominant Latinos spend 74.2 percent, slightly more than non-Hispanics. Note how shares of dry grocery vary by channel among Hispanics and non-Hispanics in Los Angeles in Figure 17.2.

TABLE 17.2

Dry Grocery Department—Non-Hispanics vs. Hispanics

Percentage of Dollar Sales by Channel

Percent of sales by channel	non-Hispanic	Hispanic	Index Hispanic to non-Hispanic	Difference Hispanic vs. non-Hispanic
$2 million-plus	72.5%	71.3%	98	-1.2%
All other Grocery	1.0	3.5	349	+2.5
All other Food	0.5	1.0	217	+0.5
Warehouse	10.0	9.5	94	-0.5
Discount	6.5	4.6	72	-1.9
Convenience/Gas	0.5	2.3	498	+1.8
Drug	2.1	1.4	66	-0.7
All other Outlets	7.0	6.5	93	-0.5

Source: ACNielsen Homescan Hispanic panel, Los Angeles, 2000

Where to place your dry grocery products

Where are the dry grocery transactions occurring? ACNielsen Homescan Hispanic panel data for other retail channels reveal an interesting story. Two other classes of trade are significantly overdeveloped—that is, they are much more common among Hispanics when compared with non-Hispanics. Los Angeles Hispanics spend 3.5 percent of their dry grocery dollars in smaller food stores (stores with less than $2 million in annual volume) as compared with only 1 percent of dry grocery purchases in these stores among non-Hispanics. This additional volume translates to $38.2 million in sales for smaller grocery stores. Similarly, Hispanics spend 2.3 percent of their dry grocery dollars in convenience stores, including *bodegas,* compared to only 0.5 percent among non-Hispanics. This additional volume translates to $27.5 million in dry grocery sales for convenience stores alone.

ACCULTURATION'S IMPACT

As is the case for $2 million-plus grocery stores, the disparity between Hispanics and non-Hispanics for share of category for these channels narrows with acculturation. For small grocery stores, it declines from 4.9 percent among Spanish-dominant to 3 percent among bilinguals to 1.2 percent among English-dominant. These shares of category for convenience stores are 4.1 percent, 1.3 percent and 0.3 percent, respectively. A review of Hispanic retail usage behavior by acculturation, based on language segmentation data, clearly shows that important differences do exist. Therefore, it is highly recommended that the cultural and acculturation backgrounds of segments be considered when, for example, targeting Hispanics with samples at the store level or in merchandising or planning for operations and distribution.

Again using the dry-foods-data example, it is clear that acculturated Hispanics' channel shares are similar to non-Hispanics, as shown in Figure 17.3. In contrast, the least acculturated segments (Spanish-dominant) buy more dry groceries in other outlets, such as convenience and gas station stores, and smaller (under $2 million) grocery stores.

Bilinguals tend to be in the middle, with the important exception of warehouse clubs, where they tend to consistently shop far more than the Spanish-dominant, not only for dry groceries but also in many other departments. Why? Bilingual Latinos in Los Angeles—and in most other Hispanic markets— tend to have higher incomes than non-acculturated Spanish-dominant consumers. They also tend to own cars, have command of English, and be familiar with warehouse clubs. In addition, they tend to have larger families than the English-dominant acculturated segments, and hence, they want shopping convenience. They also can afford to make larger purchases at one time. The more acculturated Latinos tend to have smaller households and significantly larger incomes, which also results in less time to go shopping. Therefore, they end up shopping more often in the more exclusive or non-discount stores.

In contrast, as mentioned earlier, the Spanish-dominant shoppers may not be able to get around as easily. Most non-acculturated Latina moms depend on their spouses or other relatives to take them shopping. They don't drive and warehouse clubs are often out of the way. They may also be hard to get around in if you are looking for the typical Hispanic products and staples. Non-acculturated Latinas prefer to buy in more familiar outlets, like corner stores or mom-and-pop stores. Last, their incomes do not permit them to buy large quantities of products. Of course there are many exceptions. In my qualitative studies I learned that some Latino families get together with other families and go on big shopping trips, sharing the ride, and later distributing the purchased products according to each family's investment.

Again, it is important to keep in mind that presently the less-acculturated language segments, Spanish-dominant and bilingual, are significantly larger in most Hispanic markets or regions. Hence, the marketing opportunity is generally much more attractive with the non-acculturated language segments.

TABLE 17.3

Dry Grocery Department—Acculturated and Non-Hispanic *vs.* Hispanic

Percentage of Dollar Sales

Percent of sales by channel	non-Hispanic	Hispanic	Language Segmentation			Difference English-dominant vs. non-Hispanic	Difference English-dominant vs. Hispanic
			Spanish-dominant	Bilingual	English-dominant		
$2 million-plus	72.5%	71.3%	70.0%	71.1%	74.2%	+1.7%	+2.9%
All Other Grocery	1.0	3.5	4.9	3.0	1.2	+0.2%	-2.3
All Other Food	0.5	1.0	1.7	0.6	0.4	-0.1%	-0.6
Warehouse	10.0	9.5	6.1	13.4	9.5	-0.5%	—
Discount	6.5	4.6	4.1	4.2	6.5	—	+1.9
Convenience/Gas	0.5	2.3	4.1	1.3	0.3	-0.2%	-2.0
Drug	2.1	1.4	1.2	1.5	1.5	-0.6%	+0.1
All Other Outlets	7.0	6.5	8.0	4.9	6.5	-0.5%	—

Source: ACNielsen Homescan Hispanic panel, Los Angeles, 2000

DAIRY AND FROZEN FOODS

Dairy and frozen food are two large departments. Dairy, in the Los Angeles market alone, is a $1.13 billion department ($790 million among non-Hispanics and $340 million among Hispanics) and frozen is $1.08 billion ($870 million among non-Hispanics and $210 million among Hispanics). The same channel or store (Figures 17.4 and 17.5) share pattern observed with the dry-grocery example above can be observed both between Hispanics and non-Hispanics, as well as across language segments.

FIGURE 17.4

Dairy Foods Department—Non-Hispanics vs. Hispanics

Percentage of Dollar Sales by Channel

Percent of sales by channel	non-Hispanic	Hispanic	Index Hispanic to non-Hispanic	Difference Hispanic vs. non-Hispanic
$2 million-plus	82.5%	76.4%	93	-6.1%
All Other Grocery	1.0	4.1	401	+3.0
All Other Food	0.1	0.7	986	+0.6
Warehouse	9.2	9.8	106	+0.6
Discount	0.9	1.0	117	+0.1
Convenience/Gas	0.7	2.9	438	+2.2
Drug	2.3	0.5	20	-1.8
All Other Outlets	3.4	4.6	134	+1.2

Source: ACNielsen Homescan Hispanic panel, Los Angeles, 2000

As was the case with dry grocery, channel shares for dairy products among acculturated Hispanic households in Los Angeles tend to be similar to those of non-Hispanics as shown below.

FIGURE 17.5

Dairy Department—Acculturated and Non-Hispanic vs. Hispanic

Percentage of Dollar Sales

Percent of sales by channel	non-Hispanic	Hispanic	Language Segmentation			Difference English-dominant vs. non-Hispanic	Difference English-dominant vs. Hispanic
			Spanish-dominant	Bilingual	English-dominant		
$2 million-plus	82.5%	76.4%	74.4%	75.2%	84.0%	+1.5%	+7.6%
All Other Grocery	1.0	4.1	5.3	4.0	1.6	+0.6	-2.5
All Other Food	0.1	0.7	1.1	0.4	0.3	+0.2	-0.4
Warehouse	9.2	9.8	5.7	14.2	10.1	+0.6	+0.3
Discount	0.9	1.0	1.3	0.8	0.9	—	-0.1
Convenience/Gas	0.7	2.9	4.4	2.5	0.2	-0.5	-2.7
Drug	2.3	0.5	0.4	0.6	0.3	-2.0	-0.2
All Other Outlets	3.4	4.6	7.4	2.4	2.6	-0.8	-2.0

Source: ACNielsen Homescan Hispanic panel, Los Angeles, 2000

WHAT DOES THIS MEAN TO MARKETERS?

When targeting Latinos in the retail arena, distribution and merchandising efforts must extend beyond the $2 million-plus grocery store in order to influence and increase purchases among Hispanics. In addition, Hispanic-specific channels or stores in high-density Hispanic areas need to be addressed and understood in order to best allocate sales resources and marketing funds to maximize case sales. Manufacturers and distributors need to evaluate Hispanic category data outside traditional channels. They need to understand the product mix, shopping experience and expectations, language of displays, and shelf space allocated to Hispanic-preferred brands and products.

This intelligence can persuade management of products that sell well in other channels to provide special advertising, promotion, and merchandising support in underdeveloped channels—stores not usually patronized by Latinas.

WAREHOUSE GAPS WITH HISPANICS

Warehouse clubs are a significant retail channel for many consumer goods categories in the U.S., and the Los Angeles market is no exception. In the total market, according to ACNielsen Homescan Hispanic panel data, 9.9 percent of dry grocery volume, 10.7 percent of frozen food volume, and 13.9 percent of deli volume is sold in warehouse clubs. For these departments, the shares are second only to $2 million-plus grocery stores. Even more dramatic is the fact that warehouse clubs get 17 percent of all alcoholic beverage purchases in the Los Angeles market. This share of the $596 million estimated spending in Los Angeles on alcoholic beverages translates to $60 million spent in warehouse clubs.

As mentioned above, the warehouse club channel is not a popular one among Hispanic consumers, particularly those who are less acculturated. Warehouse clubs have fewer inner-city stores and their bulky package sizes usually require the buyer to have a car and to afford the larger purchases in any case. Lastly, unless Spanish-language signs or help is readily available, the shopping experience cannot be a pleasant one.

ALCOHOLIC BEVERAGES

Where do Hispanics' purchase alcoholic beverages? ACNielsen Homescan Hispanic panel data for other channels reveals that smaller groceries, convenience, gas, bodegas and all other outlets (liquor stores included) are very popular among Hispanics for alcoholic beverage purchases.

As mentioned above, warehouse clubs' share in most categories is lower for Hispanics than for the general market, and alcoholic beverages are not the exception. For example, non-Hispanics spend 19.5 percent of their dollars in this category in warehouse clubs, but Hispanics spend only 7.8 percent. This 11.7 percentage point gap of the Los Angeles market Hispanics' $128 million spent on alcoholic beverages translates to almost $15 million in this department that is spent in other channels. As is the case in many categories, warehouse-club purchases of alcoholic beverages are highest among bilinguals. The percentage of alcoholic beverage dollars spent in warehouse clubs by both Spanish-dominant and English-dominant consumers is 5.6 percent, but bilinguals spend 12.9 percent.

FIGURE 17.6

Alcoholic Beverages—Non-Hispanics vs. Hispanics

Percentage of Dollar Sales by Channel

Percent of sales by channel	non-Hispanic	Hispanic	Index Hispanic to non-Hispanic	Difference Hispanic vs. non-Hispanic
$2 million-plus	62.3%	61.2%	98	-1.1%
All Other Grocery	0.9	2.8	317	1.9
All Other Food	0.7	1.8	269	1.1
Warehouse	19.5	7.8	40	-11.7
Discount	1.1	1.9	165	0.7
Convenience/Gas	0.8	4.0	521	3.2
Drug	7.5	7.7	103	0.2
All Other Outlets	7.3	12.9	176	5.6

Source: ACNielsen Homescan Hispanic panel, Los Angeles, 2000

Bilinguals consistently shop more in warehouse clubs than do Spanish-dominant and English-dominant Latinos. Alcoholic beverages are no exception. However, this is a unique case, beyond the classic acculturation parameter, given that shares in all other types of stores vary with acculturation (Figure 17.7).

FIGURE 17.7

Alcoholic Beverages—Acculturated and Non-Hispanic vs. Hispanic

Percentage of Dollar Sales by Language Segment

Percent of sales by channel	non-Hispanic	Hispanic	Language Segmentation		
			Spanish-dominant	Bilingual	English-dominant
$2 million-plus	62.3%	61.2%	53.5	62.1	71.9
All Other Grocery	0.9	2.8	4.1	2.7	1.1
All Other Food	0.7	1.8	3.4	1.2	0.0
Warehouse	19.5	7.8	5.6	12.9	5.6
Discount	1.1	1.9	3.2	1.3	0.5
Convenience/Gas	0.8	4.0	7.9	1.5	0.8
Drug	7.5	7.7	3.3	8.1	13.9
All Other Outlets	62.3	61.2	19.1	10.2	6.3

Source: ACNielsen Homescan Hispanic panel, Los Angeles, 2000

One high-volume alcoholic beverage that demonstrates this shopping pattern well is wine. Of all alcoholic beverages, wine has received the most attention from warehouse clubs because of its potential to attract affluent, high-potential customers. True wine aficionados buy by the case, a dynamic wholly consistent with warehouse clubs' economics. A profitable, high-volume item ($210 million in the Los Angeles market, $184 million among non-Hispanics and $26 million among Hispanics), wine is the most frequently purchased alcoholic beverage after beer (6.4 occasions per year among Los Angeles market consumers as a whole). As shown below, Hispanics not only purchase less wine than non-Hispanics in general, but also more often buy wine in supermarkets and drug stores and much less at warehouse clubs, with the exception of bilinguals, who seem to be regular patrons at warehouse clubs.

Retail-outlet preferences for wine purchases vary with acculturation. However, "wine" retail and the wine category in general has more to do with the socio-cultural realm of the Hispanic market than acculturation alone.

FIGURE 17.8

Wine—Non-Hispanics vs. Hispanics

Percentage of Dollar Sales by Channel

Percent of sales by channel	non-Hispanic	Hispanic	Index Hispanic to non-Hispanic	Difference Hispanic vs. non-Hispanic
$2 million-plus	61.2%	66.7%	109	5.5%
All Other Grocery	1.1	1.6	150	0.5
All Other Food	1.6	0.2	13	-1.4
Warehouse	20.3	10.5	52	-9.8
Discount	1.8	1.9	103	0.1
Convenience/Gas	0.1	0.6	414	0.5
Drug	6.6	11.1	166	4.4
All Other Outlets	7.3	7.5	103	0.2

Source: ACNielsen Hispanic Homescan Panel, Los Angeles, 2000

Based on proprietary studies, I have learned that less-acculturated Hispanics, particularly Spanish-dominant, tend to prefer beer and hard liquor (whiskey, tequila, rum) to wine for most of their social occasions. Both beer and hard liquor tend to be impulse purchases and are more often than not purchased at locations on the way home or to a party. Spanish-dominant Latinos rarely have cellars that need to be stocked nor could they afford purchasing large quantities. Hence, their wine dollars rarely go to warehouse clubs. On the other hand, wine is popular with the more-educated and intellectual Hispanic elite in most Latin American countries, many of which produce some of the best wines in the world (e.g., Chile and Argentina). This more-educated and sophisticated Hispanic tends to purchase wine in fine wine shops or in $2 million-plus grocery stores (see Figure 17.9). Obviously many bilinguals have discovered that "fine wine" is available at warehouse clubs—and they also seem to have time to shop these stores. Certainly, this presents a marketing opportunity for warehouse clubs to approach the Hispanic wine connoisseur.

FIGURE 17.9

Wine—Acculturated and Non-Hispanic vs. Hispanic

Percentage of Dollar Sales

			Language Segmentation		
Percent of sales by channel	non-Hispanic	Hispanic	Spanish-dominant	Bilingual	English-dominant
$2 million-plus	61.2%	66.7%	60.1%	63.1%	74.9%
All Other Grocery	1.1	1.6	5.2	1.3	0.3
All Other Food	1.6	0.2	0.3	0.3	0.0
Warehouse	20.3	10.5	5.2	16.9	4.3
Discount	1.8	1.9	3.4	1.9	1.0
Convenience/Gas	0.1	0.6	1.7	0.6	0.0
Drug	6.6	11.1	5.3	9.5	16.0
All Other Outlets	7.3	7.5	18.9	6.4	3.5

Source: ACNielsen Homescan Hispanic panel, Los Angeles, 2000

NON-FOOD ITEMS PURCHASED IN GROCERY AND DISCOUNT STORES

Packaged fare in American supermarkets extends far beyond food and beverages. Cleaning and laundry supplies, paper goods, pet-care products, and cigarettes are all profitable, non-perishable categories for retailers. Like many general-market consumers, Hispanics view the availability of these products as a convenience when doing their food shopping, and, consequently they buy many in large and small grocery stores. In fact, Hispanics in the Los Angeles market buy more of their non-food items in grocery stores than do non-Hispanics. When large and smaller grocery stores, and other food outlets are considered, Hispanic consumers buy 48.2 percent of their non-food items in food stores, compared with 43.2 percent for non-Hispanics. This 5 percent of Los Angeles Hispanics' $527 million spent on non-foods translates to $26.3 million on non-foods that is spent in "traditional" food outlets. As might be expected, the percentage of non-food dollars spent in food stores decreases with acculturation. Spanish-dominant consumers spend 51.8 percent of their non-food dollars in food stores. Bilinguals spend 46.6 percent, and English-dominant consumers spend 43.7 percent, about the same as non-Hispanics (Figure 17.11).

In addition, Latinos purchase 19.8 percent of their non-food items at discount stores, noticeably more than the 16 percent purchased there by non-Hispanics. Hispanic consumers also buy slightly more non-food items at convenience stores (including local bodegas) than do non-Hispanics (2.4 percent vs. 1.9 percent).

So, where do Hispanics purchase non-food items? The panel data show that, in addition to $2 million-plus grocery stores and discount stores, Hispanics shop at warehouse clubs, drugstores and other outlets regularly, but these are less-common shopping destinations for Hispanics when shopping for non-food purchases, compared with non-Hispanics.

FIGURE 17.10

Non-Food Product—Non-Hispanics vs. Hispanics

Percentage of Dollar Sales by Channel

Percent of sales by channel	non-Hispanic	Hispanic	Index Hispanic to non-Hispanic	Difference Hispanic vs. non-Hispanic
$2 million-plus	42.7%	45.5%	107	+2.8%
All Other Grocery	0.4	2.1	544	+0.7
All Other Food	0.1	0.6	725	+0.5
Warehouse	18.2	15.7	86	-2.5
Discount	16.0	19.8	124	+3.8
Convenience/Gas	1.9	2.4	124	+0.5
Drug	3.8	2.5	67	-1.3
All Other Outlets	16.9	11.4	67	-5.5

Source: ACNielsen Homescan Hispanic panel, Los Angeles, 2000

A similar retail usage pattern is observed for non-food products vis-à-vis acculturation. Again, retail shopping patterns correlate with acculturation. The more acculturated, English-dominant channel shares look very similar to those of non-Hispanics, and less acculturated Latino consumers, Spanish-dominant and bilinguals, show distinct non-food retail shopping preferences, as shown below.

FIGURE 17.11

Non-Foods Products—Acculturated and Non-Hispanic vs. Hispanic

Percentage of Dollar Sales

| Percent of sales by channel | non-Hispanic | Hispanic | Language Segmentation | | | Difference English-dominant vs. non-Hispanic | Difference English-dominant vs. Hispanic |
			Spanish-dominant	Bilingual	English-dominant		
$2 million-plus	42.7%	45.5%	47.2%	44.8%	43.4%	+0.7%	-2.1%
All Other Grocery	0.4	2.1	3.4	1.7	0.3	-0.1	-1.8
All Other Food	0.1	0.6	1.2	0.1	0.0	-0.1	-0.6
Warehouse	18.2	15.7	9.7	20.7	19.7	+1.5	+4.0
Discount	16.0	19.8	19.6	19.4	21.0	+5.0	+1.2
Convenience/Gas	1.9	2.4	3.5	1.3	1.7	-0.2	-0.6
Drug	3.8	2.5	2.9	2.5	2.0	-1.8	-0.6
All Other Outlets	16.9	11.4	12.6	9.6	11.8	-5.1	+0.5

Source: ACNielsen Homescan Hispanic panel, Los Angeles, 2000

FEWER HEALTH AND BEAUTY CARE PRODUCTS PURCHASED IN DRUGSTORES

In most Latin American countries, pharmacies are small, owner operated, and focused on the core business of selling prescription medicine. Therefore, Hispanics in the U.S. are less likely to think of their local drugstore as the primary shopping destination for many items beyond prescription drugs. Health and beauty care products, for example, projected by ACNielsen to be a $1.5 billion business in the Los Angeles market, are an excellent example.

Non-Hispanics in Los Angeles spend 27.3 percent of their dollars in Health and Beauty Care (HBC) in drugstores. Hispanics, on the other hand, spend only 19.9 percent. The 7.4 percent of Los Angeles Hispanics' $409 million spent on this category translates to $30 million spent in stores outside of drugstores in this one department alone (Figure 17.12). Again, as might be expected, the percentage of HBC dollars spent in drugstores increases with acculturation. Spanish-dominant consumers spend 18.6 percent of their HBC dollars in drugstores. Bilinguals spend 20.6 percent, and English-dominant spend 21.4 percent, still well below non-Hispanics.

Where are the HBC transactions occurring? A comparable look at ACNielsen Homescan Hispanic panel data for other channels reveals that two other points of distribution are significantly overdeveloped—more popular—among Hispanics. For example, Los Angeles market Hispanics spend 13.2 percent of their HBC dollars in outlets such as beauty supply stores and salons, compared to 8.4 percent of HBC purchases in these outlets by non-Hispanics. This additional volume translates to $19.6 million in sales for Other Outlets or channels. Similarly, Hispanics spend 11.4 percent of their HBC dollars in warehouse stores as compared to 10.2 percent of HBC purchases among non-Hispanics. This additional volume translates to $4.9 million in sales for warehouse stores. Hispanic consumers buy more HBC in small grocery stores and convenience stores (including *bodegas*) than do non-Hispanics.

It can be hypothesized that Latinas shop more often for their HBC products at non-traditional stores, such as beauty salons, *bodegas,* and mom-and-pop stores because of the "gestalt of the category." What do I mean by this? Again, based on my previous research, and speaking as a Latina, there may be several factors at work here. Latinas may feel more comfortable in the smaller stores. They may spend more time and experience a higher level of comfort at the beauty salon, and have the opportunity to interact with other women who can advise on these products in Spanish. Lastly, these non-traditional stores also tend to carry HBC products from other countries, not available at traditional stores.

Los Angeles market Hispanics spend 13.2 percent of their Health and Beauty Care dollars in outlets such as beauty supply stores and salons, compared to 8.4 percent of HBC purchases in these outlets by non-Hispanics.

FIGURE 17.12

Health and Beauty Products—Non-Hispanics vs. Hispanics

Percentage of Dollar Sales by Channel

Percent of sales by channel	non-Hispanic	Hispanic	Index Hispanic to non-Hispanic	Difference Hispanic vs. non-Hispanic
$2 million-plus	29.5%	29.2%	99	-0.3%
All Other Grocery	0.3	1.2	484	+0.9
All Other Food	0.0	0.4	1467	+0.4
Warehouse	10.2	11.4	112	+1.2
Discount	24.3	23.6	97	-0.7
Convenience/Gas	0.1	1.0	1300	+0.9
Drug	27.3	19.9	73	+7.4
All Other Outlets	8.4	13.2	158	+4.8

Source: ACNielsen Homescan Hispanic panel, Los Angeles, 2000

Two large categories within the health-and-beauty-care department are cosmetics and toothpaste. Cosmetics is estimated to be a $67 million category in the Los Angeles market—$49 million among non-Hispanics and $18 million among Hispanics. Toothpaste is an estimated $61 million category in this market—$38 million among non-Hispanics and $23 million among Hispanics. Each of these categories is underdeveloped among Hispanics in drugstores. These two product categories get more of their volume from Hispanics in specialty outlets and warehouse stores (Figures 17.13 and 17.14).

FIGURE 17.13

Cosmetics—Non-Hispanics vs. Hispanics

Percentage of Dollar Sales by Channel

Percent of sales by channel	non-Hispanic	Hispanic	Index Hispanic to non-Hispanic	Difference Hispanic vs. non-Hispanic
$2 million-plus	8.9%	15.4%	174	6.5%
All Other Grocery	0.3	0.4	123	0.1
All Other Food	0.0	0.1	—	0.1
Warehouse	1.0	3.8	387	2.8
Discount	40.5	35.2	87	-5.3
Convenience/Gas	0.0	0.5	1700	0.5
Drug	40.2	26.7	66	-13.5
All Other Outlets	9.2	18.1	197	8.9

Source: ACNielsen Homescan Hispanic panel, Los Angeles, 2000

While Hispanics buy more of their cosmetics in large grocery stores than do non-Hispanics, this is not the case for toothpaste. Its share in $2 million-plus grocery stores is 42.4 percent, significantly less than the 50.9 percent purchased by non-Hispanics in that particular channel. Instead, purchases of toothpaste by Hispanics take place in a wide variety of stores (Figure 17.14).

FIGURE 17. 14

Toothpaste—Non-Hispanics vs. Hispanics

Percentage of Dollar Sales by Channel

Percent of sales by channel	non-Hispanic	Hispanic	Index Hispanic to non-Hispanic	Difference Hispanic vs. non-Hispanic
$2 million-plus	50.9%	42.4%	83	-8.5%
All Other Grocery	0.2	2.5	1400	2.3
All Other Food	0.0	1.1	10600	1.1
Warehouse	12.0	14.8	123	2.8
Discount	21.7	23.8	110	2.1
Convenience/Gas	0.0	1.5	7500	1.5
Drug	9.9	5.5	55	-4.4
All Other Outlets	5.4	8.5	159	3.2

Source: ACNielsen Homescan Hispanic panel, Los Angeles, 2000

A FINAL THOUGHT ON DRUGSTORES

Since the drugstore experience as more than a pharmacy is new to immigrant Latinos, it is highly recommended that drugstore operators seek to understand the Hispanic consumer's view of American drugstores. The variety of items sold in a typical large chain drugstore in the U.S. may be daunting to someone unfamiliar with the format. Through *in-culture* marketing efforts this can be easily changed. For example, drugstores can make Spanish-speaking pharmacists or aides available, or offer vaccination clinics or other health-related programs at the store to introduce the store to the Hispanic community. Another approach is to offer classes, such as Lamaze, in Spanish.

At the store level, it would help to display new products separately and provide bilingual or Spanish-language signage as well as store maps showing where the different categories of products are located. These examples of "eye-level," personal marketing activities can successfully bring less acculturated Hispanics into drugstores.

FIND HISPANIC CUSTOMERS WHERE THEY SHOP

Manufacturers and distributors interested in placing their products in front of their target Hispanic customers can easily track the unique, yet consistent patterns in channel share within the different Hispanic market segments. The smaller language segment, English-dominant, tends to mimic the retail share patterns of the non-Hispanic consumer. The larger, less acculturated language segments, Spanish-dominant and bilingual, tend to march to a different drummer, with retail outlet shares that differ from the non-Hispanic consumer. This is consistent with most product categories and departments analyzed. Health-and-beauty-care products are not different from dry-goods, food products, and others. Therefore, manufacturers of health-and-beauty products should extend their marketing and distribution efforts beyond the drugstore channel if they wish to capture a larger share of the Hispanic market. Certainly, having a presence at Hispanic community fairs, events, and schools can help develop traffic at the drugstore and "share of heart" for both the retailer and the brands sampled. As with other types of non-food items, category-by-category shopping patterns differ.

Notes

1. A detailed description of Hispanic market segments is found in Section 2 of this book.
2. Since 49 percent and lower Hispanic population density stores are not included in the Scantrack data, caution is recommended when extrapolating data to the total Hispanic market. Channel shares may vary significantly in lower than 50 percent penetration areas.
3. All volumetric estimates are based on ACNielsen Panel numbers, based on $ per household by number of households.

Labatt USA

For more detail on this case and creative materials, go to www.incultureapproach.com

Brand or product: Cerveza Tecate

Campaign: Llegé para quedarse 2000 (Here to Stay)

BACKGROUND

For Mexican-brewed Cerveza Tecate, it has been a faster than expected climb to the top of the imported beer category in the U.S., where the whole industry has been semi-flat since the 1980s. When Tecate importer Labatt USA approached The Cartel five years ago, it wanted to break into the top 10. They embarked on an aggressive strategy to channel Tecate's marketing efforts exclusively behind the Hispanic market, namely the less acculturated Mexican American market where share had not been maximized.

The Cartel established the brand's positioning as truly authentic and the most Mexican of the Mexican beers. Sales rose, and in 1998 Tecate advanced to the eighth-ranked imported beer in the U.S. from eleventh the previous year, according to Impact Databank.

The campaign was designed to expand from within, creating a halo effect that attracted the general market and other acculturated Hispanics to Tecate—even though Labatt expended minimal advertising effort against the General Market. Along with the "Latin explosion" of the late 1990s, the brand discovered that new consumers were enjoying the point of differentiation that Tecate offers versus American brands, specifically its authenticity and trendy cache as an imported beer.

MARKETING CHALLENGE

In addition to meeting standard brand objectives (i.e., increasing volume-growth and brand awareness among the Mexican American market), The Cartel and Labatt focused on new objectives:

- Maintain the results-proven, focus strategy

- Evolve creatively and develop an authentic and genuine campaign that would resonate even more strongly among first-generation Mexican Americans

- Sustain the brand's annual double-digit growth momentum and catapult the brand to the top five

From an industry standpoint, the import category continued to experience higher than average growth rates, helping the brand to accomplish its goals. The upswing in imports was consistent with the economic boom and consumers' purchasing dynamics of the late 1990s.

From a consumer perspective, The Cartel recognized that Hispanics appreciate products from their homeland and that they did not necessarily want to be coaxed into consuming American or non-Mexican products right away. Many times they purchased U.S. name brands because they did not want to stand out from the crowd. Messages needed to support and encourage the target to consume Mexican products by evoking pride of heritage and culture already inherent in Tecate, using the *in-culture* "nostalgia factor." Respecting the halo effect, the agency also knew it was important not to alienate more acculturated Mexican Americans and Hispanics who may be inspired to drink Tecate as a way of connecting with their Hispanic heritage.

MEDIA AND PROMOTIONAL STRATEGIES

Building on the success Tecate had achieved through its initial platform, Labatt and The Cartel agreed the best course of action was to maintain the *Tecate, Llegé para quedarse* (Here to stay) positioning for 1999 and 2000. The brand's efforts continued to concentrate on the still under-tapped, Spanish-dominant Mexican American market where the most volume gains could be made with current budget levels.

To take it a step further, the team agreed to evolve or "refresh" the campaign. The Cartel developed the *Saludos desde Mexico* (Heartfelt Greetings from Mexico) campaign that genuinely depicted the target's life experiences in the U.S., which was heartily embraced by the Mexican American community.

The Cartel developed an integrated "full-circle" print, radio, outdoor, and TV campaign to drive trial and brand awareness, and at the same time generate excitement among consumers and the trade. The Cartel's media partner, San Antonio-based MediaWorks, worked closely with local Tecate brewery representatives to identify appropriate local media vehicles that would deliver messages right to the neighborhood, *barrio*-by-*barrio*. In fact, local reps from Tecate's brewer Cervecería Cuauhtemoc Moctezuma in Mexico were sent to the U.S. to positively influence volume sales in top Hispanic markets. To pitch Tecate as the "true" Mexican beer, print and outdoor ads leveraged Tecate's brand equity in the red and gold signature can. Tecate was also made the hero in all print executions utilizing humorous plays on words (double-entendres). Media was negotiated one-on-one with local radio stations and with the help of Tecate brewery reps. The reps were also enlisted to generate excitement among retailers via regional promotions at community events such as fairs, musical concerts, and sporting venues.

The authenticity positioning was maintained across the creative components. Radio spots used contemporary Mexican regional and folkloric music performed by mariachis from Mexico, as well as *corridos* (open-ended folk ballads), about the unique experience of drinking Tecate, performed by bands from Mexico. TV spots featured native Mexican people in major Mexican cities sending heartfelt greetings and good wishes to their fellow *paisanos* in the U.S. Tecate also signed on as one of the broadcast sponsors of Major League Soccer and the Mexican Professional Soccer games that aired on all Spanish TV networks.

RESULTS

Again, with absolute minimum efforts in the general market and focusing on a niche strategy, significant results in 1999 and 2000 were achieved. In summary:

- Performance growth for 1999 and 2000 was 13 percent and 23 percent, respectively.[1]

- Tecate is now the fourth largest imported beer in the U.S. after Corona, Heineken and Labatt Blue.[2]

- Awareness increased significantly across various brand and preference criteria according to proprietary measurement tools.[3]

- Also, Tecate is now the number one imported can in the U.S.[4]

Tecate has developed a solid personality and character in the U.S. Hispanic marketplace, and continues to do so while gaining respect from other segments of the market, setting the stage for a major leap that will propel the brand to new heights in the 21st century.

AGENCY: Cartel Creativo, Inc. (The Cartel), www.thecartel.com

Notes

1. Labatt USA's SADI Database for volume shipments from Mexico
2. Impact Databank Publication 2000
3. Labatt USA's Proprietary Tracking Study
4. Nielsen Food & Liquor 2000

Kraft Foods North America, Inc.

For more detail on this case and creative
materials, go to www.incultureapproach.com

Brand or Products: Oscar Mayer

BACKGROUND

Kraft Foods North America, Inc. is the largest packaged branded food and beverage company headquartered in the U.S. and the second largest in the world. Its
portfolio includes hundreds of brands, such as Velveeta, Kraft Macaroni and
Cheese, Oscar Mayer, Nabisco, Post, Kool-Aid, Maxwell House, Tombstone and
many more that are enjoyed by 99 percent of American households.

Kraft's business philosophy is deeply rooted in understanding and responding
to the needs of its consumers including the estimated 38.5 million Hispanics.
Kraft is proud of its efforts to meet the needs of a growing multicultural America.

In 1999, Kraft Foods noticed its Hispanic share was not growing as fast as its
overall share in some categories. This situation served as a strategic "call for
action" given the double-digit growth of the Hispanic population. Kraft acted
promptly by changing marketing strategies and embarking on an in-depth analysis of the Hispanic consumer and key decision-maker—the Hispanic mom.

Kraft marketing managers enlisted the support and involvement of their
senior management with the objective of developing culturally relevant marketing programs which:

• Enhance the quality of Hispanic moms' lives

• Create an emotional bond between Kraft brands and Hispanic Moms

• Are embraced by retailers as unique and value added

MARKETING CHALLENGE

The Hispanic consumer opportunity presents a classic marketing challenge for
Kraft and others—effectively applying target marketing. Kraft understands the
need for target marketing and the importance of distinguishing between consumer preferences. The cornerstone of Kraft's success is rooted in understanding
how to identify key target groups and tailor marketing efforts to the target's specific needs and concerns. The important challenge was knowing how to reach the

potential target buyer in each group, particularly when vehicles of communication are constantly evolving.

The first step in achieving these objectives was to identify valuable consumer insights about Hispanic moms. In other words, understanding not only her eating and cooking behavior but also uncovering emotional consumer insights that explain her life motivations, her dreams, and her wishes for herself and her family.

RESEARCH

Kraft thought it beneficial to communicate with several key family "decision makers" or "influencers" at the same time expanding the opportunity to reach greater numbers of consumers than in the general market. Kraft applied this insight by communicating with several Hispanic consumers at one time—crossing generations and speaking to various needs—centered on fun and nutritious foods.

Even armed with these insights, growing Kraft share depended on speaking to Hispanic women through her different roles—mother, wife, sister, daughter—positioning Kraft brands as her central allies in providing her family with their favorite foods for homemade meals and speaking to her aspirations and values.

For this task, Kraft Foods relied on leading-edge consumer insights and experts that understand the Hispanic culture. First, the company identified the Hispanic strategic-value target by using the then newly created Los Angeles ACNielsen Homescan Hispanic panel. The panel provided actual Hispanic consumer grocery purchases that were linked back to key demographic variables, shopping habits, and language preference. Second, Kraft embarked on a series of ethnographic consumer interviews with Hispanic moms, where participants spanned not only across key Hispanic geographies, but also across varying levels of acculturation.

Kraft knows that community involvement is critical when attempting to attract multicultural consumers. The Market Segment Group confirmed this recently with research indicating that Hispanics are 76 percent more likely to buy products from companies that contribute to their communities than from those that do not.

STRATEGIES FOR SUCCESS

Relevant Grassroots Presence

The company had long established important relationships with key Hispanic leaders at the national level and in key Hispanic geographies, and a history of serving as a major underwriter of Hispanic advocacy programs and organizations. However, in several areas Kraft went beyond usual sponsorships, instead negotiating brand signature programs that also appeal to the dreams of Hispanic moms. One of these programs is the National Council of La Raza's Kraft Community Service Award that honors Hispanic actors or entertainers that promote positive Hispanic roles featured at the annually televised ALMA Awards. Previous honorees include Andy Garcia and Rita Moreno. The honorees also joined Kraft in presenting a corporate contribution in their name to a local Hispanic advocacy organization.

In 2001, Kraft initiated a unique local marketing strategy in four key Hispanic geographies: Los Angeles, Chicago, New York, and San Antonio. By localizing marketing efforts, Kraft could effectively reach 55 percent of the total Hispanic segment while customizing the approach in each selling area. In addition, Kraft could also respond to retailer partnerships, specific Hispanic regional differences, and levels of acculturation. Kraft already knew the advantages of coupling these two approaches with effective local community efforts and programs.

The local development and support of brand initiatives allows Kraft to create continuity and relevance to Hispanics. Such successful corporate efforts include local public relations elements that facilitate an emotional connection with the target while building brand recognition and loyalty. This local marketing strategy has proven extremely successful for Kraft, as both share and brand sales have increased dramatically. In 2002, these efforts were expanded to Northern California, Phoenix, and Houston.

"In-Culture" Integrated Marketing

Kraft-sponsored public relations efforts were integrated with in-store retail offers and culturally relevant promotional and marketing programs at grass roots events. National programs, such as Kraft/Sears "Win a Dream Home" Sweepstakes, and

Kraft's *Comida y Familia* recipe and coupon insert were also paired with localized Hispanic retail and brand initiatives that spoke to the specific Hispanic demographic profiles and cultural practices in each target area.

For example, in Los Angeles, Kraft created promotional programs that highlighted its knowledge of Hispanic interests in family sporting events, entertainment and recreation that crossed generations, and that spoke to all of Kraft's Hispanic targets in that one geography. Although retail- and brand-focused, these programs also provided opportunities for Hispanic consumers to win college scholarships, meet Hispanic celebrities and role models, and promoted reading.

A LOOK AT A SPECIFIC BRAND: Oscar Mayer Delivers for Hispanic Moms

Oscar Mayer is a Kraft brand whose team is committed to understanding the Hispanic consumer and building cultural relevance with the brand. Although all members of Hispanic families consume hot dogs, kids are the major drivers. Because the U.S. Census 2000 projections indicate that one in every five children will be Hispanic by the year 2005, this is an important audience for the brand.

Oscar Mayer's research indicated that Hispanic moms want to maintain close family ties and be good mothers by providing for their children's success in life. The Oscar Mayer brand speaks readily to their desire to satisfy and provide fun foods for their kids. Hispanic consumers embraced the new brand positioning that Oscar Mayer products are high quality products that are family oriented, fun and pleasing to kids. This positioning was supported with a new advertising message for the Oscar Mayer brand.

CREATIVE STRATEGY

Drawings/Story Boards

The Oscar Mayer team, with assistance from its Hispanic advertising agencies, successfully launched the TV spot *Drawings* in August 2000 throughout key local selling areas (Miami, San Antonio, Los Angeles). The TV ad was supported by radio in the continuity areas and then expanded to New York.

Media and Promotional Strategies

In 2001, Oscar Mayer's media objective was to achieve effective reach levels to increase share among Hispanic consumers while increasing brand loyalty. A mix of television and radio were used to achieve this objective. The media strategy delivered the necessary brand penetration and message positioning to introduce the Oscar Mayer brand to new Hispanic consumers while local retail promotional events and radio remotes reinforced the brand with existing consumers.

This advertising strategy was executed in concert with the Oscar Mayer Hispanic talent contest nationally and in an expanded form in the top five Hispanic markets. The contest: *Singing for Fame* or *Cantando Hasta La Fama*™ invited children aged 4 to 10 to perform a rendition of the Oscar Mayer Spanish jingle at selected community organizations or at local retail locations. The program selected two finalists for $5,000 college fund awards and gave one $20,000 grand prize to a young talented performer. The program underscored the high value Hispanics place on educational attainment while Oscar Mayer facilitates the entire family's desire to make young dreams come true.

Oscar Mayer also made the program successful by selecting young college graduates to serve as Hispanic brand ambassadors. These young Hispanics promoted the brand and executed the program locally while serving as role models to the performing children. Another exciting component included the participation of Hispanic celebrities such as salsa star, Tito Puente, Jr., and the Grammy-nominated performer of traditional Spanish children's songs, El Morro.

Kraft encouraged the involvement of local retailers in Hispanic initiatives. This strategy has proven successful especially when tied to national Hispanic marketing efforts. Retailers participated in hosting Oscar Mayer's *Hasta La Fama* auditions and with local radio promotions, thereby increasing the visibility and relevance of the brand to Hispanic consumers.

RESULTS

- The messages were reinforced through the public relations program—*Hasta La Fama* contest—and additional coverage garnered through TV, radio, and print outlets. Media impressions for these efforts were estimated to reach over 25 million people in 2001, an increase of 77 percent from the previous year's program. Event highlights appeared in and on magazines.

- Radio news releases were created to promote the 2001 *Hasta La Fama* program, highlighting the 2000 contest winner and extending the program reach to 17 additional Hispanic market areas.

- The new creative and focused marketing strategy led to increases in both share and brand sales. Penetration of the Oscar Mayer brand in key Hispanic geographies increased by nearly 30 percent.

AGENCY: The Bravo Group, www.thebravogroupyr.com

California Milk Processor Board

For more detail on this case and creative
materials, go to www.incultureapproach.com

Brand or Product: Milk

BACKGROUND

In 1993, the California Milk Processor Board (CMPB) launched what was to become one of the best known campaigns in advertising history, Got Milk?® In early 1994 it expanded its efforts to include a Hispanic marketing program. One of the first questions raised was the relevance and marketing leverage of Got Milk?

MARKETING CHALLENGE

Strategic research indicated that the Milk Deprivation Strategy and Got Milk? were not a strong fit with Hispanics. Running out of rice or milk was not considered funny (quite the opposite) and Got Milk? could have been misinterpreted to mean "Are you lactating?" In addition, the foods used in the English-language campaign (peanut butter, chocolate brownies) were not always relevant for Latino audiences.

RESEARCH FINDINGS

Milk usage patterns differ between Hispanics and the General Market. The General Market strategy recognized that milk is seldom a stand-alone beverage and its consumption is linked to a select number of meals and food occasions. Research clearly indicated that Hispanics already loved milk and were heavy users of it, felt it was highly nutritious, and were drinking more than the general population, especially whole milk.

Most importantly, research revealed that Hispanics used milk extensively in scratch cooking, and passed treasured, milk-based recipes from generation to generation. Not surprisingly, grandmothers played a pivotal role in the Hispanic family.

MEDIA STRATEGIES

Thus was born the Generations Strategy and the Spanish-language theme line, "Have you given them enough milk today?" This campaign encouraged Hispanics to consume more milk by dramatizing the unique and crucial role that milk plays in the Latino family. The campaign focused on milk recipes as a way to drive incremental milk usage.

The campaign received tremendous response, from both consumers and the business press. Ongoing research indicated that it was recalled, understood and deeply appreciated. While it was not possible to break out Hispanic milk sales, comments from retailers and processors were extremely positive and a tracking study showed that consumption was stable to growing slightly.

In 2000, research indicated that the campaign needed to evolve. The tag line was changed to *Familia, Amor Y Leche* or "Family, Love, and Milk." This tag line gave the campaign a broad base, encompassed adults and young children, suggested milk as a beverage and for recipe use, and reinforced a strong nutritional message. Research indicated that this line clearly and powerfully positioned milk in the Latino family and community.

In 2001, the campaign was broadened further to include men, specifically fathers. A new TV spot featured a dad and his daughter shopping for ingredients for a milk dessert in a supermarket. This nontraditional pairing reflects the acculturation process and shifting gender roles within the Latino community.

PROMOTION STRATEGIES

Beyond the television and outdoor executions of the "Generations" campaign, a recipe booklet was developed and promoted through a direct response commercial. The response was phenomenal. The first press run of 5,000 booklets was gone in the first few hours, with 400,000 printed for additional requests. Recipe cards were also available in supermarket aisle displays where they were equally popular.

In 2000, complementing the television commercials, an outdoor campaign using the artwork of youngsters was created as a result of the new theme line. In a statewide contest, Hispanic children submitted their interpretations of the campaign tag line. The winners have had their artwork showcased in the outdoor boards and received public recognition for their accomplishments.

RESULTS

After years of steady decline, total milk consumption in California stabilized. Awareness of the *Familia, Amor Y Leche* campaign is high among Hispanics and the Milk Usage Tracking Study indicates that Hispanic milk consumption is consistently and significantly higher than the general population.

AGENCY: Anita Santiago Advertising, Inc., www.anitasantiago.com

McDonald's

For more detail on this case and creative materials, go to www.incultureapproach.com

Product or brand: Fiesta Menu "Food you love at the place you love"

BACKGROUND

McDonald's had tremendous loyalty among Hispanics, but it was lagging behind the competition in its Mexican offerings. McDonald's wanted to create a unique, customer focused event that would be proprietary to its stores, solidify its relationship with Hispanics, create new reasons for adults to visit McDonald's and expand the taste opportunities for adult Hispanics. A new Fiesta Menu was created to fulfill these goals.

Ad Américas was involved in the total process, from developing the food ideas to testing the new menu with consumers before its launch.

OBJECTIVES

- To drive business by creating a proprietary product event
- To solidify its relations with the Hispanic community and increase appeal among Hispanics
- To expand opportunities for McDonald's to compete in the full price, adult taste segment of the Quick Service Restaurant category.

TARGET AUDIENCE

Hispanic adults aged 18 to 34 and English-speaking adults, aged 18 to 49. McDonald's also wanted to attract adults who were looking for variety at breakfast time, as well as at lunch and dinner.

MARKETING CHALLENGE

McDonald's had several challenges. It needed to learn if it could offer a line of non-traditional foods not usually associated with its hamburger menu. It needed to know if customers would give it permission to try these non-traditional foods.

Research showed that the answer was Yes. Ten tasting groups of two-and-a-half hours each were conducted among Spanish-dominant and bilingual Hispanics, with two additional groups conducted in the general market. Hispanics and Anglos were positive about the concept of adding Mexican food. "It's about time," was a usual comment. Customers perceived that the added variety would be a benefit.

Products that had an 80 percent or above approval rate were chosen, including Chorizo Egg Burrito and Burrito a la Mexican for breakfast, Torta Guacamole sandwiches. Add on products were a Fiesta salad shaker, Dulce de Leche McFlurry and Shake, Sauce packets of Chipotle, Salsa, and Mexican, and wedding cookies.

Launch research included 225 in-store interviews representing all customer segments. In general, Hispanics rated the products higher across all categories.

MEDIA AND PROMOTIONAL STRATEGIES

The media strategy included television, radio, and outdoor. Promotions included Point of Purchase, in-store sampling, on-air, DJ endorsements, and press releases that provided local and national coverage.

Television and Cable was used to display and showcase the product to boost awareness and extend the current brand equity. Radio reinforced the frequency of message because it is one of the last mediums a consumer hears before entering the store. Radio also helped to maintain awareness. Outdoor helped reach customers near the point of purchase.

In-store advertising included store window decals, ceiling banners, register toppers, banners under the counters, stickers on crew members, and tray liners.

The theme of the promotional strategy was "All New and Muy Deliciouso." The introduction of a new line of products became a branded event with the Fiesta menu logo in advertisements, at the point of purchase, and on sandwich wraps.

RESULTS

The acceptance of the Fiesta Menu showed that McDonald's could add non-traditional products to its mix. Surveys found that satisfaction was high (8.8 on a scale of 10) among Hispanic customers with most of the new products. For most items, more than 80 percent of customers surveyed said they would purchase again.

AGENCY: Ad Américas, www.adamericas.com

Bayer Consumer Care

For more detail on this case and creative materials, go to www.incultureapproach.com

Brand Name: Alka-Seltzer®

BACKGROUND

Because of its strong presence in Latin America, Alka-Seltzer was the preference of U.S. Hispanics for many years as the #1 brand in the stomach aids and remedies category. Continued media support in Spanish with original creative had positioned Alka-Seltzer as the do-it-all, fun medicine for a host of gastrointestinal problems.

However, in 1992 Spanish language advertising was discontinued for several years. Alka-Seltzer's absence from the Hispanic market allowed Pepto-Bismol (the main competitor in the category) to usurp Alka-Seltzer's leadership position. In addition, acid blockers were becoming available over the counter, rather than by prescription and were rapidly gaining market share.

OBJECTIVE

In 1996 Bayer Consumer Care, owner of Alka-Seltzer, decided to re-enter the Hispanic market and regain lost market share.

RESEARCH: QUALITATIVE AND QUANTITATIVE

Aragón Advertising was commissioned to study the market situation and make recommendations. As a first step, the agency created adaptations in Spanish of General Market creative and tested them in focus groups to gain an understanding of how the market had evolved in four years. Based on consumer findings, Aragón developed a strategy with Hispanic nuances, while maintaining consistency with the new General Market positioning of Alka-Seltzer as strong, serious medicine. To further capture the mind of the consumer, a Pre/Post Attitude and Usage study was conducted.

MEDIA STRATEGIES

Based on the learning, a multi-layered, integrated marketing effort with original creative was designed and implemented. The campaign included broadcast, print media and strong promotional support.

Television

The agency developed a campaign consistent with the "strong medicine" strategy, but in keeping with Hispanic learning. Two TV ads, *Husband Knows Best* and *Older and Wiser* featured Hispanics recommending Alka-Seltzer to one another for severe heartburn with pain, while recognizing the benefits that Alka-Seltzer offers for the relief of general stomach discomfort and indigestion, the historical pre-campaign brand positioning. The ads featured a black and white flashback technique, which has become a visual Alka-Seltzer signature. The TV campaign used situations and music consistent with the Hispanic culture.

Radio

Aragón also developed a series of radio spots to feature market specific event information, in coordination with the Promotions department at Bayer Consumer Care. The radio campaign provided added value to the effort by linking together sampling, sweepstakes and product promotion at remotes and community events.

POP

Additional support was provided through the development of generic header cards with product info and sweepstakes headers with sweepstakes entries.

PROMOTION STRATEGIES

Recognizing the subtleties of each specific market, Aragón developed plans, focused on local consumer events, a Car Give-Away Sweepstakes and strong tie-in with regional sales manager to improve trade relations, including a sales kit for regional sales force.

RESULTS

Over 200,000 samples were distributed intending to propel Alka-Seltzer trial.

In the period studied, Unaided Awareness grew 76 percent. Sales grew anywhere from 5.8 percent to 12.6 percent depending on the specific markets. In a segment of the pharmaceutical industry that is stagnant and even declining, Alka-Seltzer was among the few to show positive increases. With continued media presence in the Hispanic market, refinements on the strategic planning and the launching of a line extension (Alka-Seltzer Heartburn Relief), the brand as a whole reached the number 1 position in sales for the first time since its Hispanic market relaunch.

AGENCY: Aragón Advertising, Inc., www.aragonadvertising.com

SECTION 4

HISPANIC
LIFESTYLES

Good marketing combines creative magic with science. The more marketing and advertising managers are in touch with the everyday life of the target consumer, the greater their chances of finding the key insights that will allow them to find a new angle for their marketing program. The *in-culture* consumer marketing landscape includes many facets of the Hispanic consumer. The community and the family are at the core. What we do with our families, like watching TV, reading a book or the newspaper, navigating the web, vacationing, traveling, dancing, singing, going to the doctor, or shopping, is where you find the real Hispanic consumer. Of course, there is no way this many subjects can be covered, but I have selected a few topics that relate to the strategy and planning for the marketing decision. Thanks to the many corporations and Hispanic-marketing leaders that have made their case studies available, I hope this section helps you visualize how high you can fly with your Hispanic marketing program, as well as how far it can take your business goals.

The topics are intended to be introductory in scope and to give you enough material to stimulate your "creative juices." The internet chapter (Chapter 19) and the appendix of online resources should bring to your fingertips the website information and connections you need to find more information on any of the subjects, if it exists.

In the following chapters you will find information about:

- *Healthcare and Latinos Today*

- *Travel, the Uncharted Frontier*

- *Internet and the Hispanic Online Phenomenon*

- *The Growing Hispanic Media Scene*

Chapter 18

Healthcare and Latinos Today

Despite improvements in health education and programs targeting Latinos during the past decade, there are still certain medical conditions that affect a disproportionately high share of Hispanics. Some of these have a genetic component, such as certain types of diabetes, but many other diseases, which could be prevented with regular check-ups and basic health education, correlate with cultural factors. For example, throughout Latin American countries the emphasis is on curative, not preventive medical care. The result is that medical conditions that can be prevented or alleviated at their onset are undetected or untreated until it is too late.

One of the cultural traits that supports this behavior is the belief in "fate." Some interpret it as *"está de Dios"*—if we get sick it is God's will. Conditions that affect Hispanics in the U.S. in higher proportions than non-Hispanics include diabetes, heart and cardiovascular conditions, peptic ulcers, obesity, asthma, allergy, hepatitis, and HIV/AIDS. Many times these are interpreted as God's will.

Another unfortunate cultural factor that affects non-acculturated Latina women is an extreme sense of privacy (*pudor*) that prevents them from having regular checkups. Again, the result is a disproportionately high rate of "feminine cancers." (Figure 18.1) Our research shows that many non-acculturated Hispanic women today easily adopt new products, such as infant formula or prepared baby foods as a result of successful marketing. Yet it is sad to see that so few go for regular Pap tests or breast checkups. As a result, Hispanic women are at much higher risk of developing breast cancer or cancer of the cervix than non-Hispanic women. All the conditions mentioned above are significantly more common among Mexican Latinas.

The last factor that has a negative impact on Hispanic healthcare is the limited access to healthcare for some sectors of the Hispanic market, as discussed below.

FIGURE 18.1

Barriers to Seeking Gynecological Care

in percentage

	Hispanic	African American	White non-Hispanic
Language/ cultural differences	20%	21%	21%
Discomfort with a physician	23	17	21
Cost	20	16	24
Fear of diagnosis	15	15	12
Embarrassment	18	8	9

Source: American Social Health Association, Research Triangle Park, NC.

HEALTHCARE AND *IN-CULTURE* COMMUNITY MARKETING

Some efforts have been made in both the private and public sectors to address barriers to seeking healthcare and changing healthcare habits. To succeed in addressing the prevention and education problems, *in-culture* concepts, interventions, and executions need to be implemented as in the following example.

During the past few years I have been a member of the corporate committee for a very special *in-culture* healthcare program, Latino Health Access (LHA) in Orange, California, a nonprofit, 501(c)(3) created in 1993. LHA was founded following a community assessment of the health of Latinos. The need for health education was so profound, those engaged in the study formed the Board of Directors and founded LHA. The LHA mission is to assist in improving the quality of life and health of uninsured, underserved people through high-quality preventive services and educational programs that emphasize personal responsibility and full participation in decisions affecting health. LHA trains individuals and families affected by a health condition to gain control of their health and lives. Participants that demonstrate leadership are recruited and trained to teach others. Using this peer model, LHA established the first educational program to manage diabetes and cardiovascular conditions among Latino patients. It uses Hispanic cultural values and social behaviors to change health behaviors with great success. LHA involves the target population in efforts to improve their standard of living, with reliance on their own initiative, and provides technical and other services to encourage self-help and mutual help. As a result of this participatory philosophy, diabetes and cardio-vascular programs are currently implemented in clinics, churches, migrant camps, and homes throughout Orange County. It can be done!

Latino Health Access runs another project in Orange County to help Latino families whose children have asthma. The rate of asthma-induced emergency room visits in one year was twice as high for Latinos (35 percent) as for Anglos (18 percent).[1] Latinos experience an asthma death rate which is three times greater than their non-Latino white counterparts.

Childhood obesity is another Hispanic health issue tackled by Latino Health Access. The organization reports that children of immigrants in the United States are more than twice as likely to be overweight than their foreign-born parents. The number of obese Hispanic children almost doubled between first- and second-generation immigrants. The National Health and Nutrition Examination Survey (NHANES), conducted since the 1970s, found that between 1983 and 1995 Hispanic children had the highest prevalence of obesity.[2] Overall, one-third of the entire Latino population in the U.S. was found to be overweight or at risk of being overweight compared with one-quarter of all whites and Asians. Latino Health Access developed an *in-culture* program that involves parents, schools, and the community. It teaches Latino children and their parents how to eat a more healthy diet, get more exercise, and get regular medical care.

LHA is headed by an extraordinary woman, Dr. America Bracho. With a team of dedicated Latinos and "gringos with a Latino heart," she has been able to run this award-winning program supported by corporations such as Wells Fargo Bank, Southern California Edison, Robinson's-May, Hyundai Motors America, and Bank of America. Funding from private foundations and strategic alliances with local hospitals and health-delivery organizations have succeeded in taking the concept to other areas in the Los Angeles Basin. These strategic alliances benefit all parties. The hospitals have reduced their Hispanic-patient emergency-room service demands; insurance and government programs have reduced the healthcare maintenance costs of these families. Moreover, all participants are delivering culturally sensitive health-care interventions at a fraction of the average cost. However, the Hispanic community has benefited the most by far, putting Latinos in control of their own health. The success of LHA is such that it is being emulated in other communities beyond both California and the Hispanic community.

AGAIN, IT'S "SHARE OF HEART"

Promoting your brand, product, or service through sponsorships of clinics and education programs builds the coveted "share of heart." As mentioned throughout this book, share of heart is a powerful *in-culture* marketing tool for creating and securing long-term loyalty and valued relationships with the Hispanic community. This translates into big profits for the sponsors, in addition to good corporate citizenship.

However, locating the right organization, clinic, or school program to sponsor is not an easy task. My strong recommendation is to work through established Hispanic organizations that coordinate these types of activities or through non-profits that are dedicated to this type of work and have a proven track record, such as the New York Hispanic Federation, the National Council of la Raza (NCLR), MOSAICA, and others whose online addresses are included in the appendix.

THE GOOD HEALTH NEWS

Pharmaceutical companies are realizing that the Hispanic market is a growing one that needs education about the use of drugs for various conditions. For example, Pfizer Pharmaceuticals developed a Hispanic-marketing initiative with several components. Among them, *La Guia Para la Buena Salud Para Los Hispanos*. (Guide for Healthy Living for Hispanics), a bilingual program addressing subjects such as heart disease and diabetes. The program materials include a novela-style video in Spanish that is used in popular community events, such as Calle Ocho in Miami and Fiesta Broadway in Los Angeles. In addition Pfizer developed an original *in-culture* community outreach program, based on a famous Spanish children's rhyme, *"Sana, sana, colita de rana. Si no sanas hoy sanás mañana."* (Heal, heal little toad. If you don't feel well today, you will tomorrow.) We all grew up with one or another version of the *Sana, sana* rhyme and this provides Pfizer's *Sana La Rana, Cuentos de Salud,* a wonderful *in-culture* creative platform that was developed in metropolitan New York's Hispanic areas in mid-2001.

A community outreach vehicle toured around screening for cholesterol, glucose, blood pressure, and depression; providing access to public health insurance advisors; giving cooking classes for healthier eating; and providing health education for a wide variety of diseases and stress management. The Spanish/English website, www.SanaLaRana.com, delivers the basics of health education and a toll-free number for more information in Spanish and English. This public awareness marketing program was developed by The Bravo Group in New York.[3]

In another Pfizer initiative, a pilot program took place in Miami to heighten awareness of depression and overcome the stigma associated with this illness among Hispanic women. The goal was to make more women aware of the drug Zoloft. Newspaper ads encouraged women to seek information about depression through a non-threatening and discreet telephone service.

HEALTH INSURANCE

"KidsCare" was established by the State of Arizona to provide low-cost medical insurance for children of working parents.

According to *The Commonwealth Fund 2001 Healthcare Quality Survey,*[4] Hispanics report the highest uninsured rate among all racial or ethnic groups. Just under half (46 percent) reported they had been uninsured at some time in the year prior to the survey, compared with 20 percent of non-Hispanic whites. This finding correlates with government data. For example, of the 33,863 Hispanics interviewed in the United States in March 2000, the Current Population Survey found that 68 percent were covered by either private or government health insurance, while 32 percent had no coverage. In 2000, 24.9 percent of Hispanic children under age 18 were not covered by any kind of health insurance. Among Hispanics who were covered in 2000, 47.9 percent had private insurance, the vast majority employment-based. Just over 24 percent had government health insurance. Included within that share is 8.6 percent Medicaid, 6.5 percent Medicare and 1.6 percent covered by the military.

Overall in the United States, foreign-born people are more likely not to have health insurance coverage. Low household income and low educational attainment are also characteristics of the uninsured—characteristics of many Hispanics who have recently come to this country. The Commonwealth Fund report found that Hispanics of Central American and Mexican descent were more likely to lack coverage than those of Puerto Rican descent. The report notes that Puerto Ricans who are not elderly are more likely to have Medicaid coverage than are Mexicans or Central Americans which accounts for some of the difference based on country of origin.

Lack of health insurance coverage hurts young lives especially. To promote healthcare coverage for children, the State of California launched the Healthy Families Program (HFP) and Medi-Cal for Children (MCC). The program targets Hispanic mothers, aged 18 to 49.

California Department of Health Services

For more detail on this case and creative

materials, go to www.incultureapproach.com

Brand or product: Healthy Families/Medi-Cal for Children

BACKGROUND

Healthy Families: low-cost medical, dental and vision coverage for $4 to $9 per month per child. *Medi-Cal:* no-cost medical, dental and vision coverage. Both programs are available for children aged 0 to 19 who meet income requirements.

In fiscal year 1998–99, the objective was to increase awareness about the need for healthcare coverage for children and, in particular, regular preventive services among the low-to-moderate-income Hispanic mothers aged 18 to 49. That campaign successfully increased program awareness. The new campaign in 2000-01 was designed to continue to educate the original target market, but also to attract the "harder-to-reach" market about the availability of state-sponsored services. Approximately 350,000 children had been enrolled in HFP (and an undetermined number in Medi-Cal for Children). The next phase of the campaign needed to heighten efforts in order to reach parents of Hispanic children who were eligible but had not yet enrolled in either program.

MARKETING CHALLENGE

We needed to dispel concerns and preconceived notions regarding the cost of health coverage, the difficulty of enrolling in government-sponsored programs, and the quality of service consumers would receive.

The primary target is composed of mothers, many of them recent immigrants. The majority of these women, even those who have been living in the U.S. for many years, are Spanish-dominant. These women come from a long history of using "home remedies" which have worked successfully for generations. There is fear within the target market of any government office because of potential association with the Immigration and Naturalization Service.

The secondary target includes Influencers over age 18 (friends, family, community and religious leaders, social workers, schools, and so forth); fathers or caretakers of the uninsured children; and teenagers, who could influence their parents.

MEDIA STRATEGIES

A comprehensive television, radio, outdoor and print campaign featured mothers and their children. The campaign was built around a central character, "Tía Remedios," a charismatic and active woman in her sixties whom everyone turns to for advice. Although her tea, herb and broth repertoire is quite ample, she is wise enough to know when it's necessary to go see a doctor.

In the television and radio spots Tía Remedios interacts with various family members. She has recommended Medi-Cal for Children and Healthy Families to her whole family, so she feels satisfied and happy knowing that the kids in her family have a better chance of growing up strong and healthy. Talent from the television spots were used in the print and outdoor ads to aid recall and awareness of the campaign.

The statewide campaign emphasized markets with the highest concentration of eligible Hispanic families: Los Angeles Basin, Fresno (Central Valley), San Diego, and Sacramento Valley markets. To launch new creative the heaviest emphasis was during the initial months of the campaign, January and February, 2001. There was enhanced support in priority markets with radio, and outdoor efforts were localized in high-density, low-income Hispanic neighborhoods.

The campaign allocated 70 percent of television exposure to daytime, fringe, and news, with 30 percent allocated to prime time in programming with the heaviest concentration of working women.

Radio was used in markets with the heaviest concentrations of the target audience: Los Angeles, San Diego, Fresno, Stockton and Modesto.

Outdoor placement of in-language materials was based on a demographic profile of the target audience by market.

Print was used for copy point development, public relations efforts, and advertorial support.

RESULTS

• In the initial 6 months of the campaign (January to June 2001), calls to the Spanish language toll-free line increased 14 percent compared with the previous 6 months (July to December 2000).

• 150,920 Latinos enrolled in 2001 with 74 percent of that enrollment taking place while Spanish-language advertising was running (January to September 2001).

AGENCY: HeadQuarters Advertising, Inc., www.headquartersadvertising.com

LATINO HEALTH ISSUES

On health issues, many Latinos are hit with a triple whammy. They don't have health insurance, they don't have access to a health system where Spanish is spoken, and they don't especially trust traditional medical establishments. The Commonwealth Fund report confirms each of these findings. Add to these a few Hispanic cultural beliefs, such as "fate," discussed above, and there is a high likelihood of leaving conditions untreated. Diabetes is probably the disease about which there is most concern for Hispanics, especially since it is readily treatable when medical care is available. Note how the lack of treatment leads to a high death rate from the disease as shown in Figure 18.3.

FIGURE 18.2

Incidence of Selected Conditions

Percent of adults (aged 18+) having selected conditions, by ethnicity, 1999

	Heart disease	Cancer (all types)	Breast cancer	Stroke	Diabetes
Hispanic	1.9%	2.6%	0.8%	1.1%	6.5%
Non-Hispanic white	3.5	8.5	1.4	2.4	5.2
Non-Hispanic black	2.6	3.3	0.8	3.2	8.4

Source: UCLA Center for Health Policy Research from analysis of National Health Interview Survey, 1999. Table prepared by Prepared by Mari Cantwell, UCLA Center for Health Policy Research.

Health professionals and community leaders believe that an extensive educational effort is needed to help prevent deaths from diabetes and cardiovascular diseases. Sometimes, a simple message will go a long way, saving lives and improving the quality of life for these households.

As mentioned earlier, the Hispanic community would like to find solutions to these problems, now. Both government and private and community organizations have initiated programs. There are also several national Hispanic health organizations, such as the National Coalition of Hispanic Health and Human Services Organizations (COSSHMO), the National

FIGURE 18.3

Causes of Death

1999, by ethnicity and gender

Percent of all deaths	Heart Disease	Cancer (All types)	Breast Cancer	Uterine Cancer	Stroke	Diabetes
Hispanic	24.9%	19.5%	1.5%	0.3%	5.7%	5.0%
Non-Hispanic*	30.6	23.2	1.7	0.3	7.1	2.8
White	31.1	23.4	1.7	0.3	7.1	2.5
Black	27.6	21.8	1.9	0.3	6.6	4.2
Hispanic men	23.4	18.4	–	–	4.8	4.0
Non-Hispanic* men	30.3	24.7	–	–	5.5	2.6
White men	31.0	25.0	–	–	5.5	2.5
Black men	25.8	22.6	–	–	5.4	3.3
Hispanic women	26.9	20.9	3.4	0.6	6.8	6.2
Non-Hispanic* women	30.9	21.8	3.4	0.5	8.5	2.9
White women	31.2	21.8	3.3	0.5	8.6	2.6
Black women	29.4	20.9	3.9	0.7	7.9	5.2

* Non-Hispanic includes persons of every race (e.g. White, Asian, Black) who are not of Hispanic origin

Source: National Vital Statistics Report, Vol. 49, No. 8, September 21, 2001. Prepared by Mari Cantwell, UCLA Center for Health Policy Research.

Council of La Raza (NCLR), and the National Alliance for Hispanic Health (www.hispanichealth.org) that study and track Hispanic health-related issues. The Online Resources section in the appendix provides web addresses for several organizations including universities, non-profit organizations, and government resources.

Notes

1. Latino Issues Forum, 1999.
2. "Strategies for the Primary Prevention of Obesity in PreSchool-Age Children," presentation by Christine Williams, M.D., M.P.H.; and "Weight Trends of State's Teens Worrisome," by Julie Marquis, 2000; Orange Countywide Needs Assessment, 1999.
3. Press Release, The Bravo Group, July 23, 2001
4. The Commonwealth Fund, 1 E. 75th St., New York, NY 10021-2692; www.cmwf.org.

Chapter 19

Hispanic Travel:
An Uncharted Frontier

Only recently, with the boom of American carriers flying to South America, has the Hispanic traveler gotten some attention. Despite the fact that we are assiduous travelers, very limited marketing activity takes place in this category today. With the exception of the big airline carriers that have had intermittent Hispanic target campaigns, to my knowledge Princess Cruises is the first company to target Hispanic vacationers seriously.

Think of this. Like any recent immigrant group, most U.S. Hispanics have a strong connection to another country, our country of ancestry. In addition, many of us have families also in other areas of the U.S. and we enjoy traveling, visiting, and going places with our children and extended families.

I read a while back that over 6 million people from Latin American visit Miami every year. Moreover, this number is expected to increase several times during this decade. Who are these travelers? Many times they are business people traveling North and South for business meetings. However, if you ask Hispanic-Americans, "What are you doing for Christmas?" you will find that a high percentage plan to travel with the family to visit a family member far away.

Many Latinos travel through Miami, and yet not many take advantage of this visit to stay and enjoy the unique treasures of Florida. Similarly, many pass through the airports of New York, Dallas, or Los Angeles on the way to and from family visits. Hispanics need an invitation, loud and clear, with well-managed travel packages to include the whole family, and the aunt or grandmother. We often travel year after year to visit our relatives (the exception is Cuban Latinos, who despite being so close to their homeland, don't have the luxury of hassle-free travel). Sooner or later, we want to "go somewhere else." Take the children, or the grandchildren, to the Grand Canyon, to New York, to Hawaii, to Miami, to Los Angeles beyond Disneyland and Universal Studios, to San Francisco, Chicago, you name it!

FIGURE 19.1

Traveling Together *In-Culture*

Respondents who strongly agree, by percent

	Total	Hispanic	White	African-American
I wish there were more travel packages available for other kinds of family groups such as sibling or mother/daughter trips.	61%	70%	58%	81%
Traveling with my family has become more important over the past five years.	71	80	69	80
Time is so scarce these days; traveling with my family gives us much needed time to bond.	80	84	79	82

Source: American Demographics/Zogby International.

In my limited experience on this subject, I have learned that one destination many Latinos dream of is Hawaii. However, I have yet to see a full-blown Hispanic marketing campaign inviting us to visit the Aloha State, in Spanish. *Por favor*!

The same applies to most of the other states. Hispanics are ready to embrace and get to know their wonderful new motherland, its historic sites, and discover our own historic roots from Florida to California, and we should be welcomed. If you find the *in-culture* message, there will be gold at the end of the rainbow.

Presently, limited Hispanic travel data are available. The Travel Industry Association of America conducted a study of the market which is reported in *The Minority Traveler 2000 Edition*. Based on its data, I have been able to paint a preliminary picture of the market. I hope in the future there will be as much more data and marketing activity as in other industries.

LATINOS DO TRAVEL

The volume of Hispanic travelers has steadily increased over the years, becoming an important share of total travel demand. In 1999, Hispanic travel volume accounted for 71.2 million person-trips, close to 7 percent of the total travel in the United States (including business).[1]

Although the percentage increase in travel demand from 1997 to 1999 for African-Americans (16 percent) was higher compared with Hispanics (11 percent) and Asians (7 percent), volume among Hispanics remains the largest among the three groups.[2]

THE ACCULTURATED HISPANIC TRAVELER

Note that, on average, the characteristics of acculturated, English-dominant, or bilingual Hispanic travelers are similar to those of all U.S. travelers.

Unlike the average U.S. traveler household, however, the Hispanic traveler household is a much younger parent with a larger number of children who on average spends an average of $540 on a trip compared with the $438 spent by the average household. The traveling needs and wants of Hispanic households may be different from those of the non-Hispanic traveler. Keep in mind that the non-acculturated traveler household will have an even more different set of needs.

FIGURE 19. 2

Characteristics of Traveler Households, 2000

in percent of households that have that characteristic

Characteristic	Hispanic Traveler	Total U.S. Traveler
Education of Household Head		
High school or less	19%	19%
Some college-no degree	31	24
College completed or more	50	57
Employment		
Full time	80	73
Part time	7	6
Retired	7	18
Not employed	6	3
Occupation of household head		
Managerial/professional	42	43
Technical/sales/administrative support	13	12
Other	45	46
Household Size		
One person	22	22
Two people	25	35
Three people	20	17
Four people	20	16
Five or more people	13	10
Average Household Income	**$57,200**	**$61,500**

Source: Travel Industry Association of America, *The Minority Traveler 2000 Edition*, Washington, DC, 2000.

WHY AND WHERE ACCULTURATED HISPANICS TRAVEL[3]

Traveling patterns among the acculturated Hispanic traveler households show an interesting picture:

- Most, 67 percent, travel for pleasure, of which four out of ten trips are to visit friends while fewer trips are for entertainment (15 percent) and outdoor recreation (10 percent). Only 22 percent of person-trips are business related.

- Although more Hispanic travelers tend to travel during the summer (30 percent), they also travel at a slightly lower rate than the general market during all other seasons (spring 25 percent, fall 23 percent, and winter 22 percent).

- Shopping is a favorite activity when traveling (34 percent) followed by outdoor recreation (16 percent) and visits to historical places and museums (13 percent). Twenty-two percent reported not doing any activity in particular when traveling for pleasure. The rest of the respondents usually enjoy combining two or more activities during their trip.

- More than two-thirds generally use their own car or truck when traveling. On average, they stay 4.1 nights at the homes of friends or relatives or 3.2 nights at a hotel, motel, or bed and breakfast.

DOMESTIC AND INTERNATIONAL TRAVEL

Hispanics in the U.S. travel domestically as well as internationally. Main points of destination within the United States include California, Texas, and Florida, and to a lesser extent Nevada and New Mexico. They may choose these destinations because they have friends or relatives living in these states. In addition, they often travel abroad to visit family members and friends in their country of origin. This may account for the fact that the number of personal trips by plane is slightly higher when compared to the average traveler (20 percent vs. 18 percent).[4]

Other Segments of the Hispanic Travel Market

Because family ties are strong, a transient Hispanic market exists. Hispanics in the U.S. often host family members from abroad who come to visit or study, conduct business, or are moving to the United States.

Another segment of the market that should be considered is that of wealthy Mexicans, Central Americans, and South Americans who see the United States as their main shopping destination, in particular the states of Florida, California, and Texas. Other reasons for traveling to the United States include medical needs and recreational activities such as skiing. The strong cultural and economic interdependence between the United States and Latin America makes the Hispanic travel market a very promising one.

The Inner City Hispanic Traveler

As the number of Hispanics increases in metropolitan areas in the U.S., transportation choices for non-work travel trips have changed.

Findings from the Nationwide Personal Transportation Surveys suggest that non-work travel behavior among Hispanics has changed rapidly over the last decade. From 1983 to 1995, the number of Hispanics who drove privately operated vehicles steadily increased (31 percent to 50 percent) although this proportion continued to be lower when compared to whites (43 percent to 60 percent). In particular, Hispanic men, more than women, tend to drive privately operated vehicles and most are employed workers.[5]

Hispanics with drivers licenses were likely to drive privately operated vehicles (74 percent) at almost the same rate as the white population (76 percent). In contrast, Hispanics that do not have a drivers license tend to use more public transportation or walk for non-work travel trips.

In general, Hispanics and other minority ethnic groups are more likely to use public transit or walk for non-work travel when compared to whites.[6] This is true for young adolescents under age 16 and adults aged 16 to 64. However, Hispanics who are age 65 or older tend to make less use of public transportation when compared with the white population, perhaps because Hispanic seniors are more likely to live with or near relatives who can drive them to their destinations.

Notes

1. Travel Industry Association of America, *The Minority Traveler 2000 Edition*, 2000
2. Ibid.
3. Ibid.
4. Ibid.
5. Nationwide Personal Transportation Surveys, *Mode Choice by People of Color for Non-Work Travel*, 1995.
6. Nationwide Personal Transportation Surveys, *Mode Choice by People of Color for Non-Work Travel*, 1995.

Chapter 20

Digital Marketing to U.S. Latinos

Targeting American Latinos online is possible and viable. As more reliable data emerge, it is evident that online marketing is maturing and can be a successful marketing communications venue for reaching Latinos. A larger and growing number of U.S. Latinos are accessing the internet, particularly among the Spanish-dominant where growing numbers are joining the cyber revolution. However, the Hispanic digital divide between upscale and lower-income Hispanic households is still a fact, as is the divide among generations.

PROFILING THE LATINO DIGITAL MARKETPLACE

Reported Hispanic internet-access rates vary significantly depending on the study methodology, age of the participants, and the inclusion or exclusion of Spanish-dominant Latinos. However, all studies show consistent growth in the segments of Hispanics joining the digital marketplace. In April 2002, Harris Interactive released a multicultural study, which concludes that 9 percent of all Hispanic adults wolrldwide have access to the internet today. This translates to 22 million Hispanic adults, aged 18 and older who have access to the internet.

A Tomás Rivera Policy Institute's (TRPI) study based on the National Telecommunications and Information Administration (NTIA, 2002) and U.S. census data reports that nearly 14 million Latinos own computers and over 11 million have access to the internet "from home."[1] The report also shows that U.S. Latinos have significantly outpaced Latinos in other Latin countries in internet access.

FIGURE 20.1

U.S. Households Computer Ownership

by income and ethnic background

	Under $15,000	$15,000-34,999	$35,000-74,000	$75,000 or more
White	17.5%	32.5%	60.4%	80.0%
African-American	6.6	19.4	43.7	78.0
Asian	32.6	42.7	65.6	85.0
Hispanic	9.4	19.8	49.0	74.8

Source: I. Valdés, Cultural Access Group, based on National Telecommunications and Information Administration, U.S. Department of Commerce, "Falling Through the Net: Defining the Digital Divide", July 1999.

FIGURE 20.2

U.S. Computer Households Using the Internet

by income and ethnic background

	Under $15,000	$15,000-34,999	$35,000-74,000	$75,000 or more
White	8.9%	17.0%	39.0%	60.9%
African-American	1.9	7.9	22.2	53.2
Hispanic	3.8	7.6	26.8	48.1

Source: I. Valdés, Cultural Access Group, based on National Telecommunications and Information Administration, U.S. Department of Commerce, "Falling Through the Net: Defining the Digital Divide", July 1999.

U.S. Hispanic households are adopting computer and internet technologies at a high rate of speed. A national Hispanic market study by Cheskin Research, conducted in both English and Spanish in the fourth quarter of 2000, found that 47 percent of those surveyed had a computer in their home, up from 42 percent the first quarter *of the same year.*[2] All indicators suggest this growth pattern will continue. A Consumer Electronics Association study among Hispanic non-computer owners found that 58 percent of 25-to-34 year-olds and 46 percent of 18-to-24-year-olds plan to buy a computer in the next two years. It is interesting to note that the same study shows Latinos are slightly more likely than non-Hispanics to own a stereo system, digital camera, or home security system.[3, 4] The high level of "interest in purchasing" a computer is corroborated by Strategy Research Corporation in its *2002 U.S. Hispanic Market Report.* Based on interviews conducted in June and July 2001, 46 percent of Hispanics interviewed indicated they were likely to purchase a computer within the next year versus 39 percent of African Americans and 29 percent of non-Hispanic whites.

FIGURE 20.3

Equipment for the Information Age

Percent of Hispanics who currently do not own but are planning to buy the following products in the next two years, by age

	Hispanic	18–24	25–34	35–49	50+
Camcorder	47%	59%	54%	58%	21%
Desktop/Laptop Computer	45	46	58	60	17
Cellular or PCS Phone	41	56	55	43	20
Digital Camera	36	50	41	40	15
DVD Player	36	51	38	43	16
Car CD Player	30	46	35	30	16
Personal Portable CD Player	30	43	38	35	13
Mini Satellite Dish System	27	33	35	27	14
Videogame System	27	43	38	30	7
Home Security System	26	27	31	28	17
Home Theater System	24	33	30	24	13
Personal Digital Assistant	18	24	23	18	8

Source: I. Valdés, Consumer Electronics Association, *American Demographics,* December 2001

The Department of Commerce data corroborates the dramatic growth of Hispanic computer ownership. And comScore Networks, based on its panel of 1.5 million internet users, identified Hispanics as the fastest growing internet population from 2001, growing 19 percent from 2001–2002, more than three times the growth among non-Hispanic internet users.

Roslow Research Group's (RRG) ongoing Hispanic internet tracking survey, "Hispanic Internet Tracking Studies" (HITS)[5] illustrates this high-growth phenomenon. The HITS studies, conducted since 2000, by phone, with *Spanish speakers* in the language of their choice, reveal that "among Hispanics 16 years of age and older, one-half are using the internet today." The first measurement of the HITS survey in July 2000 showed an incidence of use (in the past 30 days) at only 38 percent. By March 2001, it had increased to 43 percent and in December 2001, eight months later, to 50 percent.

FIGURE 20.4

Growth in Hispanic Internet Usage

Spanish speakers, aged 16 and over

Internet Use	July 2000	March 2001	December 2001
No internet usage	40.8%	37.1%	32.1%
No usage/ past 30 days	21.2%	19.9%	18.3%
Used in past 30 days	38.0%	43.0%	49.5%
Base	1,562	1,428	1,231

Source: Roslow Research Group, Hispanic Internet Usage Profile, 2000–002.

The same RRG study shows that use of the internet in Spanish is also increasing steadily. The average percentage in Spring 2001 of Spanish-language internet use was 39 percent. By Fall 2001, 55 percent of respondents' time on the internet was in Spanish. This dramatic change probably correlates with Univision.com's launch in 2001, with heavy advertising appealing to the large segment of Spanish-dominant consumers.

Regarding the acculturated Hispanic segment (English-dominant), the Pew Internet & American Life Project study, conducted early in 2001, reported Hispanic internet-access rates at 50 percent among Hispanics aged 18 and older. Pew's comparative figures for non-Hispanics and African-American adults are 58 percent and 43 percent, respectively.

When defining an online strategy targeted at Hispanics,

certain cities are definitely more "Hispanically wired." The chart below highlights the top 10 DMAs in terms of Hispanic internet users. New York and Los Angeles rank first and second for both overall internet access as well as Hispanic internet access, but after that significant shifts occur.

FIGURE 20.5

Internet Users by DMA

DMA	Total Hispanic unique users (in thousands)	Total unique internet users (in thousands)	Hispanic unique users as percent of total	Rank– Total internet users	Rank– Hispanic users
New York	1,656	9,241	18%	1	1
Los Angeles	1,601	6,723	24	2	2
Miami/Ft. Lauderdale	718	1,963	37	15	3
San Francisco/ Oakland/San Jose	483	3,070	16	5	4
Chicago	448	4,246	11	3	5
Houston	384	2,322	17	11	6
Dallas/Ft. Worth	339	2,786	12	7	7
Phoenix	297	1,948	15	16	8
Sacramento/Stockton/Modesto	268	1,555	17	19	9
San Diego	250	1,236	20	26	10

Source: comScore, 2002

ATTITUDES

Hispanics, who generally tend to respond more positively when asked to give an opinion, are the most upbeat when praising the positive benefits and impact of the internet. Spanish-speakers are even more positive. Internet users agree that the internet has "created more opportunities for all people," and the "internet breaks down racial and economic barriers," and also that "the internet keeps people connected." The only serious concerns voiced have to do with bad taste and pornographic content, and for some, the difficulty of navigating the web.

MORE "WIRED" YOUTH

Young and old Latinos are surfing the web. However, young Latinos continue to be more active online, the same phenomenon found across multi-cultural segments in the U.S., not only in the Hispanic market. A demographic comparison between non-Hispanic and Hispanic internet users shows interesting differences and similarities. However, Spanish-speaking Latino youth are significantly more active than their Spanish-speaking parents, with the consequent problems resulting from a technological "generational divide" that can add to the Latino family stresses. Although this situation is similar in the non-Hispanic market, the language barrier among the *non*-Spanish speaking parents aggravates the problem. Children have access to internet websites and content that Hispanic parents would never approve of and many expressed concern.

When asked if the internet should be censored for content, there was little difference by age among users, but some differences among non-users and users:

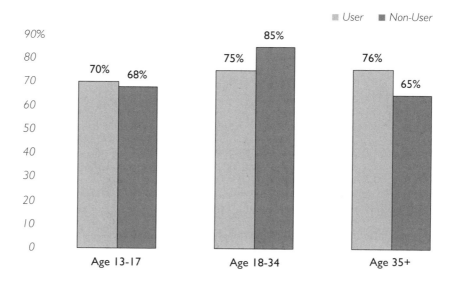

FIGURE 20.6

Hispanic Attitudes

Percent agreeing strongly or somewhat that the internet should be censored for content

Source: I. Valdés, Cultural Access Group, based on National Telecommunications and Information Administration, U.S. Department of Commerce, "Falling Through the Net: Defining the Digital Divide", July 1999.

The Census Bureau's CPS 2000 study, released in September 2001, showed that internet access among Hispanic children aged 6 to 17 is very high. Nearly 80 percent have internet access, including home and school usage.

FIGURE 20.7

Young Computer and Internet Users

Population Group	Internet Access August 2000
Total U.S.	41.5%
Hispanic*	23.6
Children aged 6 to 17	
White, non-Hispanic	94.5
Hispanic	78.9
Black	80.6
Asian and Pacific Islander	87.8

* Does not include Puerto Rico.

Source: U.S. Census Bureau, Current Population Survey, August 2000

CULTURE, LANGUAGE, AND INTERNET USE

As discussed earlier, culture plays a powerful role in how multicultural consumers respond to media messages and marketing in general. The more *in-culture* the message, the greater the affinity and consonance of its content with the mindset of the target consumers, the greater the recall and the stronger the impact on "Share of Heart."

Given that Spanish is presently the language of choice of the majority of Latino adults, most would prefer to use the internet in Spanish if they have a choice. Language choice varies significantly with the degree of acculturation, country of birth, and income of the Hispanic consumer. The more acculturated, the greater the likelihood that English is the language of choice and the higher the income. Conversely, the less acculturated the greater the likelihood that the language used will be Spanish.

Over two-thirds of Hispanics online visit websites that cater to Hispanic cultural interest and background. Culturally relevant and attuned *content* is probably the strongest hook for Hispanic online success. As Carlos Lizarralde, CEO of www.loquesea.com, a youth-oriented *Spanglish* website said, "Hispanic youth do not want refried content from Latin America and don't necessarily identify with off-line Hispanic media in the U.S." The same sentiment applies to the other age groups and acculturation segments.

Cultural Access Group (CAG)[6] conducted a study addressing the role of culture in online use. The study findings contend that only one-half of the digital divide between Hispanics and the general U.S. population is accounted for by the differences in education and income levels. The other 50 percent correlates with a perceived void of *in-culture* online content, or content specific to Latino culture. Many U.S. Latinos report that they do not find information in Spanish that is relevant to them nor do they have many alternatives. This may be due in part to the smaller number of internet websites in Spanish. A July 2000 count by the Catalan-dialect portal VilaWeb.com estimated that fewer than 3 percent of *all* websites on the world wide web are in Spanish, compared with 68 percent in English. This placed the number of Spanish-language web pages at 7.5 million in 2000, compared with 214 million pages in English.[7] However, as shown by the list in the appendix, the number of sites in Spanish is growing. It is also likely that some of the perceived gap in Spanish culture and content stems from the limited advertising and promotion activities of many existing U.S. Spanish-language websites. It is expensive to promote in broadcast media and presently only the mega players can afford it.

FIGURE 20. 8

Comparative Profile

Hispanic vs. Non-Hispanic internet use

Demographic characteristic	Hispanic*	Non-Hispanic
Male	67%	65%
Female	33%	35%
Average age	39 years	38 years
Some college education	68%	79%
Average household income	$43,800	$54,700
Own home	39%	62%
Children at home	89%	37%
Born in the U.S.	14%	92%

* Recruited from U.S. Hispanic and Spanish-language Websites

Source: Cultural Access Group (CAG), January 2001.

NAVIGATING AND USING THE WEB

Where are Latinos when they navigate the web? Information varies from source to source, similar to the penetration data presented above, but most sources tend to agree in broad terms that the home is where most of the activity takes place.

FIGURE 20.9

Primary Locations of Hispanic internet usage

Spanish speakers, aged 16 and over

Internet Use	July 2000	March 2001	December 2001
Home	71%	61%	63%
School*	13	14	10
Work*	8	13	8
Friend/Relative	4	7	11
Library	3	5	7
Internet Cafe	—	—	—

* Applies only to those in school or working

Source: Roslow Research Group, Hispanic Internet Usage Profile, 2000–2002.

Longevity—or how many years a consumer has been online—has an impact on e-commerce activity. As would be expected, the "newer" the internet surfer, the lower the e-commerce activity and credit-card use. The 2001 CAG study showed that Latinos, who as a market on average have been online a shorter time than the average non-Hispanic user, also had lower e-commerce activity (see Figure 20.10). As their internet longevity increases, Hispanic e-commerce activity will most likely increase together with the degree and comfort level of purchasing online.

FIGURE 20.10

E-Commerce Activity

years online, Hispanic vs. Non-Hispanic

	Hispanic		Non-Hispanic	
	over 3	under 3	over 3	under 3
Research products	65%	55%	78%	60%
Purchase products	42	26	75	50

Source: Cultural Access Group, January 2001.

Presently, many Hispanics tend to feel less comfortable than non-Hispanics using credit cards for purchases on the internet, 47 percent compared with 76 percent, according to the same CAG study. Vis-à-vis the purpose for using the internet, the study concludes that Hispanics use the internet in a fashion similar to non-Hispanics, with a few exceptions. These are the areas where Hispanic behavior on the internet skew higher than the non-Hispanic:

Hispanic Online Spending

Reuters reports:

• *About 38 percent of Hispanics surveyed spent more than $100 online during the three-month period (April to May 2000), compared with 16 percent of Anglos, 11 percent of Asians, and 6 percent of African-Americans.*

• *Hispanics in the U.S. will spend an estimated $42.6 million over the internet in 2002—a 100 percent increase over 1999.*

• *The leading Hispanic purchases online are CDs, 15 percent; airline tickets, 11 percent; books, 9 percent; and software, 9 percent.*

Source: Quoted in Hispanic Media and Marketing Factoids, May 2002.

• Getting information on family and relationship issues

• Researching health issues

• School research

• Chat rooms

• Looking up international, national, and local news connected to their families and the Hispanic community

The same comScore Networks study that revealed high internet growth among Hispanics also revealed that fewer U.S. Hispanic internet users bought online during a given month, with 8 percent making a purchase vs. 10 percent of non-Hispanic web users. However, Hispanic shoppers spent 7 percent ($15) more than the average non-Hispanic e-commerce shopper. It will be interesting to see how the online Hispanic shopper develops.

ADVERTISING ONLINE

With the proliferation of sophisticated websites targeted to Hispanics and the growing numbers of Latinos navigating the web, Hispanic internet advertising has grown significantly. Until quite recently, many corporations advertised to Latinos online more as an act of faith than on the basis of conclusive evidence. Some marketing managers and marketing researchers still have doubts as to the validity of data about online use, and this may apply especially to research about Hispanics' use of the internet. However, despite the lingering skepticism, Hispanic online advertising continues to grow and the data that can be gathered seem to agree that advertising online to Latinos delivers. As you can observe, many of the case studies presented in this book have an internet component.

Portals and websites targeting U.S. Hispanics and Latin Americans have opened a fascinating "Pandora's Box," alluring and loaded with magnificent data, resources, sports, music, fun advertising, and much more. The number of strategic alliances and players coming together to serve the Hispanic "surfer" grows and changes daily, creating the most unimaginable partnerships and synergies.

For example, *La Opinión* digital, the New York daily *Hoy,* the Chicago weekly *¡Éxito!,* and the Orlando daily *El Sentinel,* teamed up to create a "new news website" for the 2002 World Cup. This effort included a sales and marketing alliance. Spanish-language internet users had up-to-the minute coverage of all the tournament games in Japan, with stories specially written for the site. *Hispanic Market Weekly* reported that this is the first time four Hispanic newspapers have come together to create a joint product.

Terra Lycos (www.terra.com) offers U.S. Latinos three language options, English, Spanish, and Portuguese and operates in 42 counties with 19 languages.

Univision Online, together with its television and cable networks, is a fully integrated media powerhouse. Univision Online was designed to appeal to the less acculturated U.S. Hispanic, and the company brought many new computer and internet users to the Hispanic cyber market place when it launched.

Other giants include Yahoo! en Español, and Yupi.com, each offering a wide array of sites and programs, product information and advertising that targets Latinos. In addition, smaller portals and many websites emerge daily. Their topics are the same ones found on English-language sites. A list of Latino web sites has been compiled and is presented at the end of this section, listed by topic. It is by no means complete, but it will give you a start.

The only way to keep abreast of all these developments is, of course, by following the news online. Every Monday, *Hispanic Market Weekly,* a paid subscription newsletter, summarizes the week's U.S. Hispanic media and trade activities. HispanicAd.com, a free publication in magazine format online, covers trade information and articles on a daily basis. Other online services that provide related information include multi-cultural resources, such as *Multi-Cultural Marketing News* and the websites that also include all of Latin America and Spain in their coverage, such as www.TitularesProdu.com.

HOW TO MARKET TO U.S. LATINOS ONLINE

As we know, many Hispanic marketers are advertising on the world wide web, some targeting the less-acculturated and bilingual Hispanics, with Spanish-language websites, and others to the bilinguals and English-dominant Hispanics, with English-language websites or both English and Spanish.

The "how-to" they use is basically the same as that described in Section 5 of this book, The Integrated *In-Culture* Marketing Plan. Having a clear strategy up-front improves your ability to reach a specific target consumer segment. This brings us back to Section 2 of this book, Segmenting Latinos for Profits. The Golden Rule for success is to obtain, study, and strategize with data that will help you determine your optimal Hispanic market segments. In a perfect world, it should be easy to find reliable secondary internet-use data by key demographics and product or service data for your specific Hispanic-marketing needs. In some cases this is possible today and many internet-based research companies may have what you are looking for. This is great news, with one caveat. Do find out the *exact methodology* used to generate the sample and to gather the data. Is this a national study? Regional? What does this mean "exactly?" For some data vendors a sample of the three key Hispanic markets is "a national representative sample." And you guessed it right. It is not for most national campaigns! However, if you know precisely what the data gaps are, you can work with the magic of a marketing statistician and you may end up with a reliable estimate for your marketing plans.

Important questions are:

- Was the data gathered in English? Spanish? Or both?
- Does the sample include all Hispanics or only people who speak Spanish at home?
- Was the consumer interviewed online, by phone or in person?
- How many people were interviewed? How many men, women, teens, etc.
- What are the age breaks? That is, how many teens aged 13 to 16? And how many boys? How many girls?

There are no perfect data, so the important issue here is to become educated and find out through your peers what services they have tested and which ones have "delivered." If you need to find internet research vendors, you can call trade organizations, such as The Advertising Research Foundation and the Marketing Research Association. Both have offices in New York and also websites. Another source is through the listings in trade magazines, like *American Demographics*, *Advertising Age*, *Ad Week*, *Quirk's Market Research Review* and others. Some vendors specialize in a particular business area, food and beverages or packaged goods. These magazines usually carry ads from the latest in the field.

If the data are not available and you need to conduct a customized market study, my advice is to purchase the Agency Directory from the Association of Hispanic Advertising Agencies (www.ahaa.org). The research section lists many specialized multicultural and Hispanic-specific agencies. You can also ask the portals for user data, keeping in mind that this is "sales data." However, they may provide you with very good estimates for free. Many of these media companies are listed in the ahaa directory.

I also recommend selecting a Hispanic advertising agency with a proven track record in this area, and working with them throughout this process. You will find many high caliber Hispanic ad agencies in the *ahaa Directory* mentioned above.

Last but not least, DO NOT, I repeat, *do not* skip the face-to-face research phase with the target consumer. At least invest in a couple of focus groups. The research study cost will be a small portion of your budget, but it can save you millions of dollars. Ideally, you would want to have enough groups to learn qualitatively, first-hand, as much as possible about the website and category you are tackling. With focus groups, you can test concepts. If you have preliminary video materials for the visuals, show these to the groups and observe participants' reactions to different options. Challenge the secondary data you have by asking the "real live person" to tell you more about a particular behavior.

Then, follow the steps in the integrated marketing plan. The internet or website advertising component is an External medium that can generate "maximum ROI value" if the ad is *in-culture* and if it is synchronized with all the other External advertisement media. Whether you use direct marketing, TV, radio, print, outdoor, a community event, another online vendor, or all of the above, all should communicate the core advertising message "in consonance."

To know if your advertising campaign is working, there are excellent ways to track visits to the website ("traffic"), and how long a user visited the site, what the person bought (if applicable) and many other variables. Again, the vendors that gather this type of data are maturing and many reliable sources for the Hispanic market are available. Also, calls to your toll-free number can provide a good indication of your advertising's impact. If your toll-free lines are ringing off the hook, the results are self-evident!

DOES INTERNET ADVERTISING DELIVER?

Nielsen Media Research's New Media Services released the results of its internet usage study among Spanish-dominant and bilingual Hispanics in May 1, 2002. Univision Online commissioned the study which was conducted by telephone in 16 markets in March, with Hispanics aged 16 and older using diary samples. The results, according to Nielsen, show the "importance of the internet to Hispanics and prove the impact of advertising on Univision.com." The study found a high positive impact on brand awareness and purchase behavior for the website users.[8] The study also found that non-acculturated Hispanics visit Univision.com more than any other Spanish-language website and that the overall use of Spanish-language internet sites is growing as more Hispanics access the internet from home. A comparison of the top 5 Spanish-language websites shows that almost 3 out of 5 Hispanic households with internet access go online at least once a day, and 95 percent are online at least once a week. With these types of high exposure rates, it is no surprise that advertising effectiveness shows positive results.

LatinWebMonitor is a company that tracks advertising on Hispanic websites in the United States and Puerto Rico. It does not attempt to quantify spending or ad impressions, but rather tracks who is advertising on these sites. The company has found that 90 percent of the advertisers on websites that target Hispanics are traditional marketers of consumer brands and services. Included are automotive, financial services, telecommunications, and consumer goods, among other categories.

Non-acculturated Hispanics visit Univision.com more than any other Spanish-language website and overall use of Spanish-language internet sites is growing. Almost 3 out of 5 Hispanic households with internet access go online at least once a day, and 95 percent are online at least once a week.

La Opinión and La Opinión Digital

BACKGROUND

Ignacio E. Lozano founded *La Opinión* on September 16, 1926. Today, Lozano's vision, carried on by his children and grandchildren, has not only made *La Opinión* the leading Spanish language newspaper in the U.S., but also one of the top 100 daily newspapers in the nation. Today, *La Opinión* is the second most widely read newspaper in Southern California, averaging almost 700,000 readers per day.

During its early years, the editorial content of *La Opinión* consisted primarily of news from Mexico because most of its readers had recently emigrated from that country. However, in the last quarter century there has been an influx of Hispanics from other countries. To address the needs of Los Angeles' ever-changing Latino population *La Opinión* has devoted increased attention to reporting on issues relevant to all Hispanics.

With the advent of the internet, *La Opinión* began to closely monitor computer and internet use through both proprietary and secondary research. In 1996, *La Opinión* created an internet site with general company information. There was great external pressure on *La Opinión* to join other newspapers on the web, yet the data indicated that there was not a sufficient number of Hispanics online to support an internet site. Hispanic portals were cropping up almost daily.

In the spring of 1999, *La Opinión* saw that the number of Hispanics online was growing at an accelerated pace and began laying the groundwork for an internet site. The strategy was to lay a solid foundation which leveraged the assets of the newspaper. The site, laopinion.com, launched on March 31, 2000. It offered the contents of the newspaper online. Since that time it has continuously added features and enhanced content areas.

The primary target audience for laopinion.com is Southern California online Hispanics. Its secondary target is U.S. online Hispanics.

To reach its target, laopinion.com runs ads in its print products, *La Opinión* and *La Opinión* Direct. To reach online Hispanics throughout the U.S., laopinion.com has forged partnerships with holahoy.com, website of the New York daily newspaper, *Hoy,* and elherald.com, website of the Miami daily newspaper, *El Nuevo Herald* and Yahoo! en Español, a property of Yahoo! Inc., featuring

Spanish-language web programming. Managers of laopinion.com will continue to develop partnerships with other online companies that are complementary and have long-term sustainability.

KEY RESULTS AND FINDINGS

Since January 2001, laopinion.com has seen traffic grow by month-over-month averages of 23 percent for both unique visitors and page views. The amount of page views per user has also grown, as well as time spent per user (stickiness). Consistently, top trafficked areas within the site in order are homepage, sports, employment, classifieds, main news, city and entertainment. A study conducted by Cultural Access Group found that laopinion.com users are affluent, 38 percent with household incomes of $40,000 or more; educated, 60 percent have attended college; and young, 52 percent are aged 18 to 34.

Both users and advertisers trust laopinion.com. For many clients, interactive advertising is new. This inexperience provides both challenges and opportunities. The managers of laopinion.com work to develop comprehensive, innovative programs that meet advertisers' objectives.

As an example, HealthNet, a western regional HMO, was launching its site in Spanish. They sought to gain both brand awareness and traffic. In this case, laopinion.com developed an online health channel that leveraged its strong service journalism in health-related topics and added content unique to the website. HealthNet "owns" the channel through permanent logo placement and text links in every page. HealthNet also wanted to associate with *La Opinión*'s highly regarded brand in the community. To that end, laopinión.com developed in-paper ads, online ads and point-of-sale materials that promoted the health channel and included the line, "sponsored by HealthNet." To further strengthen the association and ensure fresh content on HealthNet's site, laopinion.com provides articles that are posted on HealthNet's site and HealthNet has links back to laopinion.com/salud.

Another example of working closely with an advertiser is the development of *Bebé BeechNut del Mes*. In conjunction with the client and its advertising agency, LatinWorks, *La Opinión* and laopinion.com created an innovative promotion. Leveraging the strengths of print and online, Hispanics were encouraged to submit photos of their babies and vote online for their favorite baby. To provide an educational element, advertorials were published in-paper and were posted online. Although at the time of printing the promotion had just begun, the response has been tremendous.

ADVERTISING ONLINE

Some Hispanic websites appear to be holding their own in advertising, despite a downward trend in web advertising for the general market. The sites are also looking for other revenue sources including subscriptions.

In December 2001, HispanTelligence, the research service of Hispanic Business, estimated revenues for 2001 for four of the largest services. It estimated Terra Lycos internet revenues at about $374 million; StarMedia Network Inc. at $67.3 million, Yupi/MSN at $9.5 million, and Univision.com at $4.8 million. Most of the successful sites have corporate backing and are part of an integrated media strategy for communications companies or other large conglomerates.

Of 500 Hispanic-owned businesses surveyed by the Minority Business Development Agency (MBDA), 42 percent had websites in 2001, but only about 10 percent of them reported participating in e-commerce that year. About 5 percent said they use the internet, but do not have a website. Altogether 58 percent of the Hispanic-owned businesses surveyed said they do not have a website.

TIPS FOR *IN-CULTURE* CYBER MARKETING SUCCESS

Site content must take into consideration not only language but acculturation issues, age groups, the importance of families, and keeping in touch with the user's ethnic community, both in the U.S. and in the country of origin.

- *In-culture* site content must take into consideration language (English, Spanish or both) in addition to age and gender of the potential users.

- Think family and keeping in touch with the user's personal community, both in the U.S. and in the country of origin.

- Integrate content for children. Hispanic online households are likely to have children, and like all parents, Latino parents have an innate desire to help their children get ahead in life.

- Provide information about education, scholarships, and opportunities for an extra-attention magnet.

- Be self-explanatory. With more newcomers to the internet, websites need to be highly self-explanatory, providing online and offline (toll-free customer service) access to help, in Spanish as well as English!

- Provide additional safety information and explanations to help overcome fears of using credit cards online, including clearly stated security measures, alternative payment methods, and easy check-out procedures.

- Create a "persona," or "meat and bones" for your website. It is difficult for Latinos and others to relate to "intangible businesses" and difficult to build loyalty with no physical presence. Plan live activity, create a "face," ideally a personality or character that can represent that persona.

- Develop alliances with established brands, companies, or sought-after activities, such as sports, music, or newspapers. For example, consider alliances with such sites as ESPN.com's Spanish-language sports site, Yahoo! en Español, laopinion.com and others. In an innovative program, Terra.com partnered with Pizza Hut in El Salvador, offering a service that allows customers living in the U.S. to order fresh pizza online and have it delivered to friends and family in El Salvador.

As more Hispanics go online, incorporating online activities in the marketing mix will become more significant. Understanding the relationship between online and offline marketing activities will take on a new level of importance.

While this section concentrates on internet usage with Hispanic consumers, the use of the internet is also growing among minority businesses, starting with the largest and gradually penetrating into smaller Latino-owned businesses. The information-technology industry has been very slow to target these microbusinesses. The opportunity is there to be owned.

SOME SITES TO WATCH

YupiMSN:
Using audience feedback to create unique content

A Spanish-language portal founded in 1996, Yupi.com was acquired by MSN in August 2001. Responding to its users, Yupi has created new channels such as CuidadFutura (City of the Future), an entertainment channel where over 250 webmasters contribute content from around the world, giving it more of an "underground" community feeling and covering topics like music, astrology, games, humor, and movies. MujerFutura (Woman of the Future) is also a popular channel, addressing the specific needs of online Latinas; it quadrupled in size a few months after the acquisition by MSN.

Mex Grocer

Hispanics are made to feel more at home in the United States by websites that bring them the foods and clothing they found at home. For example, www.Mex-Grocer.com whose taglines are:

"Bringing authentic Mexican food to your home" ™

"Tu supermercado Mexicano" ™

MexGrocer.com is the largest online grocery store for hard-to-find, non-perishable Mexican food, household products, recipes, cookbooks, and culture. MexGrocer.com streamlines the shopping process by offering authentic Mexican products not commonly in stock at conventional grocers. Amateur chefs can find authentic Mexican recipes, as well as over 100 Mexican cookbooks in both English and Spanish.

MexGrocer.com

"Bringing authentic Mexican food to your home"™
"Tu supermercado Mexicano"™

The company is positioned to capitalize on the rising volume of the $18.3 billion Mexican food market (projected for 2002 by Datamonitor) by offering an assortment of more than 1,000 items of imported and national brands through its bilingual website. Royal Crown Foods, a distributor of Mexican specialty foods, fulfills the grocery orders and UPS ensures delivery of all orders nationwide. In early 2002, the customer database of MexGrocer.com was about 80 percent non-Hispanic and 20 percent Hispanic.

The site has partnerships with several other sites that are Hispanic-targeted portals. Additionally, MexGrocer owns over 220 domain names, with such concepts as MexicanCookbooks.com and ChilesJalapenos.com, all helping to drive traffic to the site. MexGrocer continues to readjust its logistical operations, and to build affiliate partnerships to increase future business growth.

Sylvia's La Canasta Mexican

Consumers have a lot from which to choose. Last Christmas our family received delicious frozen Mexican enchiladas, and also extraordinary Mexican coffee "For the Human Bean" imported from Chiapas, ordered from a woman-owned Hispanic business with an e-component, Sylvia's La Canasta Mexican (www.sylviascanasta.com).

Peruvian Connection

Another site that I have used on several occasions, Peruvian Connection, is www.peruvianconnection.com. I am sharing this secret because I cannot get over the gorgeous Peruvian, Bolivian, and Argentinean goods they carry! Amazing! These are but two examples of what is to come. Hispanic business owners have discovered that both Latinos and non-Latinos really do go crazy when they discover, for example, a website selling genuine, good quality, fresh foods and they buy. Also, non-Hispanics have discovered a strong cultural bond, and can find beautiful garments and jewelry from a variety of South American countries.

Notes

1. *Latinos and Information Technology; The Promise and the Challenge,* prepared for IBM's Hispanic Digital Divide Task Force, April 2002
2. Q4, 2000, www.cheskin.com
3. Differences between Hispanic computer and internet usage studies can be the result of the different sampling and interviewing methodologies used in the study. For example, if only Spanish speakers are included in a Hispanic market study, the English-speaking Hispanics are not included, or if only three cities are included in the study sample, the results can vary drastically from that of a national sample, or three other Hispanic cities.
4. *Marketing to Emerging Majorities,* EPM Communications, Vol XIV. No. 3, March 2002.
5. Hispanic Internet Usage Profile, Roslow Research Group, (www.roslowresearch.com) Spring 2001 and Fall 2001
6. Hispanic Online Survey, January 2001, Cultural Access Group, (www.CAG.com)
7. www.HispanicBusiness.com, news article, July 26, 2001.
8. HispanicAd.com, April 29, 2002.

Chapter 21

The Hispanic Media Scene:
Gathering Momentum

Since I started working on this book, the Hispanic-media scene has changed, experiencing its most dramatic growth ever. Both experts and observers agree that this is just the beginning. This chapter provides an informal introduction to a complex topic, meant to provide you with a starting point on key players, trends, and issues. It is by no means a complete and exhaustive report on the Hispanic-media scene today, which could be the topic of another entire book.

The chapter begins with a brief historic perspective about the development of Hispanic television and cable in the U.S. It will give you an idea of how Hispanic media evolved and where it may go next. That summary is followed by similar summaries of radio and print.

Media is of no value without an audience, and without content, hence this chapter will also briefly cover who is watching what and where. Again, this review is by no means an in-depth treatment of the topic. However, it provides enough sources for you to know where to go for more intelligence and data.

Next in the chapter is a review of the Hispanic-advertising scene. The question is, "are major corporations *truly* taking advantage of the opportunity presented by the growing, U.S. Latino market?" As you probably guessed, the answer is no. Advertising investment is still under-used in Hispanic marketing compared with non-Hispanic advertising.

John Sinclair contributed to an earlier version of this media history section. He is Professor in the Department of Communication, Language and Cultural Studies at Victoria University of Technology in Melbourne, Australia. He has held visiting positions at the University of California, San Diego, and the University of Texas at Austin. He is author of *Images Incorporated: Advertising as Industry and Ideology* (Croom Helm, London 1987), and *Latin American Television: A Global View* (Oxford University Press, New York and London, 1999).

THE HISPANIC TV STORY

The past tells about the future

Over 40 years ago, a visionary Mexican broadcasting magnate, Emilio Azcárraga Sr., hired the young Rene Anselmo to try to sell Mexican programs to the U.S. networks. They were flatly rejected, resulting in Azcárraga's resolve to set up his own network, which we know now as Univision. Spanish-language television in the U.S. began back in 1955, but it was not until 1961 that a TV network, as we know it today, began to emerge. That year, Azcárraga's Spanish International Communication Corporation (SICC) launched its first station in San Antonio, followed over the next decade by several stations in other strategic Hispanic market locations, including Los Angeles, New York, and Miami. Programs were supplied by the network's owners in Mexico—the Spanish International Network (SIN), which was the precursor of SICC. The strategy was that entertainment programming produced for an audience in Mexico and already paid for and proven there could do double service by attracting a culturally and linguistically similar audience as an "aftermarket" in the U.S. The successful formula appealed to the Mexican, Spanish-dominant, and non-acculturated U.S. Hispanic market.

Because of the varying national origins of Spanish-speakers in the U.S., as well as their geographic distribution, the concept of "Hispanics" as a market did not exist until the 1970 Census. However, before the end of that decade, SICC/SIN had built a national network. Satellites were ideally suited to bring together into one audience—and market—the diverse and dispersed Spanish-speakers of the U.S., and SICC/SIN was the first U.S. network to interconnect all its stations and affiliates across the nation via satellite. Neither the size of the individual markets reached nor their distances apart mattered, because satellite coverage meant that they could be sold to advertisers as a national audience. From a national marketing and advertising perspective, this is when "the Hispanic market" was born.

The 1980s: Hispanic Advertising Comes of Age

The 1980s saw the beginnings of the "true" commercial development of the Hispanic audience into a more mature market. This involved the growth of the first Hispanic advertising agencies and market research companies, as well as the arrival of a competing television network, Telemundo. A few pioneers paved the road, for the next generations. For example, Luis Diaz Albertini's *Spanish Advertising and Marketing Service* (SAMS), Publicidad Siboney as well as Conill and Castor Advertising, and a few others that began operating in the 1960s and 1970s.

The 1980 Census also played a role, generating more reliable data than ever before about this growing market segment. The 1980 Census showed the kind of demographic patterns that marketers like to see: the Hispanic population was young, growing, and concentrated in specific geographical regions. Thus began a new commercial focus upon the Hispanic market.

Most national advertisers at this time were still reluctant to embrace Hispanics as a new market, because of their overall lower levels of income, education, and occupational status. However, *in-culture* market research showed Hispanics as consumers to be distinct from the general market in their spending habits. It also found the Hispanic market to be rich in many of the characteristics which advertisers seek. For example, they spend much more of their disposable income on food and packaged goods than the non-Hispanic market. They are brand conscious, and spend disproportionate amounts of their household income to purchase expensive items, such as new cars and hard durable goods. Similarly, many are willing to pay more for foods they enjoy, opening new opportunities for those in retail. In other words, they may not have the income amounts of the average American middle-class family, but, as consumers, they behave like one. Through my research, I learned that many lower-income Hispanic families worked on a cash basis, had no mortgage payments to make, and made lower monthly rent payments that were often shared among the extended family residing in the same household. Typically, two or more adults worked in the household and contributed towards the family's funds. At the end of the day, many Hispanic families could save "under the mattress," literally, the money to pay cash for very expensive goods. For those who did not have the cash available, credit became available, alas, most of the time at very high interest rates.

Neither the size of the individual markets reached nor their distances apart mattered, because satellite coverage meant that they could be sold to advertisers as a national audience. From a national marketing and advertising perspective, this is when "the Hispanic market" was born.

Marketing research and intelligence also helped Hispanic advertising-and-media planning to mature. The concept of "brand heritage," together with a couple of other tools, such as language segmentation, provided great insights for advertisers to devise sophisticated marketing-and-advertising segmentations that could easily distinguish the different types of Hispanic media users (see Chapters 10-14 for detail on marketing segmentations).

By 1987, many important changes were taking place behind the scenes. SICC/SIN was renamed Univision, and the network was in the hands of Hallmark Cards. The former Mexican owners, now Televisa, had been ordered to divest by the FCC. The new network, Telemundo, was backed by finance capital from Wall Street. Small independent Spanish-language stations in all the major Hispanic markets that emerged during the 1970s and early 1980s were acquired and formed into a second network.

Across the networks, experienced Hispanic managers and marketers were recruited, and programming was now being obtained from a greater variety of sources beyond the customary fare from Mexico. For example, Don Francisco's *Sábado Gigante*, a live national show highly popular in Chile, became a tradition on Univision, and "an expected guest" at Hispanic households throughout the United States. How did *Sábado Gigante* take off? Through the grapevine I learned that Neil Comber, the Procter & Gamble Hispanic marketing pioneer and guru was one of the first supporters of the concept and brought P&G in as the first major advertising sponsor to *Sábado Gigante*. Colgate was another pioneer charter advertiser in the program.

The new programming gave the networks more appeal to Hispanics of other than Mexican origin. Advertising grew slowly but steadily with faith that the new market would deliver, and marked the solidification of Spanish-language television as a U.S. industry.

The 1990s: Being Measured

A few companies started measuring the Hispanic market in the sixties and seventies, alas, with limited resources, and minimal credibility. For example, Strategy Research Corporation (SRC) was the first dedicated Hispanic marketing research company testing the waters. Their TV ratings started officially in the late seventies. Peter Roslow of Roslow Research Group, who today provides measurements for web usage, was one of the pioneers in the field. Other Hispanic marketing and media research by SRC dates back to 1971. Pulse, which measured Spanish language radio started even earlier, in the mid-sixties.

During the 1990s, a new standardized ratings service for Spanish-language television developed. Prior to this, networks, station owners, and marketers had not been able to provide the ongoing, consistent data needed to convince potential advertisers of the extent of Spanish-language television's reach. This was a major disadvantage in their competition with English-language networks because many national advertisers believed (as some still do) that there was no need to market and advertise in-language and *in-culture*. These advertisers believed that advertising with the mainstream networks alone was sufficient to reach a national audience. How could Spanish-language networks prove that there was a Latino consumer if its audiences were unknown and no research was available to show that advertising via Spanish-language media could deliver and "move boxes?" Hispanic market ratings did not demonstrate sales, but they certainly helped make the point there were Hispanic consumers out there that lived and consumed like everybody else!

To provide the data needed to quantify the Hispanic audience for major advertisers, Univision and Telemundo together commissioned Nielsen Media Research to upgrade the ratings measurement for Spanish-language television, and to set up the Nielsen Hispanic Television Index (NHTI). In 1992, the first national figures were produced, proving the industry's claims that the Spanish-language audience had been previously undercounted. They also documented Univision's leadership position over Telemundo. At that time, Univision had nearly two-thirds of the prime time audience, a lead that has mostly grown. NHTI superceded SRC's STARS ratings service. Abby Wool, a Hispanic media expert believes it was credibility, not size, that made the Hispanic audience real. "Major advertisers had a comfort level with good old Nielsen, whereas the SRC's numbers were not perceived as quite so impartial by many in the business and advertising world," Wool said.

That same year turned out to be a landmark in the development of the major networks. Given the high costs of local content production and its limited access to Mexican *telenovelas*, the kind of programming traditionally most popular with the majority of the Spanish-speaking audience, Telemundo was unable to compete and filed for bankruptcy. At the same time, there was a significant change of ownership at Univision. A new era began, as Hallmark sold Univision to a carefully-structured consortium which had a majority of its ownership in U.S. hands, but with significant minority shares held by Televisa, and also by the major Venezuelan production and distribution company,

Venevisión. This arrangement gave both of the Latin American companies a guaranteed outlet for their programming in the U.S. More importantly, it secured a supply of programming for Univision and assured its dominance over the industry in the United States.

Before the end of the decade there was also a significant change of hands at Telemundo, which had survived bankruptcy. With the advent of transnational capital interested in the U.S. Hispanic market and media, Sony Corporation acquired about 40 percent of Telemundo, and AT&T's Liberty Media, about 35 percent.

In the 1990s and Beyond—Hispanic Cable Comes of Age

Galavisión, Univision's bilingual programming concept, started under the strategic direction of Xavier Saralegui, who hired an extraordinary woman and pioneer, Lucia Ballas-Taynor, who later became Galavisión's general manager. Until recently, Galavisión was one of the few media venues available to reach Latino kids and teens in one of their languages. In April 2002, however, the network changed its strategy and reverted to Spanish-only programming.

In October 2001, Telemundo re-launched its GEMS Television cable network as Mun2, or MunDos ("worlds" in Spanish). The new Mun2 network targets Hispanics aged 18 to 34 in Spanish, with trendy original programming such as FuZion, a youth-oriented program that features segments on entertainment, music, and film. In addition, MunDos plans to produce original programming, with Latino casting, including novelas.

Other cable players emerged in the 1990s to appeal to the growing U.S. Hispanic audience, showing they had not only the muscle and the resources to compete, but also the brains to think Hispanic programming. Players such as MTV-S, Discovery en Español, Fox Sports Español, HBO Español, ESPN, Playboy en Español and others have broadened considerably Hispanic media horizons.

Most notable among them is Fox Sports Español that launched about five years ago in Los Angeles and grew into "the only U.S., 24-hour sports network en Español," with an impressive presence in the U.S. and Latin America. Its growth and maturity truly took off in 1999, developing an *in-culture* cable channel dedicated to sports, conceptualized to appeal to Hispanic sports fans. Fox Sports Español brings sports to millions of Hispanic and non-Hispanic fans and helps promote Hispanic sports stars in America. Under the vision of Tom Maney, a "Gringo with a Latino heart," Fox Sports Español secured contracts with sports teams throughout Latin America, filling a void for fans who wanted to watch teams from their home countries. In 2002, the cable network extended its existing reach into Latin America through a new media conglomerate. The new venture will provide access to significant sports events to the U.S. Hispanic market, including exclusive rights to Copa Libertadores, the most popular regional soccer competition.

The growth of the Hispanic-market cable industry correlates directly with the growing penetration of cable in Hispanic television households. In a few years of *in-culture* Hispanic programming, cable has been able to capture over 6.5 million subscriber Hispanic households. However, it is always important to keep in mind that subscriber households are not necessarily viewers.

Another aid in cable advertising and media planning will come from new Spanish-language ratings reports to be provided by Nielsen Media Research (NMR). Started in mid-2002, the same quarterly reports available for Hispanic broadcast media are available with the demographic and viewer profile data for Hispanic Cable Households. Fox Sports Español has contracted the services of NMR and will make these available to its advertisers.

Into the New Millennium

As of mid 2002, there continues to be mainstream corporate capital investment in the U.S. Spanish-language television industry. Other trends are the expansion of the present networks, diversification of the programming offered, and continued concentration of the industry in Miami. There also is further internationalization in the ownership of networks. In particular, TV Azteca, the competitor to Televisa in Mexico and one-time collaborator with Telemundo in the U.S., is developing a new network in the U.S., in a joint venture with Pappas Telecasting Companies. Meanwhile, Hispanic Television Network (HTVN) is up and running. A U.S. public company traded on Nasdaq, HTVN is led by a non-Hispanic businessman in Dallas and distributed by various cable companies throughout the U.S.

Both Univision and Telemundo have expanded considerably. In December 2000, Univision bought the stations of USA Networks with the intention of developing it as a second broadcast network. It launched in January 2002 as TeleFutura, with 42 stations across 27 markets, reaching approximately 70 percent of U.S. Hispanic homes.[1] As mentioned above, on the cable front, Telemundo took over Miami-based GEMS to become its cable network, renamed

Mun2 (*mun dos*). Univision has had a cable network for many years, Galavisión, but has no international cable service yet as Telemundo does with Telemundo Internacional.

As they line up in mid-2002, Univision continues to be far ahead of Telemundo and TV Azteca. Telemundo, recently acquired by NBC[2], is growing and in the process of creating a "new persona." Univision has 19 owned and operated stations and 204 affiliates, and a potential reach of 90 percent of the Hispanic audience. Telemundo weighs in with 10 full-power stations and 40 affiliates, with coverage of 88 percent of the Hispanic population. Presently, Univision has 75 to 85 percent of the Hispanic prime-time audience.

BILINGUAL, "SPANGLISH" AND ENGLISH HISPANIC MEDIA TAKES OFF

The opening of Univision's second network in 2002 raised the hopes of many marketers and advertisers that they would see more linguistically diverse programming. Whereas Univision has kept a strict policy of Spanish only on its present network (even advertising slogans have to be rendered in "correct" Spanish), TeleFutura was to allow the use of the popular bilingual vernacular often referred to as *Spanglish*. It also was expected to carry bilingual programming targeting Latinos as it had done in the past with Galavisión. This strategy would theoretically have made TeleFutura more appealing to the younger and less Spanish-dominant Latino audiences, and so extend the size of its audience among the young consumer segment. As mentioned above, Univision's management changed the approach when post-launch audience declined, and both Galavisión and TeleFutura dropped their bilingual programs for a "counter-programming" strategy and now follow the original networks' tested and proven Spanish-language format. What is "counter-programming?" In the words of Ray Rodriguez, president and CEO of Univision Networks, "The idea is to offer viewers different selections without directly competing with programs found on the original network."[3] In other words, the cable network offers programs that appeal to different viewers than those who watch the "mother network," Univision.

Presently other media companies are growing the bilingual concept. For example, as mentioned earlier in the book, Nickelodeon targets English-dominant and bilingual Hispanic youth with *Dora the Explorer* for young children, and the older youth segment, aged 12 to 24, with the *Brothers Garcia*. Mun2, Telemundos' cable company, also carries some shows and programs that are bilingual. Perhaps the newest media in the young Latino-genre is LATV, a broadcast and internet channel based in Los Angeles. It owns and operates channels 57 and 33, targeting bilingual, bicultural youth with over 10 hours of live, original, "cutting-edge" Latino music and entertainment. Judging by its explosive growth—from 3 hours of original programming in 2000 to over 16 in 2002—LATV seems to have cracked the code for this hard-to-reach market segment. Founded in 2001, LATV estimates it is available to over 3 million households via satellite and cable and another 1 million via broadcast media. LATV is majority owned by a visionary Latino, Walter Ulloa, as a component of Entravision Communications, a new Hispanic multimedia company. Advertisers such as Universal Pictures, Jack in the Box, Pollo Loco and others have supported LATV's growth.

A much more radical approach to English-dominant Hispanics is being tried by Sí TV, a non-Hispanic-owned production company based in Los Angeles which has announced that it will launch a cable network for Latinos, but with programming in English.

WHO IS WATCHING WHAT?

Not only is language—Spanish versus English versus bilingual—a challenging decision to make in any Hispanic media plan, but the way Latinos watch television also has to be considered. For example, it is common for Hispanic families to watch TV together. Teens may watch novelas in Spanish, with their parents and perhaps grandparents, and then watch English-language programs with their siblings or friends.

FIGURE 21.1

"A Family Affair"

Percentage of Hispanic Teens who say they usually spend time watching TV with . . .

	Spanish-language TV	English-language TV
Mom or Dad	62%	21%
Brothers or sisters	23	64
Other adults in the home	11	2
Friends	9	17

Source: Starcom Worldwide's Kidscope Study, quoted in *American Demographics,* April 2001.

WHO IS WATCHING

Through the courtesy of a Nielsen Media Research subscriber, the tables below describe the universe of Hispanic media watchers for the 2001–2002 season.

FIGURE 21.2

Hispanic Media Watchers, 2001–2002

in thousands

Hispanic Households	Total	Spanish-dominant
2+ persons	34,405	18,784
Working women (30 or more hours per week)		
Age 18+	5,278	2,461
Women Total 18+	11,447	5,855
18 to 24	1,931	910
18 to 34	4,519	2,484
18 to 49	8,298	4,266
21+	10,602	5,479
21 to 49	7,453	3,890
21 to 54	8,321	4,296
25 to 49	6,367	3,356
25 to 54	7,235	3,762
35 to 64	5,767	2,715
55 +	2,281	1,183
65+	1,161	656
Females 15 to 24	2,810	1,400
Men total 18+	11,605	6,581
18 to 24	1,923	1,212
18 to 34	4,917	3,056
18 to 49	8,840	5,108
21+	10,787	6,054
21 to 49	8,022	4,581
21 to 54	8,870	5,026
25 to 49	6,917	3,896
25 to 54	7,765	4,341

Hispanic **Households**	Total	Spanish-dominant
35 to 64	5,813	3,064
55 +	1,917	1,028
65+	875	461
Males 15 to 24	2,820	1,712
Persons 18 +	23,052	12,436
18 to 24	3,854	2,122
18 to 34	9,436	5,540
18 to 49	17,138	9,374
21+	21,389	11,533
21 to 49	15,475	8,471
21 to 54	17,191	9,322
25 to 49	13,284	7,252
25 to 54	15,000	8,103
35 to 64	11,580	5,779
55 +	4,198	2,211
65+	2,036	1,117
Teens (12 to 17) Total	3,724	2,036
Male	1,909	1,043
Female	1,815	993
Total 12 to 14	1,948	1,046
Total 15 to 17	1,776	990
Children (2 to 11) Total	7,629	4,312
Boys	3,912	2,211
Girls	3,717	2,101
Children (6 to 11) Total	4,376	2,462
Boys	2,257	1,270
Girls	2,119	1,192
Children 2 to 5	3,253	1,850
Children 6 to 8	2,179	1,220
Children 9 to 11	2,197	1,242

Source: Table reports Nielsen Media Research universe estimates provided by a third party.

WATCHING WHAT?

In the tables below, through the courtesy of Arturo Villar, publisher of *Hispanic Market Weekly*™, the complex issue of what is being watched can be addressed candidly and with reliable data.

FIGURE 21.3

Most-Watched Programs, Hispanic Adults 18 to 49

Total U.S. Adults 18-49 Ratings, Q4 2001 through Q1 2002

Rank	Program Name–Day	Network	NHTI
1	*Amigas y Rivales*–Tue	UNIV	14.7
2	*Amigas y Rivales*–Mon	UNIV	14.5
3	*Amigas y Rivales*–Wed	UNIV	14.0
4	*Por un Beso*–Wed	UNIV	13.9
5	*Amigas y Rivales*–Thu	UNIV	13.8
6	*Por un Beso*–Tue	UNIV	13.6
7	*Por un Beso*–Thu	UNIV	13.4
8	*Salome*–Mon	UNIV	13.2
9	*Por un Beso*–Mon	UNIV	13.0
10	*Derecho de Nacer*–Mon	UNIV	13.0
11	*Amigas y Rivales*–Fri	UNIV	12.8
12	*Derecho de Nacer*–Tue	UNIV	12.7
13	*Por un Beso*–Fri	UNIV	12.5
14	*Derecho de Nacer*–Wed	UNIV	12.3
15	*Cristina*–Mon	UNIV	12.3
16	*Salome*–Tue	UNIV	12.1
17	*Carita de Angel*–Mon	UNIV	12.0
18	*Derecho de Nacer*–Thu	UNIV	12.0
19	*Derecho de Nacer*–Fri	UNIV	11.9
20	*Carita de Angel*–Tue	UNIV	11.9
73	*Friends*–all day parts	NBC	4.0
81	*El Clon*–Fri	Telmnd	3.6

Source: NHTI.9/24/01-3/03/02, Regular Programming, All Broadcast Networks From *Hispanic Market Weekly*, April 1, 2002

The Hispanic TV Universe At-A-Glance

Prepared for this book by La Fuente de Informacion de la Prensa Hispana's *Hispanic Media Directory*, (www.hispanic-media.com), below is a summary of the "Hispanic TV media universe" targeting the US Hispanic market late 2001, including the U.S./Mexican border.

These are the number of stations in each state or territory:

U.S.				Mexico	
Arizona	6	New Jersey	2	Chihuahua, MX	7
California	32	New Mexico	6	Coahuila, MX	5
Colorado	7	Nevada	4	Nuevo León, MX	3
Connecticut	1	New York	1	Tamaulipas, MX	16
Florida	8	Oregon	5	Baha California, MX	9
Georgia	1	Pennsylvania	1	Sonora, MX	2
Hawaii	1	Puerto Rico	5		
Idaho	1	South Carolina	1		
Illinois	3	Texas	47		
Indiana	1	Utah	4		
Massachusetts	5	Virginia	1		
Maryland	1	Washington	2		
		Wisconsin	1		

Source: Hispanic Media Directory, www.hispanic-media.com.

WHAT NEXT?

In early 2002, *The Hollywood Reporter* commented, "2002 is shaping up as a year of bruising competition among Spanish-language broadcasters in the United States, who are anxious to exploit the increasingly sizable demographic in search of enormous potential returns." In the same issue, media industry analyst William Blair & Co., was quoted as saying, "Spanish-language media is probably going to grow 2 to 3 times faster than the general media market over the next 5 to 10 years."[4]

I predict more mergers, more acquisitions, and more single station purchases in the near future in the Hispanic media world. The changes in the
industry are so profound and so many new players are joining the Hispanic
media momentum, that it is almost impossible to follow them in detail without
help. Fortunately, as I said earlier, there is *Hispanic Market Weekly*
(www.hmweekly.com) that does the job extraordinarily well with its Monday
summaries and Special Recap issues, and HispanicAd.com with reports on the
trade and the Hispanic media world, on a daily basis.

SOME SPECIFICS

A few examples of what is to come, with special thanks to *Hispanic Market
Weekly*.

- Univision continues its long-term relationship with Mexico's Televisa and
  Venezuela's Venevisión with "a landmark rearrangement" of its relationship
  with both networks, giving Univision's three networks exclusive rights in
  the U.S. and Puerto Rico for all programs produced by Televisa and
  Venevisión—among others.[6] Univision announced at its 2002 up-front presentation, where it presents its new programming, that it will maintain its
  well-tested Spanish-language programming, as discussed above, for both
  networks, Univision and TeleFutura.[6]

- With the acquisition of WQHS, Channel 61, to broadcast in Spanish in Cleve-
  land, Ohio,[7] Univision shows the road to yet another trend, the addition of
  new emerging Hispanic markets to the giant network's reach. This type of
  acquisition will probably be one of the most common occurrences in the
  decades to come.

- Telemundo merges with G.E.'s NBC Network for $2 billion in what analysts
  agree is the largest price ever paid in the history of Hispanic media.[8] The
  question is what will NBC/Telemundo's merger bring to the table? The slo-
  gan, "We've Got the Power," suggests Telemundo feels strong with NBC's
  backing. With new reality shows, original novelas, and the benefit of its new
  owners, it is expected to become a strong competitor for Univision. For
  example, through NBC Network connection, Telemundo announced recently
  it will air new sports programming, including the 2004, 2006, and 2008
  Olympic Games and Golden Globes.[9]

- Almost simultaneously, and some would speculate in response to the NBC deal, Univision announced in June 2002 that it will acquire HBC, the biggest Hispanic radio company, for $3.5 billion in stock. This would make Univision an "integrated" multi-media giant, with countless cross-promotion opportunities to offer its advertisers.[10]

- On the audience front, it is still too soon to know how TeleFutura will impact the Hispanic market audience in the long run, especially now that it has changed direction in programming.

- Expect to see more venues to reach one of the most challenging, and sought after Hispanic media segments today, the Tween and Teen Latino youth segments. The language preferences and media use by the tidal wave of young Latinos are still being sorted out.

- The newest emerging network, Mexico's TV Azteca's, Azteca America acquired minor stakes in several stations in California and a station covering Houston. This move gathers under one network roof most of the Hispanic markets experiencing the effects of the tremendous inflow of recent Mexican immigrants in the past two decades. It is also unclear how Azteca America will evolve and how many of its innovative, award-winning programs it will import from Mexico.

- New joint ventures between U.S. and international investors will create new networks. For example, Mexican and west-coast investors launched VidaVision, a cable network based in Miami reaching areas in Texas, Georgia and Latin America.[11]

- New "fully integrated" media marketing companies are forming, such as Entravision (EV) Communications, which describes itself as "a diversified Spanish-language media company that employs a combination of television, radio, outdoor advertising, and publishing operations." Entravision Communications owns 23 Univision-affiliated television stations and plans to acquire several more TeleFutura affiliates. It is estimated that EV covers about 80 percent of U.S. Hispanic consumers. EV also owns 58 Spanish-language radio, and 11,200 outdoor faces or billboards in key Hispanic markets. It also owns *El Diario/La Prensa*, in New York.[12]

FIGURE 21.4

Spanish Language Tiers

Launched by major cable and satellite providers

AT&T	Canales Españoles
Adelphia	Adelphia en Español
Time Warner	Nuestros Canales en Digital
Cox	TeleLatina
Direct TV	Para Todos
Echostar	Dish Latino and Dish Latino Dos

Source: Fox Sports Español

- We will see more English-language programming for Latino audiences either in mainstream media or in new, targeted media. For example, Latin Access, a syndicated 30-minute "magazine-style" weekly show about Latino entertainment, launched early in 2002. It is broadcast in English through the major networks' affiliates in large Hispanic markets, with an estimated 95 percent coverage of the U.S. Hispanic television market. Advertisers sponsoring the launch included M&M/Mars, Taco Bell, and Goya, among others.

- There will be stronger integration of Hispanics in the continental U.S. and those on the Island of Puerto Rico, at least in media and marketing. Until recently, very few Hispanic clients included Puerto Rico in their marketing plans, relegating this 4-million-strong market to the international department.

- Last, expect new ventures and synergies between the U.S. Hispanic market and Latin America and Spain. It is highly probable that during this decade we will get to see a "Global" Spanish-speaking network that talks to the almost 400 million Spanish-speakers around the globe. How about Vision-Global?

HISPANIC RADIO MATURES

The Hollywood-style glamour of television and the power of its visual image sometimes cast a shadow over radio, a powerful broadcast media that plays a vital role in the advertising success of an integrated Hispanic marketing campaign. As with television, Hispanic radio has experienced explosive growth, maturity, and change over the past couple of decades. Moreover, as in television, new mergers and acquisitions take place almost weekly. For example, recently Univision acquired HBC, the largest Hispanic radio company.

This exponential growth is not by chance, but reflects the fact that Hispanic radio is a medium with a growing audience that reaches most Hispanic market segments. Sometimes radio is the only Hispanic broadcast medium in small emerging Hispanic markets. In addition, since the number of radio stations in Hispanic cities in the U.S. outnumbers the television and cable channels in these markets, radio has the potential to deliver to precise targets of the Hispanic market *simultaneously*. For example, a specific campaign or message can be broadcast to several sub-segments of the same age group that are reached through very different programming styles.

The out-of-home reach of radio is also important when designing a Hispanic media strategy. Latinos tend to drive more often than non-Hispanics do with family and friends and commute less by themselves. The radio may be on all day in workplaces as well as in many homes.

Today, radio networks and independents offer a wide range of programming, musical styles, and language mixes for all tastes and preferences and are included in most integrated marketing strategies. A more recent strategic development combines Hispanic-oriented websites, radio, and mega-events. However, the advertising effectiveness of radio has been more than proven alone or in partnerships, depending on the product and strategy. As the case study on page 274 illustrates, the results can be highly profitable. As with the review of television, use this section as an introductory review to help you find more information.

Since the number of radio stations in Hispanic cities in the U.S. outnumbers the television and cable channels in these markets, radio has the potential to deliver to precise targets of the Hispanic market simultaneously.

BEING MEASURED

The present day Hispanic radio scene is rich and diverse, with a wide variety of styles of programming for all consumer segments. Arbitron tracks Hispanic radio use based on panelists who complete a diary, and provides the "best estimates" available today. However, in my years evaluating research methodologies with the Hispanic market I learned that Latinos tend to be "more forgetful" than other populations, particularly Spanish-dominant, less-acculturated segments. Therefore, the Arbitron data are probably underrepresenting the true picture of the Hispanic media audience. To improve on this, Arbitron is currently experimenting with a "Portable People Meter" which would eliminate the memory problem. Nielsen Media Research is providing financial support as well as its television survey research expertise in the U.S. market trial of the Portable People Meter.

ARE WE LISTENING?

The results of studies conducted by telephone rather than door-to-door, in person, can vary drastically, particularly with certain segments such as Spanish-dominant young Hispanics.

Media use data vary considerably, depending on the source of the data, the method used to gather it and, in the Hispanic market, the language used to collect it. If you compare two studies, one conducted by telephone and one door-to-door, in person, the results can vary drastically, particularly with certain segments such as Spanish-dominant young Hispanics. How do I know? My obsession with measurements in diverse markets led me to conduct several studies using both methodologies simultaneously. All factors were equal, except that half the study was conducted by telephone and the other half door-to-door. Including the sample area, both were conducted in the same zip codes. Guess what? The data varied significantly in some categories and media was one of them. For example, more Spanish-language radio listeners were found among the door-to-door sample. This reflects the socio-economic characteristics of the people that participate or refuse to participate in one or another method.[13] This is just one small example of how much variation you can find in any body of data. Therefore, it is extremely important to evaluate the source and reliability of the data you use to plan your media strategy.

Back to radio usage data. In April 2002, *Hispanic Market*

Weekly reported on a media study by the San Francisco-based New California Media group (NCM) an association of more than 200 print, broadcast, and online "ethnic" organizations. Miami-based firm Bendixen & Associates, a public opinion firm, conducted the study in California. The survey report states, "Fifty-percent of Hispanics indicated that they mostly listen to Spanish-language radio, and 43 percent said they watch Spanish-language television."[14] Another report that touches on this issue is The *MSR&C Ethnic Market Report* from Market Segment Research & Consulting. This study reports that Hispanics spend considerably fewer hours listening to radio than watching television, 16.6 hours per week with radio versus 25.4 hours with television.[15]

Which one is correct? Probably both. The "most often" question only suggests frequency of exposure, "more or less often," but not the length of listening each time the radio is turned on. In some markets, such as Los Angeles and New York, due to the distances and heavy traffic, it is possible that a consumer listens to the radio several hours a day while in the car. But the majority of Latinos, nationwide, probably do not. However, since we are a "wheeled" society and we get in the car even for the smallest chore, it is possible that we do turn the radio on in the car "more often" than we turn on the TV set. In sum, it is possible that Latinos turn to radio many more times a day than to television, or to print media, for that matter. However, the length of time in front of the television can easily be longer since we tend to watch for blocks of time —from the beginning to the end of a program—versus a car ride that can be brief.

Which insight should you use to prepare your radio and television buy? Is the answer "Both"? Depending on the integrated strategy you have created for your campaign, and which segment you are targeting, you can decide the optimal time to use each medium. You can study—or guesstimate— the times when different consumer segments will most likely be in a car whether going to work or shopping. For example,

In markets such as Los Angeles and New York, a consumer may listen to the radio several hours a day while driving.

Latino youths will likely be in a car late at night whereas the working Hispanic parent who has children to care for at home, or the *Abuelita*, in her 40s or older who is shopping for her family are more likely to be in the car during the day. You know the mom will be preparing her family's meal at certain hours, or she will be cleaning the house, with the radio on. She may not be able to watch television while she is cooking, although I have seen many who do.

Back to the question of how to prepare your TV or radio buy. You can only buy an ad with an audience and a schedule of ads with a reach. Nielsen Media Ratings and Arbitron ratings measure these quantities. A good media planner at a Hispanic advertising agency can help you develop a successful radio and TV media plan.

CHANGING LIFESTYLES

As with non-Hispanic Americans, Hispanic lifestyles are changing, with growing family and work-related demands. This results in more and longer hours driving in the car. Usually in the Hispanic market this means listening to the radio. A 2001 Arbitron study shows that Los Angeles' four-county area residents, Hispanic and non-Hispanic, are spending considerably more time in traffic and less time at home, with the expected higher number of hours listening to the radio. The 1,000 participant sample base for the study was drawn from the Arbitron diarykeepers, the people who inform the industry about their radio usage behavior and preferences.

Some highlights of the Arbitron study follow, which apply to the entire sample in the Los Angeles area, not just Hispanics, except where noted:

- Two years ago only 14 percent of adults aged 18 and over were in vehicles by 6 A.M.; today, 20 percent are.

- Hispanics made 3.8 trips on average each day in 2001 *vs.* 3.1 in 1999.

- We stop and shop even more on the way home, or go home and then leave again to shop. More buying decisions are made each day, many at the last minute.

- More hours are spent in cars earlier, longer (over 1.5 hours per day) and more often, and are usually alone—except for radio. That affects how listeners feel about radio, how radio is used, and how listeners respond to the radio.

The same was found to be true in most markets in the U.S.

• Media use is shifting. Thirty-nine percent of adults aged 18 and older said their radio use was greater than the year before, while only 15 percent said it decreased; 53 percent of Hispanics said they are listening "more often."

• Eighty-two percent of adults aged 18 and older said they now use radio every day. Seventy-six percent use TV and only 41 percent read a newspaper every day. Most people under age 65 spend more time each day with radio than with any other medium.

• When in the car, 84 percent said "listening to radio" was their number one activity, and 96.5 percent listen to some radio in the car.

• At work, 61 percent said they have listened to radio and 35 percent said they do so on a regular basis.

• Fifty-four percent of adults aged 18 plus said they shopped at a store they "heard about on radio," in 2001 compared with 48 percent in 1999. The same patterns were observed for restaurants.

• Thirty-eight percent of adults aged 18 and older said they have bought a product or service recommended by their favorite personality on the radio.

@ Excerpts from The Los Angeles Lifestyles Study, Arbitron, 2002, quoted in HispanicAd.com, 02/17/02

In the first quarter of 2001, Arbitron released Arbitron 101 en Español a Spanish-language version of the Arbitron 101 web-based training module that will allow Spanish-speaking media planners to learn more about using Arbitron radio ratings. To find out more, go to www.arbitron.com and click on support and training.

RADIO AS THE MEDIUM

Some advertisers tend to feel at a loss when budgetary limits do not include the costs of television advertising.

However, radio, as the lead medium in an *in-culture* advertising campaign, can deliver excellent results. The Franklin Electronic Publishing case study that follows clearly demonstrates this scenario.

Franklin® Electronic Publishers

For more detail on this case and creative materials, go to www.incultureapproach.com

Product or brand: Spanish-English electronic dictionaries, Electronic Translator

BACKGROUND

Franklin Electronic Publishers is the worldwide leader in handheld electronic books, and the creator of the handheld electronic reference category. Three of its electronic products are offered in both Spanish and in English—two handheld Spanish-English dictionaries, and an electronic translator. All instructions and packaging for the three products are bilingual, making them as easy to use for Spanish speakers as for English speakers.

The company had strong sales in Latin America for several of its bilingual Spanish-English electronic dictionary products. However, sales were practically non-existent in high-Hispanic U.S. markets, apparently due to lack of product awareness. In mid-2000, Franklin hired Español Marketing & Communications, in Cary, NC, to analyze the potential for its products and develop a market program test for the U.S. Hispanic market.

RESEARCH

Strategy Research Corporation reports that the Spanish language is the most important factor in unifying Hispanics of differing ethnic backgrounds. Due to an increase in immigration over the past few decades, an overwhelming majority (86 percent) of Hispanics indicated Spanish as their first language.

When comparing comfort of speaking English with frequent use of English, there is a wide gap between the typical Hispanic's proficiency and necessity of using English at work—an ideal opportunity for a Spanish-English dictionary.

However, the Yankelovich Hispanic Monitor found that of U.S. Hispanic adults, 89 percent consider the Spanish language the *most important* aspect of Hispanic culture to preserve. This means that many parents with children growing up in an English-speaking environment make an extra effort to keep their children fluent in Spanish.

Parents and educators want their children to learn English, because it is essential for success. Educators are trying to determine the best way to teach children English, and are actively looking for tools to help them learn. The U.S. Department of Education has made successful Hispanic education a primary area of focus. In bilingual, ESL, and dual-literacy classrooms, the electronic dictionaries could easily become a staple learning tool. It also can become an individual tool for youngsters at school and at home, just like a calculator.

HISPANIC MARKET TEST

In order to test a program which would be expandable to the rest of the U.S. Hispanic market, representative test Metropolitan Statistical Areas (MSAs) were selected: Houston-Galveston-Brazoria in Texas and Phoenix-Mesa in Arizona. They are described in the table below.

Houston-Galveston-Brazoria	Phoenix-Mesa
#7 U.S. Hispanic market	#9 U.S. Hispanic market
1,348,588 Hispanics (29% of total pop.)	817,012 Hispanics (25% of total pop.)
73% Mexican country of origin	82% Mexican country of origin
$37,894 mean HH income (1998)	$36,555 mean HH income (1998)

Source: U.S. Census 2000

CREATIVE STRATEGY

Target Consumer: Spanish-dominant Hispanic women aged 18 to 54, with school-age children living at home, who are actively interested in learning English.

CREATIVE CONSIDERATIONS

Create memorable name and tagline for the product which can be used in all communications.

Whenever possible, distinguish between the two featured models, both visually and in copy points. The DBE-1440 has 2 million translations and does not pronounce words, while the deluxe BES-1940 has 2.5 million translations and can pronounce words.

MEDIA AND PROMOTIONAL STRATEGY

The media and production budget ruled out Spanish-language TV. The product description and benefits are complex, and require time and visuals for a potential consumer to fully understand them. Additionally, the client wanted to offer co-op advertising to all participating retailers, in exchange for the purchase of incremental cases of product and set-up of in-store displays or point-of-sale materials. The agency therefore recommended a combination of Spanish-language radio and bilingual direct mail.

Radio stations were selected based on their market rankings, cost-effectiveness, and their interest and creativity in featuring the Franklin dictionaries above and beyond traditional advertising. A strong co-op advertising schedule ran for six weeks, featuring two 60-second commercials, with the tagline:

> Mejor inglés al instante con el diccionario electrónico Franklin . . . es como tener un profesor de inglés en la palma de su mano!

> *Improve your English instantly, with the Franklin electronic dictionary . . . it's like having an English teacher in the palm of your hand!*

Each market created an on-air contest called *La Frase Que Paga* (The Phrase that Pays), where clues to the winning phrase were "spoken" each day by the Franklin Dictionaries, with heavy promotion, live DJ endorsement and elaboration of benefits. Consumer callers who knew the phrase of the day won the deluxe Franklin dictionary.

For the direct mail portion, ADVO was chosen as the supplier, due to its cost-effectiveness and to its ability to precisely target high-Hispanic neighborhoods. Since there was no way to guarantee that only Spanish-speaking consumers would receive the inserts, the direct mail piece was a bilingual one. In early December, in Houston, more than 200,000 full-color, 2-sided inserts were distributed in the highest density Hispanic zones. The insert featured the benefits of the two key products, encouraged the purchase of a Franklin dictionary for Christmas, and featured participating retailers. In Phoenix, over 90,000 inserts were distributed in the highest density Hispanic zones.

RETAILER PARTICIPATION

Five national retailers participated in the test program—RadioShack, Staples, Best Buy, Circuit City, and Service Merchandise. Retailers received co-op radio tags based on their relative support in each market, as well as logos included in the direct mail piece. Retailers ordered extra product to be prepared for increased consumer demand, displayed bilingual point-of-sale materials, and provided sales data to Franklin.

TRACKING AND RESULTS

Participating retailers were asked to submit monthly sales data by product SKU, for the year preceding the program through the month following the program (16 total months of data). Additionally, stores with a high share of Hispanic population within 10 miles of their location were considered core stores, while stores with low share of Hispanic populations were considered secondary stores. Several retailers also provided control market data—corresponding data from similar MSAs which did not have any Spanish-language marketing activities.

The following conclusions are based on analysis of that data:

• Overall, unit sales increased 153 percent during the test period compared to the previous year.

• In Houston, unit sales increased 192 percent. The deluxe model accounted for 60 percent of total sales.

• In Phoenix, unit sales increased by 91 percent. The deluxe model accounted for 56 percent of unit sales.

(Author's Comment: It is also likely that the Houston market performed better than the Phoenix market because the Houston market is more Spanish-dominant.)

In 2001, Franklin expanded its Hispanic-market efforts nationwide, with a co-op program with key retailer RadioShack. Franklin is running an advertising schedule and promotional campaign on Radio Unica network, and expanding its direct mail program to additional markets.

The Hispanic market test exceeded the expectations of the Franklin management team. According to Maritza Lorge, marketing manager at Franklin, "The test showed Franklin and our retail partners the power and influence of the U.S. Hispanic market."

The Franklin case also shows the impact of a well-planned and well-executed in-culture radio-based strategy!

AGENCY: Español Marketing and Communications, www.espanolmarketing.com

BIG PLAYERS IN RADIO

Two major players dominate Hispanic radio audiences in the largest markets. Hispanic Broadcast Corporation, (HBC) owns and operates more than 40 radio stations in 12 of the 15 Hispanic markets. Spanish Broadcasting System (SBS) is the other large Hispanic-owned radio-ratings leader in five of the largest markets. Both giants entered the new millennium forming strategic alliances and partnerships with the satellite-radio players, considerably increasing their coverage and businesses. Two others, Entravision and Radio Unica are also leaders in market coverage and numbers of major-market stations owned.

NEW PLAYERS FOR GROWING CHALLENGES

Hispanic radio is definitely well prepared for the challenges created by the growth of the market of urban and Hispanic listeners. A radio industry report reads, "The Urban and Hispanic radio formats already rank second and third among all radio formats. In addition, radio research shows above-average time spent listening among both of these groups. As these groups grow in importance for advertisers, radio is positioned well to benefit from the burgeoning ad dollars. Spot radio will be particularly important in reaching those "pockets" of high concentration, as metros vary significantly in their ethnic and racial composition."[16] New players are investing in increasing the power and reach of some stations.

For example, between the end of 2000 and early 2002 two digital-quality satellites—XM Satellite and Sirius Satellite Radio—launched more than 100 radio channels each, including several targeting Hispanics in traditional as well as non-traditional "emerging" Hispanic markets. Sirius is carrying 10 channels with Hispanic-oriented programming, some with commercial-free music and others licensed to Hispanic Radio Network (HRN). One is even carrying BBC Mundo, from London. HRN provides programming that appeals to Hispanic youth as well as the traditional Hispanic market segments like the Mexican Ranchera crowd. It also offers news and information, sports, and shows for Latinas.

XM Satellite Radio system and Hispanic Broadcasting's five Spanish-language music channels also appeal to different segments of the Hispanic market, with rock en Español, salsa, romantic, tropical/Caribbean, and Regional

Mexican, plus 18 hours of live programming.[17] In addition, HRN produces Spanish-language programs for syndication, with 120 stations in the continental U.S.A. and Puerto Rico, not counting its 22 affiliates in Latin America. Another notable example is the case of Entravision, described above in the Television section. Entravision presently owns the largest centrally programmed radio network in 26 markets with 56 radio stations. Together with its other media properties and partnerships, such as those mentioned above, Entravision is a compelling integrated marketing partner in today's competitive world.

LATINO RADIO FORMATS

It is a challenge to talk about Hispanic radio formats because there is so much variety, and within each genre there's even more variation. However, the formats can be categorized into a set of styles:

- Contemporary Youth oriented (Hip-Hop, Hispanic Rock, etc.)
- Contemporary Adult oriented
- News
- Talk
- Sports
- Regional Mexican (Tejano)
- Spanish "Oldies"
- Tropical (Caribbean music, salsa, cumbia, etc.)
- American Tex-Mex
- Christian

According to *Hispanic Media Directory*, approximately one-third of all U.S. Hispanic radio stations have a "Regional Mexican" format. Others can be grouped as follows:

- Over 100 Hispanic radios stations are Christian
- Over 100 are "Adult Spanish Contemporary"
- Over 70 are "Talk"
- Over 50 are "Tropical"

FIGURE 21.5

Top Billers for Spanish-language Radio

HBC=Hispanic Broadcasting Corp   SBS=Spanish Broadcasting System

Rank	Stations	Format	Location, owner	Gross billings, 2001 (in $millions)
1	KLVE-FM KTNQ-AM KSCA-FM KRCD-FM KRCV-FM	Contemporary Spanish News/talk/sports Regional Mexican Spanish oldies Spanish oldies	Los Angeles, HBC	$84.00
2	WSQK-FM WPAT-FM	Tropical Romantic favorites	New York, SBS	$60.00
3	KLAT-AM KTNL-FM KOVE-FM KRXT-FM KOBU-FM	News/talk Regional Mexican Adult contemporary Hip-hop Regional Mexican	Houston, HBC	$37.00
4	WAMR-FM WRTO-FM WQBA-AM WAQI-AM	Adult contemporary Salsa hits News/talk News/talk	Miami, HBC	$35.90
5	WRMA-FM WXOJ-FM WCMQ-FM	Adult contemporary Tropical All-time classics	Miami, SBS	$30.50
6	KLAX-FM KXOL-FM	Regional Mexican Adult Contemporary	Los Angeles, SBS	$20.47
7	KDXX-FM KDXT-FM KHCK-FM KESS-AM KLNO-FM KDXX-AM KDOS-FM	Regional Mexican Regional Mexican Tejano News/talk/sports Regional Mexican Regional Mexican Regional Mexican	Dallas, HBC	$20.00
8	KCOR-AM KROM-FM KXTN-FM KBBT-FM KCOR-FM KXTN-AM	Regional Mexican Tejano Hip-hop Spanish memories Tejano News/talk	San Antonio, HBC	$19.23
9	WLEY	Regional Mexican	Chicago, SBS	$15.00
10	WOJO-FM WIND-AM WIXX-AM	Regional Mexican News/talk Tropical	Chicago, HBC	$15.00
Total				$338.10

Source: Hispanic Business Magazine, December 2001.

Hispanic Radio in Summary

These were the Hispanic Radio organizations in January 2002:

Spanish Broadcasting System	Entravision Radio
Moon Broadcasting	Radio Unica
Hispanic Broadcasting Corporation	Uno Radio Group
World Radio Network	Mega Communications
La Radio Cristiana	

The following table shows in which state these broadcast and how many in each state. The U.S./Mexican border is considered "one media market," hence the Mexican stations are also included.

State	#	State	#	State	#	State	#
Alabama	1	Kansas	4	Nevada	7	Virginia	1
Arkansas	6	Louisiana	3	New York	9	Washington	13
Arizona	25	Massachusetts	11	Ohio	2	Wisconsin	2
California	150	Maryland	5	Oklahoma	5		
Colorado	13	Minnesota	2	Oregon	6	Baha California, MX	53
Connecticut	8	Montana	1	Pennsylvania	6	Sonora, MX	58
Delaware	1	Missouri	1	Puerto Rico	98	Chihuahua, MX	76
Florida	45	Mississippi	1	Rhode Island	2	Nuevo León, MX	21
Georgia	15	N. Carolina	10	S. Carolina	1	Tamaulipas, MX	79
Idaho	6	Nebraska	2	Tennessee	5		
Illinois	18	New Jersey	2	Texas	150		
Indiana	2	New Mexico	26	Utah	3		

Source: Hispanic Media Directory, (www.hispanic-media.com)

NOVEL FORMATS

How can you capture the Hispanic listener on an ongoing basis? Hook their attention and loyalty? Many formats have tested successfully and new concepts are emerging. For example, last year the first interactive radio novela, *La Herencia* (*The Inheritance*) was launched by Radio Televisa in Mexico and Radio Unica in the United States. The one-hour program invited listeners to participate and enter a sweepstakes. The program in Mexico was a huge success, "attracting up to 400,000 participants to its sweepstakes and prizes during the 13 week run."[18] In the U.S., participants could call an 800 number and participate in talking about the script and vying for $100,000 in prize money.

Proven and tested formats are reaching new audiences. That is the case with a radio event in June 2002 in Chicago. A radio station owned by Entravision Communications broadcast *Parranda 2002* live from Skyline Stage at Chicago's Navy Pier. The Spanish-language station's first major concert promotion included the hottest entertainers in Latin music.[19] Who could have guessed only a few years back that a big Latin Parranda would one day be the party at the Pier?

Hispanic Radio network (HRN) is bringing a new approach with its community-oriented "cause marketing" radio programs. This format, growing in popularity, discusses a social topic relevant to the Hispanic community or presents an educational theme. Sometimes these are built into the sponsorship of a corporate ad campaign. This can be a highly successful tool for creating "Share of Heart" for your brand. Hispanic Radio Network is championing the concept under the guidance of Jeff Kline, its CEO, who said, "the goal is to create world peace. We created HRN to educate and empower U.S. Hispanics, and when we get advertising support, it gives us a better chance to promote health, education, and economic opportunities for them."[20] Halleluiah! This is what I call "Hispanic Share of Soul" marketing.

PRINT'S UNIQUE ROLE

Print targeting U.S. Hispanic readers is also gathering momentum after having witnessed major changes in the past decade. As was the case with TV and radio, Hispanic newspapers, magazines, and books have also experienced dramatic growth and maturation, and are still experiencing a steep growth curve.

The role of print in the integrated Hispanic-market strategy is unique because it is a "tangible and permanent medium." Broadcast media does a terrific job raising consumers' awareness and enticing them to try products or services. However, in these highly stressful times and in a cluttered advertising environment, it is hard to make the impact necessary for potential customers to retain your message.

Hence, tangible and long-shelf-life messages, printed in newspapers, magazines, direct mail pieces, and coupons act as mnemonics. They help consumers remember a message. Immigrants tend to need more mnemonic or visual memory aids than native consumers. A piece of paper with the core message—and visuals—helps both in the decision-making and in closing the sale. Moreover, print ads can also provide more in-depth information and the possibility of re-visiting the message as many times as needed. In addition, the "pass along" factor gives print the potential to reach larger audiences.

Print is also extending its marketing services to the Hispanic market. Presently, several Hispanic newspapers offer services such as door-to-door product sampling that add value to the marketing mix. Hence, print media play a unique and powerful role in Hispanic marketing today.

Newspapers

The leading U.S. Hispanic newspapers have not only increased their circulation in the past decade, but also have embraced the cyber age with creativity and ingenuity. They have expanded into new areas of real-time services and information, strategic partnerships, marketing alliances, and entertainment. Most large Hispanic urban markets now have a Spanish-language daily publication and an integrated website.

LANGUAGE

Print media can be used to target very specific Hispanic market acculturation segments, and their editorial tends to cover issues that are relevant to the different target groups. For example, a typical small Spanish-language publication will target the less acculturated, recently arrived Latino immigrants. Larger daily publications usually target the bilingual Spanish reader including acculturated and non-acculturated Latinos. English and bilingual publications target the more acculturated native and U.S.-born populations.

According to *Hispanic Media Directory*, U.S. Hispanic publications can be grouped by language roughly as follows: 40 percent bilingual, 30 percent Spanish, and 30 percent English.

As the list above shows, there are many newspapers and publications targeting Latinos in the U.S., beyond the scope of this brief summary. The Online Resources section of this book lists several organizations that either group or represent the majority of these publications. Among these, the

Preferred Language
for Hispanic Print

in percent
Based on responses from 19,106
readers of Hispanic print

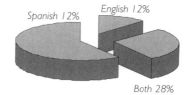

Spanish 12%   English 12%

Both 28%

Source: Western Publication Research,
Carlsbad, CA 760-434-7474

Hispanic Print Media At-A-Glance

Compiled by La Fuente de Información de la Prensa Hispana's Hispanic Media Directory, (www.hispanic-media.com) below is a summary table of the "publications universe" targeting the U.S. Hispanic market in late 2001, and numbers by states.

Summary of Hispanic Publications:

Classifieds	12	Magazines	25
Community newspapers	435	Newsletters in database	30
Daily Newspapers (English, Spanish, and both)	22	Publication chains	8
Journals in www.hispanic-media.com database	17	Hispanic Yellow Pages in database	4

Publications by state, including Mexican border states

Alabama	1	Kansas	3	New York	63	Washington	8
Arkansas	1	Louisiana	4	Ohio	5	Wisconsin	5
Arizona	13	Massachusetts	7	Oklahoma	5		
California	217	Maryland	1	Oregon	9	Baha California, MX	21
Colorado	6	Minnesota	5	Pennsylvania	11	Sonora, MX	8
Connecticut	7	Montana	3	Puerto Rico	46	Coahuila, MX	11
District of Col.	12	Missouri	10	Rhode island	1	Chihuahua, MX	14
Florida	141	N.Carolina	6	S. Carolina	3	Nuevo León, MX	16
Georgia	13	Nebraska	2	Tennessee	5	Tamaulipas, MX	21
Idaho	1	New Jersey	23	Texas	97		

There are 14 daily Spanish-language-only newspapers. Of those, four submit their circulation data for audit by the Audit Bureau of Circulations (ABC).

National Association of Hispanic Publications (www.nahp.org) is the largest trade organization that both markets and represents its many members. Periodically it publishes a *Hispanic Publications Media Kit and Resource Book* listing over 200 publications with over 10 million in combined circulation. Below the largest newspapers and national magazines are mentioned in a brief, introductory fashion to illustrate the breadth and scope of Hispanic print today.

HISPANIC DAILY NEWSPAPERS, KEY PLAYERS

New York

Two daily Spanish-language newspapers, *El Diario/La Prensa*, "the nation's oldest major Spanish-language newspaper," and *Hoy*, the newest entry in the market, cover the extended New York market area. Both *El Diario/La Prensa*, now owned by media conglomerate Entravision Communications, and *Hoy* show healthy audited circulation growth. The 1997–2000 *ABC Newspaper Circulation Trends* report shows *El Diario* increased its audited circulation by 1 percent between 2000 and 1999, and the new *Hoy* shows promising growth as well, recently surpassing *el Diario*'s circulation. Testing new approaches that might appeal to New York's Hispanic youth aged 18 to 34, *El Diario/La Prensa* and *Urban Magazine* joined forces to launch *Urban Sofrito*, a bilingual entertainment and cultural insert. This approach gives Generation Ñ and Latinas/Latinos in New York a reason to read the Spanish-language publication. The same approach worked well with Los Angeles-based *La Opinión* that implemented the strategy in the mid-1990s.

Los Angeles

Calling itself "the country's leading Spanish-language daily newspaper," *La Opinión* was founded in Los Angeles in 1926 by Don Ignacio Lozano Sr., an industry icon. It grew to become one of the top 100 daily newspapers in the U.S., and in the early 1990s *La Opinión* sold a large stake to *Times Mirror*. During the past few years *La Opinión* broke several marketing and sales barriers, increasing its daily circulation to about 100,000 in the 1990s. Its ABC audit shows circulation growth of 9 percent between 1999 and 2000, reaching 128,000 in its most recent audit. Including pass along readership, *La Opinión* easily reaches two to four times this number of readers per day. In early 2000, *La Opinión* opened a full-service internet site, www.laopinion.com, that today offers a wide variety of features and services, in addition to the newspaper's content, online.

Leading in the print media integration model, *La Opinión* established marketing partnerships with KMEX-Television, Radio Unica, and Grupo Gigante Supermarkets in the early 1990s to fully penetrate the Hispanic market. Additional partners of the newspaper and its website include, among others, www.holahoy.com, website of the *New York Daily News*, and www.elherald.com, website of the Miami daily newspaper, *El Nuevo Herald*, and Yahoo! En Español, a property of Yahoo! Inc., featuring Spanish-language web programming.

Miami

Founded in 1987, *El Nuevo Herald de Miami*, owned by *The Miami Herald*, targets the Hispanic community of South Florida. The ABC audit shows 8 percent growth for the newspaper between 1999 and 2000. A Knight-Ridder publication, *El Nuevo Herald* recently received the Jose Ortega y Gasset award, a prestigious honor in Spanish-language publishing given by Spain's *El Pais*, for "overall quality and reporting, noting the importance of providing information to a multi-faceted Spanish-reading audience." Other Hispanic publications owned by Knight-Ridder are *Nuevo Mundo*, serving the San Francisco and Silicon Valley area, and *la Estrella*, for the Dallas Fort Worth Hispanic market. All three newspapers have their websites, www.elherald.com, www.nuevo mundo.com and www.laestrelladigital.com.

Chicago

In Chicago, *¡Exito!* newspaper was founded in 1993 as "the most valuable source of relevant information for Spanish speaking Latinos in Chicagoland." With the growing presence of Latinos in Illinois, *¡Exito!* has succeeded in penetrating the diverse Hispanic readership market.

Many other newspapers are maturing across the Hispanic market. To learn more about these publications and their potential for you as advertising and promotions vehicles, ask your Hispanic media planner to consider a comprehensive plan that includes not only the big players, but also many grassroots periodicals that reach the Hispanic family. As mentioned earlier, their trade organization, the National Association of Hispanic Publications publishes a comprehensive directory that includes "big and small" (www.nahp.org).

HOW DO WE READ?

The Media Audit conducted a study among 10,000 Hispanics and addressed a variety of issues, among them, newspaper readership patterns. For example, the audit found that Hispanics don't read the front-page section of newspapers as regularly as the non-Hispanic population, 35.8 percent versus 51.4 percent. However, they read the sports section almost as much as non-Hispanics, 24.8 percent versus 28.7 percent. Curiously, the study concluded, Latinos are more inclined to read the classified ad section, 12 percent compared to 10 percent.[21]

THE HISPANIC MAGAZINE BOOM

In 1994, bilingual *Latina Magazine* started its fundraising to "create a vehicle that would talk to the soul of the U.S. Latina." It was followed by *People en Español* in 1995. Other smaller titles, like *Latina Style!*, that also covers the political scene and civic world of Latinas, followed during the next decade. Presently, however, *People en Español* continues to lead in circulation and readership.

I have strong emotional ties with both *Latina Magazine* and *People en Español* as I had the pleasure to collaborate in their launches. The battle was not an easy one because many advertisers were under the false belief that "Hispanics don't read." History has proven that this was a serious misperception and these new magazines opened one of the most prolific new media venues in Hispanic marketing.

Before the 1990s, the largest Hispanic magazines created in the United States tended to be in English targeting the business community, e.g., pioneer *Hispanic Business Magazine* and later *Hispanic Magazine*. Both continue to cover the growth and success of the Hispanic market, reaching corporations and Hispanic professionals alike. *Hispanic Business Magazine* (HBM) was founded and is still directed by Jesus Chavarria, whom I consider one of our Hispanic marketing pioneers and an unsung hero. Based in Santa Barbara, California, HBM tracks the Hispanic market and business scene in detail. Its December issue, with advertising expenditures, and others tracking the growth of the Hispanic business sector are eagerly awaited, used, and quoted in the Hispanic market. *Hispanic Business Magazine* pioneered many Hispanic trade activities, such as trade-specific Hispanic marketing conferences, like the Se Habla Conferences, and the corporate Round Tables in Washington, D.C. Today the magazine offers a suite of Hispanic services both online and offline.

Similarly, *Hispanic Magazine* covers the political scene in detail, as well as business and the corporate world. Targeting acculturated Latinos in the business community, *Hispanic Magazine* also offers up-to-the minute news coverage through www.Hispaniconline.com.

Ahead of its time was *Vista Magazine*, the Sunday newspaper insert carried by many general market newspapers nationwide. *Vista Magazine*, founded by Arturo Villar (now publisher of *Hispanic Market Weekly*) 17 years ago, was the first mass-market, crossover Hispanic magazine, in English. Owned today by Hispanic Publishing group, that also owns *Hispanic Magazine* and Hispanic Online, *Vista* recently launched a bilingual boxing and baseball insert targeting Hispanic males to increase appeal and circulation. The first issue of *Vista* with the *Boxing* insert had a circulation of one million in April 2002.

TRACKING ADVERTISING PAGES

The *Hispanic Magazine Monitor*, a service that tracks advertising sales in the Hispanic press launched in September 2001. The June 2002 *Monitor* listed 28 magazine titles in its comprehensive report, compared with only 17 titles in the January issue, showing the *Monitor* will most probably succeed in capturing the complete mass circulation market in the near future.

The vast majority of the new magazines that emerged after 1990 are mass circulation magazines. For example, *Cristina La Revista*, predating *O*, Oprah Winfrey's magazine concept, since 1991 provides an extension to Cristina's famous television show. Cristina Saralegui is one of the most popular and beloved media personalities in the U.S. Hispanic market. Several of the new titles are the "en Español" version of existing well-established American magazines, such as *National Geographic en Español*, *Men's Fitness en Español*, *Marie Claire en Español*, and *Teen en Español*. Most magazines "en Español" are close direct translations of the Anglo version or titles produced for a Latin American reader. An exception is *Selecciones* (*Reader's Digest*) that has been available both in English and Spanish in the U.S. and Latin America since I can remember. It now caters to the U.S. Hispanic with a re-directed focus to our market, rather than the Latin American market.

FIGURE 21.6

Ad Page Counts and Estimated Dollars for April, 2002

Title (frequency)	Issue Date	Ad Pages 2002	Ad Pages 2001	% Change prev yr	Est. Dollars[1] 2002	Est. Dollars[1] 2001	% Change prev yr
BuenHogar[2] (m)	April	4.00	9.66	-58.59%	$22,825	$57,472	-60.29%
Cosmopolitan en Español[2] (m)	April	19.65	na*	na*	$174,724	na*	na*
Cristina la Revista[2] (m)	April	27.81	na*	na*	$289,060	na*	na*
Estylo (bi-monthly)	April/May	31.66	na*	na*	$198,200	na*	na*
Glamour en Españo[l2] (m)	April	32.66	na*	na*	$114,310	na*	na*
Harper's Bazaar en Español[2] (m)	April	5.00	na*	na*	$13,250	na*	na*
Hispanic Business (m)	April	33.83	47.32	-28.51%	$584,705	$817,326	-28.46%
Hispanic Magazine (m)	April	30.33	61.50	-50.68%	$458,535	$850,880	-46.11%
Latina (m)	April	63.65	83.15	-23.45%	$928,530	$1,172,747	-20.82%
Loft[2] (m)	March/April	24.00	na*	na**	$47,940	na*	na**
Marie Claire en Español[2] (m)	April	4.00	na*	na*	$10,750	na*	na*
Maxim en Español[2] (bi-monthly)	April/May	14.66	na*	na**	$91,200	na*	na**
Men's Fitness en Español[2] (m)	April	9.00	na*	na*	$34,020	na*	na*
Mira! (bi-weekly)	April 9	13.66	na*	na*	$80,025	na*	na*
Mira! (bi-weekly)	April 23	11.66	na*	na*	$68,640	na*	na*
National Geographic en Español[2] (m)	April	3.00	na*	na*	$11,200	na*	na*
People en Español (m)	April	55.32	57.50	-3.79%	$1,952,467	$1,564,700	24.78%
Selecciones[2] (m)	April	27.00	20.00	35.00%	$541,150	$363,800	48.75%
Ser Padres (bi-monthly)	April/May	19.00	na*	na*	$725,000	na*	na*
Teen en Español[2] (m)	April	19.00	na*	na*	$47,880	na*	na*
TV y Novelas[2] (weekly)	April 6	14.16	na*	na*	$169,195	na*	na*
TV y Novelas[2] (weekly)	April 13	14.50	na*	na*	$169,842	na*	na*
TV y Novelas[2] (weekly)	April 20	14.16	na*	na*	$170,993	na*	na*
TV y Novelas[2] (weekly)	April 27	12.33	na*	na*	$150,363	na*	na*
Vanidades[2] (bi-wkly)	April 2	48.00	na*	na*	$544,295	na*	na*
Vanidades[2] (bi-wkly)	April 16	13.82	na*	na*	$164,520	na*	na*
Vanidades[2] (bi-wkly)	April 30	25.65	na*	na*	$294,595	na*	na*
Vista (m)	April	12.50	na*	na*	$472,750	na*	na*
Totals		604.01	na	na	$8,530,964	na	na

1. Estimated dollars based on rate cards from magazine publishers and/or S.R.D.S.;
2. U.S. edition. Dollars estimated at U.S. Hispanic gross rates.
* Monitoring for these titles began in Jan, 2002. **Title not published this period.

Source: ©2002. Media Economics Group, All Rights Reserved. Used by permission. www.HispMagMonitor.com

In comparison, *Latina magazine* was created *in-culture* and completely from scratch. Talking to the soul of the Latina immigrant *caught between two cultures,* Latina has a loyal readership base that, as a bilingual magazine, talks to the "complete *familia.*" The younger generation in the family can read it in English, and the older generation in Spanish. Now also linked to a website and marketing arm, *Latina* continues to talk to the Latina and her extended family. *People en Español* has captured the lion's share in the magazine trade, not only in circulation, but also in advertising pages. *People en Español*, created to bring American popular culture to the non-English reader, both men and women, and Hispanic popular culture to the Hispanic community at large, has developed a large following of acculturated and non-acculturated Hispanic readers, even when some of the readers' Spanish is a bit "rusty." *People en Español* and *Latina magazine* each created a genre with its own unique editorial content.

BEING MEASURED: WHO IS READING?

Several Hispanic magazines have their audiences tracked on an ongoing basis by Simmons Hispanic. The need to know how many readers magazines have—from an unbiased third party—is as important as the circulation. Most magazines conduct marketing research studies with their target readers to provide a useful "live picture" of the reader. However, the best audience measurement source is always a third party with standardized methodology, independence, and the ability to compare with other magazines in the trade, or with the general market. If the data are "self-reported" there is always the risk of misrepresentation. However, nobody truly understands the mindset of the reader better than the magazine editors and their teams. Occasionally they share this research with advertisers. *People en Español*, for example, tracks its readers on an annual basis and publishes selected results in its HOT study (Hispanic Opinion Tracker) that gives marketers a clear picture of the readers. This study is available to the trade, and by request. Through the courtesy of Lisa Quiroz at *People en Español* I have quoted data from these studies in other sections of this book. See the index.

Some Hispanic magazines are also audited for circulation, depending on whether they are clients of Audit Bureau of Circulation (ABC) or Business Publications Audit (BPA). These audits simply count circulation, not the quality of readership, while Simmons looks at the readership and not the circulation numbers.

New Magazines

Almost every month a new magazine for Hispanics debuts. A few examples:

- *Latino Impact*, targeting Generation Ñ and the young Latinos and Latinas, covers music, television, and film. Presently it comes out four times a year in tabloid size, published by Emanon Entertainment, Inc. in New York City.

- Another player targeting the male audience, aged 25 to 45 is *Loft*, U.S. edition, by Zoom Media Group. Initially a bimonthly magazine targeting the "affluent cosmopolitan Hispanic man" *Loft* is distributed in the U.S. and Latin America. Featuring prominent personalities from the international scene, plus lifestyle, travel, entertainment, and sex, of course. The magazine will use popular people as columnists, including Diego Armando Maradona, the famous Argentinean soccer player.

- Focusing on the accomplishments and lives of successful Latinos, *Latino Leaders*, "the magazine of the successful Hispanic American" covers topics ranging from business and the arts to healthcare and politics. Targeting the "mature" segment of the market, *Latino Leaders* has been able to talk successfully to both the soul and heart of the Hispanic Boomers. Published six times a year by Ferraez Publications of America, this magazine fills a need as well as an information gap.

Multi-media Magazines

Batanga, "America's largest Latin Internet Radio Network" offers under one roof not only a quarterly magazine reaching, they claim, 10,000, but also internet radio, e-mail marketing campaigns, and street teams to reach 12-to-34-year-olds. This integrated media package can be highly effective if the strategy and messages are launched in synergy and *in-culture*. It seems to be working well. For example, Americatel, a telecommunications company, used Batanga to promote its free ISP service 123.com. Americatel concluded that the internet-radio ads were "among the most effective ways to deliver traffic to its web site." It also used Batanga's e-mail database to promote its advertising messages and finally, it used the street team on a Cinco de Mayo event to deliver a CD-ROM with an ISP offer and to collect data in five markets.

Another example was the Interscope campaign promotion to drive traffic to an Enrique Iglesias autograph-signing event. Batanga promoted the event on its internet radio, sent e-mail messages to listeners in the Los Angeles and Houston areas, and used its street teams in both places to drive traffic to stores where the events were being held. Interscope sold 4,000 copies of the CD in one store alone. A relatively new media player and concept, Batanga has the potential to combine state-of-the-art marketing strategy with state-of-the-art technology to reach the Hispanic market today.

Urban Latino Magazine also combines different media to reach young Hip Latinos with a "magazine lifestyle show," in English, combining a television series and *Urban Latino Magazine*. The 110,000-circulation magazine has editorial control of the TV show. To appeal to the young hip Latino, the magazine leverages popular artists, such as J-Lo (Jennifer Lopez) who shared her fashion line during her appearance. The co-production launched in New York in April 2002. Given the trend in Hispanic industry, it would not surprise me that many more combined and fully integrated media strategies emerge in the next couple of years.

OTHER MEDIA

The past decade has seen the creation and growth of all kinds of marketing and communications media. With the maturation of Hispanic marketing and larger budgets, more corporations are incorporating these as a component in their *in-culture* integrated marketing strategy.

To provide you with a flavor of these activities, I include a brief description of some of the most useful of these growing and exciting "other" media. The Online Resources Guide in the Appendix should point you to the sources to locate these companies, along with Hispanic marketing and advertising agencies, or consultants.

• *Telemarketing* to the Hispanic market has grown into an effective, sophisticated and complex industry. In-bound and out-bound services in both English and Spanish are available. These services can track to the minute the effectiveness of your ad, and also can be used to close the sale or application for your product or service. Because most Hispanic households are "traditional" and appreciate a kind caller, the out-bound response tends to be high. The Hispanic in-bound caller market has matured to the point that campaigns I have been involved with have had to use multiple vendors to handle the in-coming volume of calls from advertising campaigns. This has been especially true from Spanish-language television commercials where a toll-free number is made available, in large print on the screen, and repeated a couple of times, or included in a jingle. Providing a toll-free number helps close the sale, and places the buyer in a proactive role, rather than reactive. What does not work so well, in my experience, is the use of words rather than numbers for the telephone number. Like most consumers these days, Latinos are busy, and if you want us to connect with you and call you, you must make it very, very easy! *Gracias!*

- *Direct Marketing:* It used to be that Hispanic households received almost no direct mail solicitations or catalogs. That has changed, but the amount of direct mail is still not even close to parity with the non-Hispanic market. *Target Marketing*, a trade magazine that covers the direct mail industry states, "Hispanic households presently receive an average of 20 direct mail pieces a year, compared with 300 or so received by the general U.S. population." They also report that a direct mail campaign with Hispanics can get anywhere from 25 percent to 100 percent greater response from the Hispanic market than from the population at large. You may be thinking that Hispanic households are fortunate receiving fewer unsolicited mail pieces. However, this feeling generally does not apply to the Hispanic market, which I learned first hand in many research studies and in ethnographic observations. The truth is many Hispanic householders enjoy watching commercials, listening to radio ads, and receiving direct mail letters. For many, particularly the foreign-born and less acculturated, Spanish-dominant consumers, these are well received—"a blessing." A well executed, emotionally and culturally attuned, Spanish-language or bilingual mailer communicates to this segment that your company and your brand care about the Hispanic community. To increase response, you should include a discount coupon, especially if you are advertising your brand to consumers that may have never heard about it. Beyond that, a mnemonic component, as mentioned above, can be extremely useful to those of us who migrated as adults and have to learn everything from scratch. The well-designed direct mail piece will not only "tell me" but, more importantly, "show me" the benefit of your product or service, "invite me" to try it, and "give me" a discount to help break the ice.

- *Out-of-Home Advertising:* Spanish, bilingual, "cross-over," *in-culture*, English, or no language at all, out-of-home advertising can be found in many places with high-to-medium concentrations of Hispanic population. Be it large billboards, on buildings, stadiums, buses, or at bus stops, the beauty of out-of-home is that it has the capability of creating a "physical reality" in the mind of the consumer. In addition, out-of-home is available everywhere your target consumer travels. For example, several years ago a client of mine, a bank that in the past had worked mainly via direct mail, was having trouble getting Hispanic consumers to reply to a credit card offer in a new market. We learned in the focus groups I conducted that many targeted Latinos did not feel comfortable applying for a credit card offered by the well-known bank, "because the bank did not have local offices." The respondents felt a need to see and "touch" the place where their money was going, to help dispel the natural distrust so common in our culture when it comes to large and impersonal institutions, banks included. This bank was planning to become a nationwide bank, as it did a few years later; however, at the time, they did not have offices in Hispanic markets in the West and South. The client chose to use large, well-placed billboards to create a local presence. By showing large bank buildings in the outdoor signs, with clearly visible signs of the bank, the client was able to establish a presence in the target market. These well-done, *in-culture* out-of-home advertising signs helped change the low response rate and successfully change behavior.

  Another clear cut example is the use of large visual boards in political campaigns, where a potential voter can perceive the "look" of the candidate from afar. Again, the *in-culture* marketer will know that the candidate must be looking into your eyes, conveying trust, but also friendliness. A "smile," well executed, can mean many thousands of new votes. The $5.5 billion out-of-home industry however, has room to grow when it comes to the Hispanic market and some are already moving in this direction. For example, Clear Channel Outdoor went Hispanic creating a new Hispanic marketing division in 2001.

- *Product Sampling:* Presently, you can home deliver product samples and track effectiveness in Hispanic-specific zip codes with companies such as Latin-Pak, a Hispanic market-specific-sampling company. Another option is to deliver in partnership with newspapers that offer Hispanic-market-specific socio-demographic profiles from their subscriber bases. They can usually drop samples to their entire subscriber base or to a sub-segment that includes only those households with the desired profile. In-store sampling is popular in Hispanic marketing and for a good reason. It delivers sales. We love testing and trying samples of new products at the supermarket or any store. Our husbands, our children, and *la Abuelita* will all test the product. If we like it, (which we should, since you did all your marketing research and technical corrections before deciding to approach the Hispanic market), we will buy it.

- **Event Marketing:** Several companies specifically targeting Latino market events have emerged in the past decade. Events include such festivities as Calle Ocho in Miami, Cinco de Mayo in Los Angeles, Fiesta de Mayo in Chicago, or the Puerto Rican Day Parade in New York. These companies can also leverage non-Latino events for your product or service. An advertising executive at The Cartel Creativo ad agency told me, "We Latinos have a party gene." Every occasion is a good occasion to party. In addition to having fun, dancing, and singing, if we can receive gifts, see our favorite stars, enjoy a free lunch, test new products, learn about health or other things, all *en familia*, these events are close to Hispanic heaven. It is no surprise that mega-events continue to grow, and smaller, customized events are taking place everywhere. For example *Tarde de Oro*, an event created and sponsored by AARP, drew a massive crowd of the Latino Senior segment, "Los Grandes" in Puerto Rico, and also to its stand at the Cinco de Mayo event in Los Angeles. Procter and Gamble launched its "Explosion Musical" concert series in 2001 in Los Angeles and toured to four other Hispanic markets. On a serious note, the annual conference of National Council of La Raza tackles civic and political issues for Latinos.

- **College Fairs:** As the demand for Latino youth marketing becomes higher, college fairs to connect with Generation Ñ are emerging. These annual events bring together potential college candidates with the schools. With the support of colleges that want to attract Latinos—and other multicultural students—college fairs get in touch with and distribute samples and direct mail pieces to young Latinos and Latinas. The organizers also have some of the most complete and up-to-date Hispanic youth databases and in many cases, not only the basic demographics but also other information of interest to the advertisers. Such is the case of National Hispanic College Fairs, Inc., a company that is adding fairs in new Hispanic markets every month.

ADVERTISING TO U.S. LATINOS: STILL UNDER UTILIZED

The Hispanic advertising industry has grown at a healthy rate since the late 1990s, but analysts suggest there is still room for healthy growth during the next decade.

FIGURE 21.7

Hispanic Advertising Industry Growth

Year	Billings	Percent Change
1997	$1.4 billion	—
1998	1.7 billion	+22%
1999	1. 9 billion	+11
2000	2.4 billion	+27

Source: Hispanic Business Magazine, quoted in ahaa's on-line,Hispanic Media & Marketing Factoids, May 2002

A 2002 study released by the Association of Hispanic Advertising Agencies (ahaa) reveals that the majority of America's top advertisers are significantly under-investing in their efforts to reach Hispanic consumers. At a time when corporations are looking for new markets to supplement slow growth in mature industries, many are missing a major opportunity when it comes to reaching Hispanic consumers. The study *Missed Opportunities: Vast Corporate under investing in the U.S. Hispanic Market,*[22] indicates that in the past three years nearly two-thirds (64 percent) of top companies *targeting Hispanic consumers* invested on average less than 3.2 percent of their overall advertising budgets on reaching this market. Corporations in the study that received the top scores are approaching or exceeding the recommended target of eight percent of their overall advertising budget.

The study found:

- Hispanics represent about 13.6 percent of the U.S. population. However, in the past three years, in aggregate, America's leading advertisers (including those who do not target Hispanics specifically) have allocated an average of only 2.4 percent of their measured media advertising resources to target Hispanics.

- Relative to their overall advertising resources, on average, food and beverage products, food services, personal care, general merchandise, insurance, and telecommunications companies have invested the most in marketing to Hispanics, while computer makers, software, travel, entertainment, pharmaceuticals, the U.S. government, auto makers, securities, and specialty retailers have invested the least.

- With heightened awareness of the value of the U.S. Hispanic market, since 1999 leading advertisers have almost doubled their allocations of advertising resources to Hispanics from 1.8 percent of total advertising dollars in 1999 to 3.2 percent in 2001.

- By 2001, the number of leading advertisers still grossly under investing relative to the threshold needed to be effective in reaching the Hispanic market had dropped to 42 percent.

The study conducted by Santiago & Valdés Solutions confirmed a longtime belief among Hispanic marketers that corporations that are serious about turning a profit when marketing to Hispanics need to invest more in advertising.

THE TOP 60 ADVERTISERS

As mentioned earlier, every year *Hispanic Business Magazine* (HBM) publishes in its December issue the advertising and media investments in the Hispanic market. Below are highlights from the December 2001 issue. I strongly recommend you visit their website, www.HispanicBusiness.com, to learn about the magazine's many services and data sources.

FIGURE 21.9

Hispanic Market Advertising Expenditures, 2001

gross expenditures ($ millions)

Medium	
Network/National TV	$845.0
Local TV	$461.3
National Radio	$159.0
Local Radio	$410.8
National Newspapers	$ 86.1
Local Newspapers	$129.2
Magazines	$ 60.0
Out-of-Home	$ 69.1
Total	$2,220.45

Source: *Hispanic Business* Magazine, December 2001. Used by permission.

Even in a challenging year like 2001, Hispanic advertising expenditures grew. The HBM article calls it an "anemic 4 percent" compared with 13 percent in 2000, 11 percent in 1999 and an "impressive 21 percent in 1998."[23] My analysis is more positive. The non-Hispanic advertising industry experienced a more severe contraction following the dot.bomb economic crises and September 11, 2001. Comparatively speaking, the Hispanic market fared very well. As can be observed in Figure 21.9, several new players entered the market and few left.

FIGURE 21.9
_____

Hispanic Business Magazines

Top 60 Advertisers in the Hispanic Market, 2001

Rank	Company	Gross Media Expenditures ($ millions)	
		2001	2000
1	Procter & Gamble	$55.0	$46.2
2	Ford Motor Co.	51.0	14.0
3	AT&T	42.0	35.0
4	MCI Worldcom	41.3	37.5
5	Sears, Roebuck & Co.	38.0	35.0
6	Americatel	30.0	25.0
7	Miller Brewing Co.	30.0	25.0
8	General Motors	29.5	16.2
9	McDonald's Corp.	27.0	27.0
10	Philip Morris	25.0	25.0
11	Colgate-Palmolive	25.0	16.2
12	Johnson & Johnson	23.0	17.0
13	Toyota Motor Corp.	22.0	22.0
14	Anheuser-Busch Co. Inc.	22.0	22.0
15	U.S. Army	20.0	9.2
16	Burger King Corp.	20.0	12.7
17	Kraft Foods	18.7	17.1
18	Coca-Cola	18.7	*
19	J.C. Penney Co. Inc.	16.0	9.1
20	Home Depot	16.0	15.7
21	PepsiCo	16.0	10.1
22	Hyundai Motors	14.2	5.5
23	Western Union	12.6	12.0
24	Tricon Global Restaurants Inc.	11.4	14.6
25	Kmart Corp.	11.4	9.9

Rank	Company	Gross Media Expenditures ($ millions) 2001	2000
26	Lexicon Marketing Corp.	10.3	*
27	Nestlé	10.0	7.5
28	The Pillsbury Company	10.0	3.0
29	Gruma Corp. (Mission Foods)	10.0	10.0
30	Coors Brewing Co.	10.0	10.0
31	DaimlerChrysler	9.9	*
32	Wal-Mart Stores Inc.	9.8	5.0
33	American Home Products Corp.	9.5	9.9
34	Honda Motor Corp.	9.0	9.7
35	Goya Foods	9.0	8.0
36	Walt Disney	8.5	7.0
37	General Electric	8.3	*
38	Quaker Oats Co.	8.0	12.0
39	Kellogg Co.	8.0	6.5
40	Domino's Pizza LLC	7.5	*
41	Bank of America	7.0	*
42	General Mills	6.4	*
43	State Farm Insurance	6.3	*
44	Washington Mutual	6.0	*
45	Toys "R" Us	6.0	6.0
46	Greyhound Lines Inc.	5.9	5.6
47	Sprint Corp.	5.9	5.2
48	Clorox Co.	5.5	4.0
49	Mars Inc.	5.5	*
50	Labatt U.S.A. (Tecate Beer)	5.1	*
51	Nabisco	5.0	5.0
52	Allstate Corp.	5.0	11.3
53	Avon	5.0	5.0
54	American Airlines	4.5	4.5
55	Unilever Bestfoods	4.3	3.6
56	Target Corp.	4.1	*
57	Florida State Lottery	3.6	2.4
58	California Lottery	3.2	4.1
59	Pennzoil/Quaker State	3.0	*
60	United Distillers & Vendors (Cuervo)	1.5	*
Total		$862.4	$871.9

* Did not appear in 2000 list. All numbers are rounded.

Source: Hispanic Business Magazine, December 2001, p. 40 Used by permission.

TWO-THIRDS OF MAJOR ADVERTISERS ARE MISSING OPPORTUNITIES

The low scores in the study mentioned earlier demonstrate that companies are not placing a proper value on the opportunities the Hispanic market offers. Shareholders should be concerned with corporate America's inertia in failing to seek out Hispanic consumers. The companies with the best understanding of the Hispanic market's contribution to profitable revenue growth will be in the best position to thrive over the long-term.

Using SRC 2002 data tracking Hispanic adults' language-preference and media consumption, Santiago & Valdés Solutions—now the Santiago Solutions Group—determined that for optimum effectiveness in reaching the Hispanic market, advertisers should devote at least 8 percent of their advertising dollars to Hispanic advertising and marketing. Results in this report were obtained by comparing the percentage of measured media spending on Hispanic Spanish and bilingual advertising and comparing this to the 8 percent optimum-spending ratio.

IN CONCLUSION

The evidence is everywhere. Hispanic media are finally making a true debut on the U.S. marketing and media scene. In the next decade we anticipate that many more mergers and acquisitions will take place. Expect to see new players both from within the United States as well as from abroad. Spain and Mexico have much to contribute, and growing wealth among American Latinos is surely going to play a role in future media development and ownership.

Contentwise, there is no doubt that as the Hispanic markets' new youth and Latino and Latina segments mature, they will demand more representative, Hispanic-friendly programming in mainstream media. The present players will have to adjust to the demands of these age groups if they don't want to lose their trade.

As we become a more diverse nation, expect to see in the near future simultaneous programming in mainstream media and Spanish language media; co-productions of cultural and political programs that can be broadcast simultaneously in both English and Spanish.

Advertising dollars will surely grow as measurements and tracking systems continue to mature. The decision will be based less on "pleasing cultural groups" that demand a fair share, and more on the healthy return on investment that the Hispanic market brings to those who have learned to market *in-culture*.

Notes

1. *Hispanic Market Weekly*, January 14, 2002.
2. The Telemundo/NBC merger raised concerns from the National Hispanic Media Coalition that serves as an umbrella for many Latino media and civil rights organizations. The coalition asked the FCC to deny permission for the merger and filed a notice of appeal of the FCC's decision with the U.S. Court of Appeals on several concerns, "since it did not know how NBC planned to serve its Latino audience." However, the FCC did not rule against the merger, now confirmed.
3. Quoted in *Los Angeles Times*, Home Edition, C-1, January 14, 2002
4. *Hollywood Reporter*, January 14, 2002.
5. *Hispanic Market Weekly*, January 7, 2002.
6. *Hispanic Market Weekly*, May 20, 2002.
7. *Hispanic Market Weekly*, February 4, 2002.
8. *Hispanic Market Weekly, January 27, 2002.*
9. *Hispanic Market Weekly*, May 20, 2002.
10. HispanicAd.com, June 12,2002.
11. *Hispanic Market Weekly*, October 8, 2001.
12. Latino Leaders, April-May 2000
13. Valdés, M. I., HMC Hispanic Database studies, 1982–1984, unpublished papers.
14. *Hispanic Market Weekly*, April 29, 2002.
15. "Growth of Spanish Language Television Viewership," paper presented by Univision, IQPC conference, 2001.
16. "Impact of Census 2000 Data on Radio Industry, "December 2001. Interep Research, quoted by HispanicAd.com, December 9, 2001.
17. *Hispanic Market Weekly*, January 28, 2002.
18. *Hispanic Market Weekly*, September 18, 2001.
19. HispanicAd.com, May 22, 2002.
20. *Hispanic Market Weekly*, April 15, 2002.
21. Quoted in Hispanic Market Radio Check, September/October 2001. Katz Hispanic Media publication closed in early 2002.
22. Conducted by Carlos Santiago, Santiago&Valdés Solutions, (now Santiago Solutions Group) courtesy of ahaa.
23. "Spending Spree," *Hispanic Business Magazine*, December 2001.

SECTION 5

AN
INTEGRATED
STRATEGY
FOR HISPANIC
MARKETS

Chapter 22

The Integrated *In-Culture* Marketing Strategy

You are now ready to create an *in-culture* integrated marketing plan to successfully target Latino consumers in the 21st century.

First, as you probably now know by heart, "If you want your Hispanic plan to see profits, with a healthy return on investment (ROI,) you need to approach the Hispanic marketing program with the same commitment, business principles, and investment parameters as you would if this were a general market (GM) initiative." In other words, if you would not launch a brand new GM product or service without a well-developed integrated marketing plan, why should you do it for this 40-million-person market? You need to determine which is your optimal Hispanic market segment at the onset of your marketing strategy. You can find in Chapters 10-14 of this book several simple, low cost market segmentation tools for this purpose.

Knowing which is your best Hispanic consumer segment will ensure that your marketing strategy focuses with surgical precision on the best business opportunity for your company. To do so, you *must* have solid market information, target-consumer data and insights, and you must test your concept or product before moving ahead with a multi-million-dollar initiative. You would be surprised how often I find Hispanic-marketing programs that were launched with none of this information—unplanned, unsupported, and with no long-term budgetary commitment. Moreover, if the program fails, the typical conclusion is "the Hispanic market does not

I am indebted to my colleague and former partner, Carlos Santiago, for his many contributions to this chapter. The integrated Hispanic strategy and the AARP case study are based on earlier work of our former company, Santiago & Valdés.

work!" We call this "the vaccine approach, " a great way to kill your corporate Hispanic-marketing opportunity.[1]

As you should conclude after reading this book, success in marketing to Hispanic consumers usually requires a fresh new approach, different from the general market approach. Lack of *in-culture* sensitivity and awareness can result in a flawed marketing plan.

This approach has many similarities to marketing to the general population. Having said that, I must bring to your attention that Hispanics are among the cultures that tend to be on the lower end of the "adoption scales." This means that, as a population, we tend to take longer to adapt and begin using new products or services. Of course, this varies from product to product and from urban to less-urban environments. Hence, depending on your particular product or service category, you also need to factor this *"cultural variable"* into your timeline and include the extra time needed to see the full results of your plan, before you pull the plug.

Some companies believe they can simply appear on the Hispanic radar screen with a new product or service and be accepted by the Hispanic consumer from day one. They believe it is enough to advertise on Spanish-language media, translate a general market direct mail campaign or brochure into Spanish, or simply offer a promotion that worked well with the non-Hispanic market. However, rarely are such one-dimensional efforts successful with this market.

What is needed is a fully integrated *in-culture* strategy that:

- Aligns the internal infrastructure and functional areas, and

- Aligns external marketing strategies, at the same time. (Figure 22.1)

- Is executed in a way that the initiative creates, communicates, and delivers long-lasting high-value relationships, *in-culture*.

FIGURE 22.1

External Integrated Stratgey

360° In-Culture Marketing Wheel of Fortune™

Copyright © 2002 Santiago Valdés Solutions

THE INTEGRATED STRATEGY

External Elements of an Integrated Strategy

To compete effectively in an increasingly crowded marketplace, corporations designing integrated Hispanic strategies need to address external elements such as the following:

- What sort of competitive edge should you strive for?

- Which customer needs, acculturation level, and Hispanic sub-segments should you serve? Not all Hispanic customers have the same lifetime value or potential.

- How should you position the brand against rival brands in the market-place?

- What actions should you take in light of industry trends, language and acculturation patterns and behavior, community and political changes, and distinct levels of economic power?

The integrated model below (Figure 22.2) will help you explore how you can use various "external" strategies in a product introduction that is designed to be sustained over a long period.

FIGURE 22.2

Integrated Strategy Alignment

Internal Strategy (Back-End/Infrastructure) and
External Strategy (Customer Facing)

© Santiago & Valdés Solutions (SVS)

Some Application Examples

There are many approaches to building a relationship with Hispanic consumers.

Food Industry: For example, how would this model help a food company positioning a new product targeted to the Hispanic market?

In the food category, the tried-and-tested strategy for competing relies on product differentiation and market segmentation. Suppose a new line of replacement meals for Hispanic tastes (*Sabor Hispano*) is introduced. The targeted market segment might be bilingual, professional, acculturated Hispanics. The product would have to be differentiated by a variety of strategies including substantial brand advertising via print and television, exciting promotions and prizes, more shelf space, free samples, demonstration booths at events and stores, and an end-aisle display targeted to the segment in large supermarkets and warehouse clubs. Compare this integrated strategy with the 360° *In-Culture* Wheel of Fortune approach and you can see how many elements need to work together to help establish the brand.

Branding is the platform on which to build other strategies to acquire new customers and retain old ones. Awareness of brands, especially unaided, can vary widely within the Hispanic market and it can differ from awareness in the non-Hispanic market. In order to take your brand "seriously," the Hispanic segments (mom, dad, or the children) need to see the brand at the dinner table. You must be sure they know how to talk about the brand to their family and friends. Remember that networking is an integral part of our culture, and if we like something, we recommend it with enthusiasm. This recommendation by friends and family is the *"Vecina* Standard"—like a gold standard, that can add major marketing value to your brand. In short, Hispanic consumers are more likely to buy your brand if they consider it "a friend," not a stranger.

In a nutshell, the well-executed 360° *in-culture* Wheel of Fortune helps build an image of a friend with whom the Hispanic customer would like to do business. All of this takes time and the payoff is rarely immediate.

Consumer electronics retail chain: Assume an electronics retailer is new and unfamiliar to Hispanics. The retailer should be armed with:

- An initial phase of break-through branding activities through broadcast advertising and public relations.

- Familiarization and building trust through events and community involvement.

- Optimized direct-response television and targeted direct mail.

- Location of retail outlets on the "right corners" properly designed and merchandised, with a well-trained bilingual staff.

- *In-language* fulfillment, superior service, and payment options.

- Database systems for tracking and establishing two-way communications that create an intimate personal relationship, and

- Subsequent mailers to up-sell and cross-sell by meeting customers' specific unmet needs in a culturally relevant manner.

DO NOT TRY THE STAND-ALONE APPROACH

A stand-alone Hispanic-marketing strategy is simply too short-lived in today's crowded marketplace to capture the attention and change the habits of prospects. Hispanic consumers have become increasingly wiser, less trusting, more guarded, and more aware of value choices. The marketplace and competitors require Hispanic marketers to up the ante by becoming more sophisticated, employing emerging technologies and new methodologies, and combining these with the traditional "tried and true."

Marketers can reach consumers through dozens of marketing strategies and tactics. Not all industries use all strategies all the time, but most Hispanic marketing industry leaders use most of them most of the time. Each effort pulls in the same direction and creates synergies that connect brand advertising to direct response, websites, public relations, in-store displays, events, and intelligently targeted feet-on-the-street programs.

As shown in Figures 22.1 and 22.2, above, marketing strategy and management requires a 360-degree process. The effort must aim at the right target and be backed by a comprehensive plan of attack. Unfortunately, many firms trivialize Hispanic marketing to a one-dimensional strategy equivalent to Spanish media segmentation rather than aiming for specific age cohorts, consumer behavior and needs segments among Hispanics. By contrast, Hispanic market experts start by targeting their integrated strategy directly at the core user segment. Equally importantly, they make sure their integrated strategies have the necessary investment to reach the right primary target and allow time for word-of-mouth marketing to kick-in, taking into account the slower adoption rate of Hispanics.

"EYE LEVEL" OR COMMUNITY MARKETING

Hispanic marketing is much more than generating brand awareness through events and media relations. A drug manufacturer with only a public relations campaign in Spanish, a bank with just Spanish brochures in some locations, or a grocery chain with several Hispanic products on the bottom shelf of an aisle are not doing Hispanic marketing, much less following an integrated Hispanic market strategy.

Eye-level or community marketing is a powerful boost that leapfrogs your effort into the right Hispanic-target group. For example, you can rely on a grassroots or affinity marketing strategy to help capture the Hispanic market. Affinity marketing and cause-related marketing focus on businesses and non-profit Community Based Organizations (CBOs) joining in win-win-win efforts. Although affinity marketing is only a small part of the overall strategy, it is important because it can reinforce positions and build strong relationships with customers on a personal level. This is especially true when brands are new to certain Hispanic segments and the Hispanic non-profit promoting or sponsoring your business has broad awareness, credibility, and a tight network of members. Affinity marketing provides corporate America with "foot in the door" access to Hispanic-consumer homes. However, as discussed earlier, other marketing strategies building from the initial affinity introduction are crucial for gaining trust, and creating stand-alone 'stickiness' or recall for your brand.

Investing in a sponsorship of the World Cup, or Calle Ocho, or Fiesta Broadway is like investing in the Super Bowl. These events can be very successful if integrated and fully maximized on broadcast and print *before and during* the event, as well as at the retail level, but this investment alone is insufficient.

In sum, the Hispanic media market may not be as cluttered with competitors as the general market, and that has been an argument in the past in favor of "not doing a lot more than advertising." However, advertising alone will not work instant miracles, nor give you the "big bang" ROI you could achieve if you boost your strategy with your presence at CBOs. Advertising can change attitudes over time, but when executed in combination with other "eye level" marketing activities, as a part of the integrated strategies plan, you can also generate the coveted 'Share of Heart' which precedes share of pocket, and solidifies the long-term relationship of your brand with the target Hispanic consumer segment.

INTERNAL ELEMENTS OF THE INTEGRATED STRATEGY

The internal aspects of an integrated Hispanic strategy are, in most cases, more important than the external because they "interact behind the stage" to deliver the brand promise to the target consumers. What is the point of executing the best possible external integrated marketing strategy if, when your client is ready to buy, your product or service is not ready, or "falls apart" or fails to deliver what you promised? In the best of cases, the different functional pieces of the business, R&D, manufacturing, IT, human resources, distribution, service, finance, etc., will be aligned internally and responsive to the factors on which the external Hispanic marketing strategy depends. An important point to keep in mind is that the integrated Hispanic marketing strategy should be consistent with and supportive of the overall non-Hispanic corporate strategic objective, and not in conflict.

SOUNDS TRIVIAL? ONLY IN THEORY!

In reality, the external ("customer facing") and internal (back-end) elements of Hispanic initiatives are seldom in alignment. Strategic and operational misalignments often plague corporate Hispanic initiatives. Under these circumstances it should not be a surprise to find that many Hispanic tests have been launched, just to crash shortly after take off.

The typical legacy that Hispanic market managers inherit and senior executives recollect is "Someone tried that once and it didn't work." Sadly, they wrongly conclude that the market opportunity is not there. In reality, the effort was treated as a tactic, unaligned with key functional groups, ill conceived, poorly executed, or both. Often, multicultural marketing programs cannot shake these ghosts even when the external and internal strategic thrusts are better aligned. Labels stand between opportunity and what shareholders ultimately crave—success in new growth markets.

FIND A CHAMPION

An integrated Hispanic marketing strategy must have access to internal resources and influence over their allocation. If it does not, the initiative typically is not funded adequately or disappears before a good ROI has time to emerge. One of the best ways of dealing with this challenge is coordinating and unifying the various functional areas that must support the strategy under a senior-level champion with overall accountability to the CEO and Board of Directors.

The Hispanic initiative champion leads the creation of the holistic integrated strategy, the business-wide game plan. The champion has the experience and seniority to cross functional lines, lead a successful strategy execution, manage deviations from plan, and recalibrate the strategy. Team members from relevant functions across the organization flesh out the overall strategy and give it more substance, realistic deliverables, and timelines as applied to their specific part of the business.

Among Hispanic market leaders it is common practice to name the integrated Hispanic strategy as one of the top five deliverables of the senior-level champion. Over the long-term, integration, passion, and focus on results against changing corporate agendas, leads to a Hispanic strategy that is capable of creating sustainable advantages. When all the elements of the integrated

Hispanic strategy are mutually supportive, there is little room for confusion and distraction.

The right communication and quantitative skills and experiences are essential at the core of an Integrated Hispanic management process. However, cooperating across functional lines, business units, or competing products, brands, or segments, rarely happens naturally in corporate environments. Thus, often such cross-functional teams "spin their wheels" rather than readily adopting the implementation of the corporate-wide Hispanic initiative. It takes a special kind of seasoned leader with smooth style and determination to set aside time and energy to referee apparent conflicts, negotiate additional resources or uncover existing ones, and rally support for a winning attitude and a unified approach.

THE INTERNAL STRATEGY ELEMENTS

The internally focused elements of a successful corporate-wide integrated Hispanic initiative boil down to change-management principles, that is, transforming the corporate culture to assume an *in-culture* Hispanic mindset across the entire organization's functional areas and managerial levels by:

- Empowering employees through training and development,

- Making the initiative a priority,

- Identifying a vocal and engaged senior level champion,

- Setting realistic corporate and departmental objectives,

- Providing fair accountability and proper rewards,

- Officially aligning, timing, recalibrating, and planning across functional areas on an ongoing basis.

Through the courtesy and support of AARP's management, I present below a detailed example of the entire introductory integrated Hispanic-marketing strategy. During the past couple of years, both Carlos Santiago and I worked with AARP as their consultants and had the honor and pleasure to partner with this extraordinary client to bring AARP to the "Los Grandes" Hispanic market segment. This case study demonstrates the value and application of the integrated Hispanic-marketing strategy and how it is implemented from top to bottom—from executive management to customer care and local chapters—in a committed organization.

AARP

Initiative: Integrated Hispanic Strategy

BACKGROUND

AARP is a nonprofit, nonpartisan membership organization for people aged 50 and over. AARP provides information and resources; advocates on legislative, consumer, and legal issues; assists members to serve their communities; and offers a wide range of unique benefits, special products, and services for its members. These benefits include AARP webplace at www.aarp.org, *Modern Maturity* and *My Generation* magazines, and the monthly *AARP Bulletin*. Active in every state, the District of Columbia, Puerto Rico, and the U.S. Virgin Islands, AARP celebrates the attitude that age is just a number and life is what you make it.

MARKETING CHALLENGE

After reaching 40 percent penetration among all U.S. adults aged 50 and over, AARP's challenge focused on relating the AARP brand to the aging boomer segment. Early in 1999, AARP reorganized in order to create more value for current and prospective members. Upon further analysis, it was determined that in order for AARP to continue delivering on its mission of enriching the lives of Americans aged 50 and older, it was crucial for the organization to meet the needs of all underdeveloped segments. It began with a focus on Hispanics in that age group.

A CHAMPION AT THE HIGHEST LEVEL

AARP demonstrated a strong commitment to building and serving an increasingly diverse membership. In 1999, the executive director, Horace B. Deets, and the Board of Directors established the Hispanic Membership Development initiative as one of the association-wide priorities, one of the annual objectives for every employee at AARP. Dawn Sweeney, associate executive director of membership, who reported directly to Deets, was assigned the lead facilitating role. One of Dawn Sweeney's direct reports, Nancy Franklin, director of membership development and value management took on the role of the senior level champion of the ambitious initiative.

UNDERSTANDING THE TARGET MARKET AND THE PERCEPTION OF AARP

A national quantitative study designed by AARP Knowledge Management, Isabel Valdés, and the Cultural Access Group was conducted to help AARP:

- Target groups according to acculturation,

- Identify opportunities for Hispanic membership recruitment and retention,

- Analyze AARP's mission, advocacy, information, products and services, and determine their relevance to the U.S. 50+ Hispanic market,

- Identify U.S. Hispanics' 50+ market needs and interest and determine language and information delivery channels and media usage.

The results, among self-identified Latino boomers and the Los Grandes age segment (aged 45 to 64) with incomes of more than $25,000, showed wide variations among five major Hispanic markets in education, years in the U.S., and most importantly, acculturation. This finding was crucial for strategy design. The five markets were Los Angeles, Miami, New York, Houston, and San Francisco.

Each market showed distinct acculturation levels. AARP membership and awareness was about three times lower among Spanish-dominant respondents than among those who were English-dominant. Hispanic AARP members, who had been enrolled through general market efforts and word-of-mouth, were unsurprisingly, more English-speaking and bilingual, had higher incomes, were older, and more likely to renew their memberships than Spanish-dominant. On the other hand, Spanish-speaking and bilingual non-members who were aware of AARP were about 20 percent more likely to join than English-speaking Hispanics. Furthermore, the study found that family focus, rather than personal pursuit, was strongly correlated with the less acculturated sub-segment.

Common across all acculturation levels was the importance of financial security. While learning that AARP already offered products and services that were important to them, especially access to discounted insurance products, the majority of Hispanics did not feel AARP related products were for them. Thus, it was clear that there was a need to create relevance among all Hispanics, as well as significant brand awareness among less-acculturated Hispanics.

Determining the Market Size

AARP also needed to learn how many Hispanics were also present within its membership. Previously, AARP used census block data to try to reach Hispanic members while most other companies relied on Spanish-surname lists to flag Hispanics in their file; however this proved only partially useful and often problematic. In response to this challenge, Geoscape® International,[2] a Miami-based firm specializing in multicultural market-intelligence data, systems, and consulting services was selected to apply a system they call DirecTarget®. This system combines a proprietary name-based set of algorithms with precise geo-demographics and household level data to perform identification, and segmentation.

FIGURE 22.3

DirecTarget Map of Houston

The map below illustrates member AARP households against a backdrop of geo-demographic data. Combining the identified households with a map revealing their residential characteristics helps reveal patterns in the data and identify related characteristics of their neighborhood which can later be applied to a variety of marketing and customer strategies.

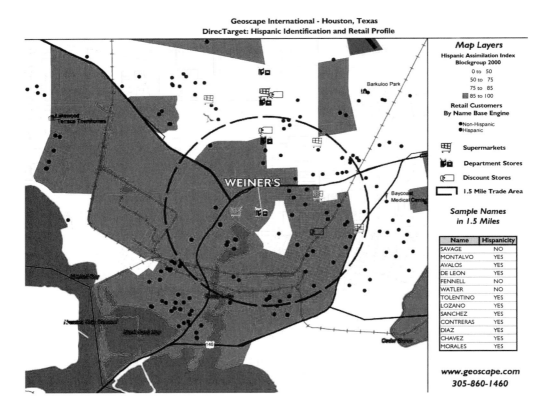

Geoscape applied DirecTarget® successfully to AARP's membership database. In addition, AARP management and its consultants validated and refined the ability to focus resources specifically toward those individuals who were most likely to desire AARP's information, products, and services in the Spanish language.

While Hispanics make up about 7 percent of all U.S. adults over age 50, the refined Geoscape International analysis indicated that AARP already had about 500,000 Hispanic members, or 12 percent of the Los Grandes segment of Hispanics aged 50 and over. Thus, it was decided that in order to achieve significant progress in its mission, the Hispanic Membership Development (HMD) initiative would target Los Grandes and aim at adding 370,000 new members by 2006 while significantly increasing awareness levels.

PLANNING AARP'S INTEGRATED HISPANIC STRATEGY

Santiago & Valdés Solutions (SVS) assisted AARP in the development of a marketing strategy, overall planning, and project management. It also assisted in the selection of agencies to provide advertising, public relations, community affairs, and call center management. A seasoned SVS project manager worked on a day-to-day basis to complement the dedicated AARP project management team. Based on the research described above, the project management team created an integrated Hispanic strategy that included:

- Understanding cultural preferences,

- Assessing current readiness to meet the HMD objective,

- Identifying critical success factors,

- Developing functional unit business plans,

- Counseling the units and orchestrating cross-functional integration, and

- Integrating their areas with the external, member-facing portion of the Hispanic initiative, focusing on membership development planning.

A national advertising agency search led to the selection of HeadQuarters Advertising in San Francisco, based on the strength of their vision for the brand, their ability to understand the challenge, and their recommended communications strategy.

Selecting the Right Target Segment and Geographic Market for a Launch

AARP and its consultants defined four criteria in relation to the geographic markets chosen to launch the membership and acquisition goals of AARP:

- A Spanish-dominant Hispanic population had to be well represented in each market.

- The target demographic of Hispanic adults aged 45 to 64 had to be a significant portion of the population in both absolute and percentage terms.

- The markets chosen had to have strong Spanish-language broadcast media, but at the same time be affordable.

- There had to be an opportunity for AARP to increase membership quickly.

New York and Miami were selected based on the following analysis:

- There was an indication that non-members in New York and Miami who were aware of AARP had a higher likelihood of joining (according to AARP research).

- The interest ranking and ratings for the top products and services offered by AARP were similar in each market (according to AARP research).

- There was an opportunity to make significant and measurable inroads in these markets.

- They were affordable markets considering the budget.

More specifically, for Miami, HeadQuarters determined:

- It was the third largest Hispanic market in the country, and the sixteenth largest television market, according to Nielsen Universe Estimates for DMA.

- One-quarter of the Hispanic population in Miami is aged 45 to 64 with 82 percent of Hispanics foreign born, that is, "on target."

- While Cubans make up the largest Hispanic group in the metropolitan area, recent years have brought large numbers of Nicaraguans, Colombians, Mexicans, Hondurans, and Guatemalans who are participating in business and politics.

- More than 2 out of 3 Hispanics in Miami speak Spanish mostly or only at home, according to 1999-2000 Nielsen language enumeration estimates.

Specifically for New York HeadQuarters determined:

- The New York DMA is the second-ranked Hispanic market in the U.S. with a Hispanic population of more than 3 million persons, equivalent to 11 percent of the total U.S. Hispanic population.

- Nineteen percent of New York's population is aged 45 to 64 with 77 percent of the Hispanic population being foreign born, also highly on target.

- Hispanic culture in New York has been well preserved because of a continuous influx of Dominicans, Mexicans, South Americans, and Central Americans. In addition, a long-established Puerto Rican community is more familiar with mainstream activities for people over age 50.

POSITIONING AARP

With low awareness and significant cultural differences, the monumental Hispanic-marketing challenge was to deliver a broad idea of what AARP is and yet try to complete a sale with a 60-second or 30-second television spot. Introducing AARP was not a simple task. There was much to say and explain. It is a reputable non-profit organization. The breadth and depth of benefits it offers are real although membership is only $12.50 a year for a married couple. It is safe and reliable. It has been around for a long time and has more than 35 million members and only members benefit from its discounts and other opportunities.

In relation to potential Hispanic members, it was important to acknowledge the *in-culture* approach, the particularly strong phenomenon among Hispanics of a lack of planning, the preference to avoid facing certain things in life, and the lack of familiarity with this type of service organization. The effort, to be successful, had to be synergistic with all other membership development, public relations, and grassroots efforts. There was no single selling point to communicate. AARP's new target audience required a 360° introduction, awareness, establishment of a brand, and education about the brand in a very short period of time. The target segment was culturally diverse, many times facing barriers like language, a low level of education, and overall distrust in institutions and unfamiliar brands.

ADVERTISING STRATEGY

The advertising strategy was carefully structured to take advantage of the research learnings and to fit into the integrated Hispanic strategy AARP was developing:

Communication Objective: To introduce and generate awareness of AARP, but also to entice the target audience *in-culture* to call for more information and join, increasing the Hispanic membership base.

Target Audience: Spanish-dominant Hispanic adults aged 45 to 64.

TARGET PERCEPTIONS

• Initially, neither younger (45-55) nor older (55-64) groups of the Los Grandes senior segment identified with AARP. It was seen as "not for me" or "for the old." Some had received mailings but discarded them, perhaps due to lack of awareness about the organization, as well as a lack of cultural understanding of its services and benefits. As mentioned above, non-acculturated Latinos had very little awareness of AARP. Also, research showed that there was a stigma attached to old age and that the target audience did not want to be reminded that they were not young anymore. Lastly, lack of planning ahead is a common practice among many Hispanics, more so among the non-acculturated.

THE CONCEPT

"La segunda juventud es mejor que la primera"
(The second youth is better than the first)

Creative Rationale for the Campaign: The target audience needs to see and feel this new phase of life in a positive way, making it desirable, showing its advantages as a second chance of living their lives to the fullest. The target must identify with the people to be shown in AARP's Hispanic advertising. They enjoy their second youth; they have the freedom that comes with having grown children; they are allowed to think of themselves. They are invited to dream of doing all the things they could not in their youth due to lack of time and the responsibilities. AARP is presented as a second chance in life for the couple—family—but with the benefits of the wisdom and maturity acquired along the way.

The campaign informs the Hispanic target that there is an organization that helps them get the most out of life. The agency proposed to base the image and brand communication of the campaign on a well known poem called "Instantes" (*Instants,* sometimes attributed to Argentinean writer and poet Jorge Luis Borges, some but scholars say it is not his work).

In some instances, the words were rewritten to fit the messages' particular needs, but maintained the concept:

If I could live my life again I wouldn't try to be perfect.

I wouldn't take too many things so seriously. I would take more risks.

I would travel more. I would be thankful for each sunrise . . .

. . . and I would admire each and every sunset. I would climb
more mountains . . .

. . . to see what's on the other side. I would swim in more rivers.

I would go places I've never been before.

I would eat more sweets.

I would take more care of real problems and less about imaginary ones..

I would always remember that life is made of moments.

I would fall in love more often . . .

. . . I would visit my loved ones more often.

I would take more rides on the carrousel at the fair . . .

The Tagline: Created in Spanish first, the tagline was thoroughly thought out in order to arrive at a long-lasting and faithful representation of a concept which AARP could own with time:
"La segunda juventud es mejor que la primera"
(The second youth is better than the first)

Basic Promise: With its resources and strength, AARP assists you in making smart choices, reaching your goals and dreams, and making the most of your life after 50. Discounts and offers that were top-of-mind were travel discounts, vision care and pharmacy, medical and life insurance, and retirement planning information.

Desired Consumer Take Away: "Rather than a stigma, AARP membership affords me entry to, and participation in a wide variety of relevant benefit and support programs designed to meet my needs."

Tonality: Establish a warm relationship between the member and the organization. The copy was to be communicated in an uplifting and positive manner, taking care to be celebratory, informative, and educational.

Communications Architecture:

Phase 1: Brand advertising and awareness building: During this phase, the message was intended to create an affectionate link between the prospect and AARP using visuals and words that would touch the prospect's emotional fibers. HeadQuarters also attempted to quickly build AARP's brand personality making it recognizable and approachable, leveraging overall membership services and benefits, and maintaining brand message.

Phase 2: Direct response and membership promotion: The creative message would be reinforced with concrete benefits information and target high opportunity segments through selected membership attributes and benefits through direct TV and direct mail. In this phase, AARP would also operationally track results, adjust messages and channels as appropriate, and generate brand ubiquity through targeted communications and promotional opportunities such as events, associations, and media-driven activities.

INTEGRATED EXECUTION AND INTERNAL ALIGNMENT

The integrated Hispanic strategy aligned the customer touch points elements in bilingual and or Spanish fulfillment pieces such as Bill Me statements, Welcome Kits, and informational brochures which were created to fit within the usual processes of the association.

Making it Work Within AARP

Telemarketing: To ensure "culturally sensitive" and effective customer-care solutions to Hispanic AARP prospects and members, AARP's consultants chose a call center based on specific variables, identifying a vendor that provided the latest in contact center technology with "best practices" in functionality and one that would provide creative, cost-efficient options to serve the AARP-member base. Based on stringent evaluations, Technion Communications was selected as the call center for the Hispanic market. They provided optimal results and statistical data to assess continuously the efficiency of the specific programs and make daily adjustments. Technion's ability to provide "state-of-the-art" technology and "boutique" management solutions helped AARP deliver on its customer-care promise of respect and efficiency while building a relationship with the Hispanic market.

Customer care: Staff in AARP's customer care center were trained to ensure that Hispanic members received appropriate cultural and age sensitivity as well as the same amount of attention and care as the non-Hispanic member segment. This step optimized relationship building in conjunction with the launch of direct TV and direct mail efforts.

ADDITIONAL INTEGRATED EXTERNAL CUSTOMER-FACING ELEMENTS

Joint Efforts:

Through AARP Services Inc. (ASI), the services coordination arm of AARP, a joint member development strategy was created and aligned with The Hartford Financial Services Group, Inc.,one of ASI's key service providers. Research had shown that their auto and homeowners' insurance products and services were of special interest to the Hispanic target seniors.

Events:

An events strategy was developed by headquarters and state offices integrating specific community needs in the top four Hispanic states: California, Texas, New York, and Florida. In California, for example, sponsorship of Fiesta Broadway was selected as a primary event to build brand awareness, to recruit volunteers, to test on-site member acquisitions, and to strengthen relationships with other Hispanic community organizations. At Fiesta Broadway AARP targeted Hispanic attendees aged 50 and over with incentives to draw them to AARP's Supersite.

Media: Television served as the main medium for creating awareness, image, and generating direct responses. Dr. Isabel's show on Radio Utica, a national Spanish radio network, expanded the reach and key messages of the effort. In addition, radio was used by states for promotions before major events like Fiesta Broadway, as were newspapers. Additional newspapers were integrated in states like New York adn florda where research indicated tht the target segment wanted additional detail and there existed strong newspaper offerings in the market.

Community-service advocacy: In-depth plans for each state focused on community service advocacy and relationship building and included volunteer recruitment, training, and development events.

Community relations/public affairs: With the assistance of a consultant, AARP developed a public-relations/public affairs agency search with specific criteria and review process. Comunic-Ad/MAPA Communications, a D.C.-based firm, was selected to provide grassroots issues, and relationship management, public affairs and public relations, public policy, and community and media relations expertise and to ensure integration into the overall Hispanic Membership Development initiative. The primary focus was to provide relationship management expertise with the Hispanic community to AARP executives and eventually leverage media and outreach efforts to expand the branding, acquisition, and retention strategies.

Segunda Juventud

Since one of the most tangible and frequent benefits of AARP is its award-winning publications, *My Generation, Modern Maturity,* and *AARP Bulletin,* it was essential to extend AARP's mission in an *in-culture,* deeply relevant print vehicle to serve the particular needs and interests of the Latino 50+ community. The publication strategy led to the selection of *La Opinión* to provide editorial suport in the creation of a new quarterly publication. In a record 12 weeks from concept to distribution, AARP's Publications unit created *Segunda Juventud,* the new sibling to its family of magazines.

With an initial distribution to 250,000 Latino member households in target states, *Segunda Juventud* became the largest Hispanic magazine launch ever. The publication currently reaches more than 350,000 Latino member-households and an estimated total audience of 1.5 million readers each quarter. It delivers to AARP Latino members the promise of great resources and strength, assisting them in making smart choices to reach their goals and dreams and helping them make the most out of their "Second Youth." Like AARP's broadcast branding efforts, the magazine presents the maturing stage of life in a positive, desirable light. In addition, *Segunda Juventud* provides an effective channel to directly reach the Latino segment over age 50 in a powerful marketing vehicle. It has become a key component of AARP's integrated strategy to add value and establish warm relationships between the Latino AARP member and interested service providers. Latino AARP members' reaction to *Segunda Juventud* has been exceptional. It has become an influential, high quality publication, not only making a significant difference to mature Hispanics, but also creating an advertising venue to reach the Los Grandes age segment.

Internet: An online strategic component could not be missed. The first phase, leveraging the magazine, was to create its parallel presence on the internet, www.segundajuventud.org, to keep members and potential members informed about the latest developments on a monthly basis. In Puerto Rico, Populi Com.com, the interactive arm of Lopito, Ileana & Howie's advertising agency created the *in-culture* website for Los Grandes. Its content supports the general information of the magazine but also serves as a public relations tool to keep solidifying AARP's commitment with the community. Areas like entertainment, food, and profiles skew more towards Hispanic-specific relevance. The second phase of the online stragegy focuses on strengthening the general site of AARP.org for Spanish-preferred members and prospects. This area focuses on explaining what AARP is, explains in detail the many benefits of becoming a member, and even issues new memberships for individuals or their parents.

RESULTS

Although the program continues, the following are preliminary results:

- In the first 4 months after launching the image and direct TV efforts, awareness of AARP among Hispanics in New York and Miami increased by 50 percent and 70 percent, respectively. At a national level, December 2001 over Fall 2000 awareness of AARP among Spanish speaking Hispanics jumped 61% while it remained relatively stable for English speaking Hispanics and non-Hispanic whites. Among specific brand attributes that describe both current and desired AARP equitites, *"AARP is a vital and important organization,"* also showed strengthening.

- A thorough analysis of the database after the first six months of the launch indicated that there were approximately 38,000 new Hispanic members.

- In the first twelve months after the campaign was launched, the direct response effort alone generated over 33,000 inquiries resulting in nearly 20,000 new members, a conversion rate of over 60 percent.

- With ongoing monitoring, training, and development, the quality assurance at the call center increased from 74 percent initially to 97 percent at the end.

AARP's model illustrates the tremendous impact that a strategic, *in-culture* integrated marketing approach can have in a complex and aggressive campaign. Each element builds on the other, multiplying the synergistic effect of the emotional-cultural elements, the well-supported and sustained corporate commitment, the strategically, hand-picked elements of the plan, and superb execution. I wish we could talk about the financial investment. Let me only say that the ROI—the new members acquired and the increase in brand awareness in the plan's time frame—exceed many I have witnessed in other corporate efforts with similar or more resources.

In any integrated Hispanic-market strategy, advancing team members along the learning curve is critical. The focus on the Hispanic segment has to become a living strategy, a second soul of managers regardless of functional area, and an integral way of conducting business in the future. Corporations that maintain their Hispanic strategy at a single advertising agency and have few internal champions face the loss of years of experience when any of the champions decide to depart from the company. It is critically important, therefore, to spread and transfer the knowledge, cross-pollinate skills, develop a network of experts across functional areas and managerial levels, provide fair accountability and proper rewards, and update succession plans with human resources.

AGENCIES: Santiago & Valdés Solutions (now the Santiago Solutions Group), www.santiagosolutionsgroup.com, and
HeadQuarters Advertising, www.headquartersadvertising.com.

Notes

1. "The vaccine approach" was coined by Hector Orci, La Agencia de Orci & Asociados, Los Angeles
2. Geoscape, DirecTarget, HomeBase and GeoBase are trademarks of Geoscape International, Inc. Geoscape International, www.geoscape.com.

Online Resources

This is not an exclusive list, but rather an attempt to show the variety and depth of websites now available with information and entertainment for Latinos. Many of these websites are bilingual, and many offer several different kinds of services or information. I apologize in advance for any glaring omissions.

ESPECIALLY FOR LATINAS

Chicanas	http://chicanas.com	*Women*
De mujer.com	www.demujer.com	*Portal for women*
Latin Girl Magazine	www.latingirlmag.com	*Magazine for teens*
Latina Mami	www.latinamami.com	*Women*
MANA	www.hermana.org	*A national Latina organization*
Mujer Web	www.mujerweb.com	*Portal for women*
Mujerfutura.com	www.Mujerfutura.com	*Portal for women*

ACADEMIC

California Latino Net	http://clnet.ucr.edu	*University of California*
Hispanic College Fund	http://hispanicfund.org	*Funds, Grants & Scholarships*
LAMP: Latinos and Media Project	www.latinosandmedia.org	*University of Texas at Austin*
Latin American Network Information Center	www.lanic.utexas.edu	*University of Texas at Austin*

ADVOCACY ORGANIZATIONS

Association of Hispanic Arts	www.latinoarts.org	*Media advocacy*
Hispanas Organized for Political Equality	www.latinas.org	*Political advocacy*
Hispanic Association on Corporate Responsibility	www.hacr.org	*Advocacy with corporations*
Hispanic Scholarship Fund	www.hsf.net	*Education funds*
Hispanos Famosos	http://coloquio.com /famosos.html	*Information about famous Hispanics*
Latino Issues Forum	www.lif.org	*Advocacy organization*
League of United Latin American Citizens	www.lulac.org	*Advocacy organization*
MALDEF	www.maldef.org	*Mexican American legal defense and education*

National Council of La Raza	www.nclr.org	*Advocacy for low-income Hispanics, publications and research*
National Hispanic Foundation for the Arts	www.hispanicarts.org	*Media advocacy organization*
National Latino Children's Institute	www.nlci.org	*Advocacy for Latino children*
Nosotros	www.nosotros.org	*Advocacy organization for Latino performers*

ARTS AND CULTURE

Aztlán Net	www.aztlannet.com	*Art*
Barrio Life	www.barriolife.com	*Art*
Frida Kahlo	www.fridakahlo.com	*Art*
Global Music Directory	www.dgolpe.com	*Music*
HispanicArt.com	www.arteamericas.com	*Art*
La Música	www.lamusica.com	*Music*
Los Mestizos	www.losmestizos.com	*Art*
Museo de las Amerécas	www.museo.org	*Museum*
Museo del Barrio	www.elmuseo.org	*Museum*
Smithsonian Center for Latin Initiatives	http://latino.si.edu	*Information on and photos of exhibits, job opportunities, research, all for Latinos*
The Library of Congress Hispanic Reading Room	www.loc.gov/rr/hispanic	*What the Library of Congress offers on Hispanics and Latin America*
Virtual Diego Rivera Web Museum	www.diegorivera.com	*Art*

BUSINESS AND FINANCIAL

Bloomberg Latin America	www.bloomberg.com/sa	*Financial news*
Business News Americas	www.bnamericas.com	*Business news*
Dr. Tango	www.drtango.com	*Online content and applications consulting for healthcare companies*
Hispanic Business	www.hispanicbusiness.com	*Magazine and research on line, primarily on business*
Hispanic Journal	www.hispanicjournal.com	*Business*
Hispanic-Market	www.hispanic-market.com	*Business in Hispanic market*
Invertia	www.invertia.com	*Market news in Spanish*

Latin American Newsletters	www.latinnews.com	*Latin American business news*
Latin Business Association	www.lbausa.com	*Business association*
Latin Trade	www.latintrade.com	*Latin Trade Magazine's on-line presence*
Latino Reach Northwest	www.latinoreach.com	*Business network in the Pacific*
Latinvestor	www.latinvestor.com	*Latin Investor's online site*
Mundo Latino	www.MundoLatino.com	*Weekly business news*
US Hispanic Chamber of Commerce	www.ushcc.com	*Equivalent of U.S. Chamber of Commerce for Hispanics businesses*
Viajo.com	www.viajo.com	*Business & leisure*
Zona Financiera	www.zonafinanciera.com	*Latin American finance*

E-COMMERCE

El Coqui Gifts	www.ElCoquiGifts.com	*Gifts*
Español.com	www.espanol.com	*E-Commerce*
Fiera.com	www.fiera.com	*E-Commerce*
Mercado Libre	www.MercadoLibre.com	*E-Commerce*
Que rico.com	www.querico.com	*E-Commerce*
The Human Bean	www.thehumanbean.com	*Zapatista coffee from Chiapas, Mexico plus politics*
Todito.com	www.todito.com	*E-Commerce*
Yavas	www.yavas.com	*Books and music*

ENTERTAINMENT AND FILM

American Latino Connection	www.am-latino.com	*Entertainment*
Cine Las Américas	www.cinelasamericas.org	*Film*
Cinemaluna	www.cinemaluna.com	*Film*
CineSol Latino Film Festival	www.cinesol.com	*Film*
Es Más	www.EsMas.com	*Entertainment*
Galán Incorporated Television and Film	www.galaninc.com	*Film*
Hispanico.com	www.hispanico.com	*Entertainment*
Latino Film Festival	www.latinofilmfestival.org	*Film*
Los Angeles Latino International Film Festival	www.latinofilm.org	*Film*
Miami Latin Film Festival	www.hispanicfilm.com	*Film*

National Alliance for Media Arts and Culture	www.namac.org	*Film*
New York International Latino Film Festival	www.nylatinofilm.com	*Film*
San Diego Latino Film Festival	www.sdlatinofilm.com	*Film*
Tulipanes Latino Art & Film Festival	www.tlaff.org	*Film*
Vivahollywood.com	www.vivahollywood.com	*Entertainment*

HEALTH

Buena Salud	www.buenasalud.com	*Health information for Spanish-speakers*
Hispanic Health	www.hispanichealth.org	*Health information and advocacy*
Office of Minority Health Resources Center	www.omhrc.gov	*Links to health services for Hispanics; listings for every state*
SAMHSA'	www.health.org	*Clearinghouse for alcohol and drug information*

JOB SEARCH

Bilingual Jobs	www.Bilingual-Jobs.com	*Job Search*
Hispanic Employment Program	www.hepm.org	*Job Search*
Job Latino	www.joblatino.com	*Job Search*
Lat Pro	www.LatPro.com	*Job Search*
Saludos	www.saludos.com	*Job Search*
U.S. Navy	www.elnavy.com	*Recruitment*

LITERATURE

Criticas magazine	www.criticas.com	*Reviews of Spanish-language books in Spanish*
Hispanic Culture Review	www.gmu.edu/org/hcr	*Journal published by students of George Mason University, poetry and stories*
Isabel Allende	www.isabelallende.com	*Literature*
Latino Lingo	www.latinolingo.com	*Literature*
Libros Latinos	www.libroslatinos.com	*Literature*
Nuestra Palabra	www.nuestrapalabra.org	*Literature*

MARKETING AND MARKET RESEARCH

All Access Entertainment — www.AAEevents.com — *Events marketing, creators of Fiesta Broadway*

Cheskin — www.cheskin.com — *Market research company*

Cultural Access Group — www.accesscag.com — *Market research company*

Geoscape International, Inc. — www.geoscape.com — *Lists and maps for multicultural direct marketing*

HispanicAd.com — www.hispanicad.com — *Advertising and media news and information*

Hispanic-Research Co. — http://hispanic-research.com — *Marketing consultants*

Informania!com — www.informania.com — *Subscriptions available in Spanish. Information on the internet economy, bilingual dictionary, resource center*

La Fuente de Información della prensa Hispana — www.hispanic-media.com — *Information and analysis about Hispanic media*

Latin American Research Group of the Federal Reserve Bank — www.frbatlanta.org/econ_rd/larg — *Finance and economic research in Latin America*

Latin Visión — www.latinvision.com — *Marketing consultants*

Media Economics Group — www.LatinWebMonitor.com — *Monitors advertising spending on Hispanic web sites*

Media Economics Group — www.HispanicMagazineMonitor.com — *Monitors advertising spending in the U.S. Hispanic print market*

National Association of Hispanic Media — www.nahp.org — *Media kit*

Roslow Research Group — www.roslowresearch.com — *Market research company*

SRDS — www.srds.com — *Publishers of Hispanic Media & Market Source*

Strategy Research — www.strategyresearch.com — *Marketing consultants*

The Tomás Rivera Policy Institute — www.trpi.org — *Mentioned many times in this book, TRPI publishes excellent research on the Hispanic middle class among other things*

U.S. Newspaper Links — www.usnewspaperlinks.com — *Includes links to Hispanic papers published in the U.S.*

MEDIA

American Latino	www.americanlatino.net	*News*
Annuario Hispano (Hispanic Yearbook)	www.hispanicyearbook.com	*Excellent directory of Hispanic radio and tv stations, publications, and organizations*
Batanga	www.batanga.com	*Internet radio and other services*
CNN en Español	www.cnnenespanol.com	*News*
Contacto Magazine	www.contactomagazine.com	*Newsmagazine*
Dos Mundos	www.dosmundos.com	*Bilingual newspaper from Kansas City*
El Conquistador Newspaper	www.conquistadornewspaper.com	*News*
El Extra News	www.extranews.com	*Newspaper*
El Heraldo	www.elheraldo.com	*Newspaper*
El Nuevo Herald	www.miami.com/elnuevoherald	*Newspaper*
El Sol de Texas	www.elsoldetexas.com	*Newspaper*
Enlace	www.enlacelink.com	*News in Spanish*
Galavisión	www.galavision.com	*Television network*
Hawaii Hispanic News	www.hawaiihispanicnews.com	*Newspaper from Hawaii*
Hispanic Broadcasting	www.hispanicbroadcasting.com	*Radio and television*
Hispanic Online	www.hispaniconline.com	*Hispanic magazine's web site*
Hola!	www.hola.com	*Celebrity newsmagazine*
La Conexión	www.LaConexionUSA.com	*Newspaper from North Carolina*
La Oferta	www.laoferta.com	*Newspaper*
La Opinión	www.laopinion.com	*Newspaper in Spanish from Los Angeles*
La Prensa San Diego	www.laprensa-sandiego.org	*Bilingual newspaper from San Diego*
La Raza	www.laraza.com	*Newspaper in Spanish from Chicago*
LA Ritmo	www.laritmo.com	*Latin American rhythm magazine in English*
Latina	www.latina.com	*Magazine for women*
Latina Style	www.latinastyle.com	*Fashion magazine for women*
Latino News Network	www.latnn.com	*Newspaper*
qvMagazine	www.qvmagazine.com	*Magazine for gay Latino men*
Telemundo	www.telemundo.com	*Television network*
Univision	www.univision.com	*Television network*

Urban Latino	www.urbanlatino.com	*Magazine for urban Latinos*
Zona Latina	www.zonalatina.com	*Links for all kinds of media in Latin America*

ONLINE COMMUNITY

Barrio	www.barrio.net	*Chat rooms, e-mail, and news*
CiberPaís	www.cyberpais.org	*Mexican-American online community*
Spanish Pride	www.spanishpride.com	*Spanish and English, pen pals, message board, games, shopping, music*

PORTALS

Asociados	www.Asociados.com	*General*
Ciudad Futura	www.ciudadfutura.com	*General*
El Sitio	www.ElSitio.com	*General*
Hispanic Dot Com	www.hispanic.com	*General*
Hispanic Vista	www.hispanicvista.com	*General*
Latino.com	www.latino.com	*General*
LatinoLA	www.latinola.com	*Los Angeles Latinos*
LatinoWeb	www.latinos.com	*General*
Lo Que Sea	http://us.loquesea.com	*Teens*
MuyBueno.net	www.muybueno.net	*Bay Area*
Qué Pasa	www.quepasa.com	*General*
Starmedia.com	www.us.starmedia.com	*General*
Terra.com	www.terra.com	*General*
To2	www.todos.com	*General*
Yahoo en Español	www.espanol.yahoo.com	*General*
Yupi	www.yupi.com	*General*
Yupi/MSN	www.yupimsn.com	*General*

MISCELLANEOUS

Despegar.com	www.despegar.com	*Online Travel*
Diversity, Inc.	www.diversityinc.com	*News and analysis about diversity in the workplace and in the U.S. in general*
Preciomania.com	www.preciomania.com	*Price Comparison Site in Spanish*

PROFESSIONAL ORGANIZATIONS

National Hispanic Real Estate Professionals   www.nahrep.org
   Real estate professionals

American Association of Hispanic CPAs   www.AAHCPA.org
   Hispanic CPAs

Association of Hispanic Advertising Agencies   www.ahaa.org
   Hispanic advertising agencies

California Chicano News Media Association   www.ccnma.org
   Advocacy for Latino journalists and diversity in the news media

Hispanic National Bar Association   www.hnba.com
   National association for Hispanic lawyers

Hola! Hispanic Organization of Latin Actors   www.hellohola.org
   Organization for Latino actors

Latino Professional Network   www.lpnonline.com
   Association of Latino professionals and students from a variety of professions

National Association of Hispanic Federal Executives Inc.   www.nahfe.org
   Organization of Hispanics who work for the federal government

National Hispanic Business Association   www.nhba.org
   National organization of students and alumni interested in
   education and business issues for Hispanics

National Hispanic Corporate Council   www.nhcc-hq.org
   Information on Hispanics, primarily for Fortune 1000 companies

National Hispanic Employee Association   www.nhea.org
   Professional Organization

National Latino Communications Center   www.nlcc.com
   Professional Organization

National Society of Hispanic MBA's   www.nshmba.org
   Professional organization for Hispanic MBAs

Professional Hispanics in Energy   www.phie.org
   Professional Organization

Society of Hispanic Professional Engineers   www.shpe.org
   Professional organization for Hispanic engineers

The National Association of Hispanic Journalists   www.nahj.org
   Professional organization for Hispanic journalists

National Association of Hispanic professionals   www.nshp.org
   Network organization for Hispanic professionals

SEARCH ENGINES

Las Culturas	www.lasculturas.com	*Links with many sites that offer information on a variety of topics including health, celebrities, news, and religion*
Latin World	www.latinworld.com	*In English and Spanish with lots of links*
Internet Resources for Latin America	http://lib.nmsu.edu/ subject/bord/laguia	*Links to many other internet resources, especially for librarians and researchers*
Latindex.com	www.latindex.com	*In Spanish, with links country-by-country*

INDEX

1990 U.S. Census, xvii

AARP, 136, 314–327
ALMA Awards, 206
acculturation, 33–34, 68,
    94, 116, 136, 143, 154,
    182, 239
    definition of, 34
    impact on shopping
    behavior, 187–200
    of seniors, 133
ACNielsen's Homescan His-
    panic Panel, 56, 68,
    143–152, 153–178,
    180–200, 205
Ad Américas, 211–212
Ad Age, 245
Ad Week, 245
advertising, 296–301
    agencies, 109, 245
    online, 242–246, 249
    outdoor, 245, 294
    print, 245
    radio, 245
    sales, 288, 289
    strategy, 202–203, 207,
    210, 213–214
Advertising Research
    Foundation, The, 244
advertisements, 82, 122
affluence, 130
affluent Hispanic house-
    holds, 28
African-Americans, 36, 41,
    43, 133, 229, 236
    households, 30
    women, 118

youth, 94
age-compression phenom-
    enon, 138
age distribution, 8
aging, 133
Agriculture, Department
    of, xvii
air travel, 114
airline tickets, 242
Albertini, Luis Diaz, 255
Albertson's grocery stores,
    91
alcoholic beverages, 31,
    92, 191–194
Alka-Selzer, 213
allergies, 219
alliances, 250
allowances, 95
American Baby Group, 82
American Demographics,
    86, 245
American dream, 56, 123,
    124
Americatel, 291
Amigas y Rivales (TV pro-
    gram), 103
Anheuser-Busch, 91, 107
Anita Santiago Advertis-
    ing, Inc., 210
Anselmo, Rene, 254
Anthony, Mark, 95
antidepressants, 121
AOL Time Warner, 107
apparel, 117, 118, 253
Aragon Advertising, 213
Arbitron, 269, 272

Arbitron 101 en Español,
    273
Arce, Carlos, 60
Argentina, xvi, 11, 252
Army, *see* U.S. Army
Asians, 36, 43, 230
Associated Press, xvii
Association of Hispanic
    Advertising Agencies
    (ahaa), 39, 48, 86,
    109, 245, 296–297
Asthma, 219, 221
Astrology, 250
automobile
    sales, 109
    ownership, 127
    use, 232
automotive industry, 27
Avanzando con tu Familia
    (magazine), 121–125
average American family,
    255
Azcarrága Sr., Emilio, 254

B-vitamin, 83
babies, 83
baby boomers, 104
baby contests, 248
baby food, 117, 145–152
Ballas-Taynor, Lucia, 258
banking, 114
Bank of America, 221
Bank One, 129–130
barriers to seeking health-
    care, 220
"barrio teen" culture, 108

Batanga, 291

Bauer Consumer Care, 213

beach soccer, 102

Bebé BeechNut Del Mes, 248

beer, 91, 174, 193, 201–203

Bendixen & Associates, 271

Bendixen, Sergio, 48

Best Buy, 276

beverages, 171–175
  fruit-flavored, 173

biculturalism, 87, 106, 120

bilingual consumers, 66

bilingual Latinos, 187

bilingualism, 87

Bill and Melinda Gates Foundation, 107

birth
  defects, 83
  rate, 79
  weight, 79

births to older women, 117

blended culture, 94

blood pressure, 222

bodegas, 144, 149

Bolivia, 11, 252

books, 242

bouillon, 168–171

Bounty, 123

Bracho, Dr. America, 221

brand heritage, 71, 159, 256

branding, 136, 309
  emotional, 204–208

brands, 60, 88, 147
  loyalty, 160
  passion, 90
  recall, 108
  shares, 168

Bravo Group, The, 208,

223

breakfast food, 161–165

Bush, George W., 48

businesses, Hispanic owned 43–46

business-to-business opportunities, 115

butter, 153–158

buying power, 22
  by state, 24–26

CDs, 242

CD players, 235

cable programming, 82, 267

Caliente (TV program), 103

California Department of Health Services, 224–225

California Milk Processor Board (CMPB), 209–210

Calle Ocho (event), 222

camcorders, 235

cameras, 127

Canada, xvi

Canal Teen, (Terra.com web channel) 103

cancer, 226–227
  breast, 219, 226–227

Cancer Registry, The, 134

canned Mexican foods, 181

canned soup, 168–171

Cantando hast la Fama (Singing for Fame), 208

car insurance, 117

carbonated beverages, 171–175

cardiovascular disease, 134

Caribbean countries, 11–12

Carina Su Mejor Amiga (call-in show), 121

Cartel Creativo, Inc., 112, 203

Cartel Group, The, 110, 201–203

case studies
  Bayer Consumer Care, 213–214
  California Department of Health Services, 224–225
  California Milk Processor Board, 209–210
  Franklin Electronic Publishing, 274–277
  Kellogg's, 90–91
  Kraft Food North America, 204–208
  Labatt USA, 201–203
  La Opinión and *La Opinión* Digital, 247–248
  McDonald's, 211–112
  March of Dimes, 83–84
  PepsiCo, 98–101
  Procter & Gamble, 121–125

cash basis, 255

Castor Advertising, 255

Catalan-dialect portal, 234

cause marketing, 282

causes of death, 227

Central America, 10, 11

Central Americans, 15

cereal, 90

Cerveza Tecate, 201–203

cervical cancer, 134

cesarean section, 79

cigarettes, 194

Chayanne (music artist), 100

Chvarria, Jesus, 287

checking accounts, 16

Cheskin Research, 234

Chiapas, 251

Chica Teen (online model-search contest), 103

Chicago, 129–130, 181, 182

chicoismo, 88, 106

child-bearing years, 117

children, 35, 82, 86, 127, 239, 249
and parents, 105–107
as marketers, 88
language fluency, 102

children's television, 82

Chile, xvi, 11

cholesterol, 155, 222

Christmas, 228

Cinco de Mayo, 291

citizenship, 34

Coca-Cola, 97, 107

coffee, 158–161

cold remedies, 165–168

Colgate, 256

college, 36–39
enrollment, 10
fairs, 295

Columbia, 11, 252

Comber, Neil, 121, 256

Comida y Familia, 207

Common-law marriage, 113

Commonwealth Fund 2001 Healthcare Quality Survey, The, 223

community, 218, 242
involvement, 205
marketing, 109

computers, 127, 233–246

computer literacy, 86

comScore Networks, 235

Congressional districts, xvii

Conill, 255

consultants, 109

consumer electronics, 309–310

Consumer Electronics Association, 234

consumer products, 131

Control (TV news and entertainment show), 103

convenience stores, 149, 185–200

cooking, *see also* Food preparation
classes, 222

cooking oil, 154

Coors Brewing Company, 115

Copa Libertadores, 259

corridos, 203

Corona, 203

corporate boardrooms, 47–48

corporate sponsorships, 39

cosmetics, 117–119, 196–199

Costa Rica, 11

costs of selling to Hispanics, 57

cotton, Inc., 118

country of origin, 11

coupons, 207

credit, 255

credit cards, 114, 116, 127, 249
use, 241

Crest, 123

Cristina La Revista, 288

cross-border transactions, 12

cruise travel, 228

cruz/kravetz:IDEAS, 27

Cuba, 11

Cubans, 14, 37, 46, 50, 72, 75

cultural nuances, 72

cultural values, 87, 137

Cultural Access Group, 240, 248

Circuit City, 276

customer services, 182–184

customs, 103

D'Alesandro, Giuseppi, 108

DVD players, 127, 235

Datamonitor, 251

data samples, 244

dairy, 189–190

dandruff, 102

"Deep Roots", 60

Democrats, 49

dental care, 224

department stores, 149

depression, 120, 222, 223

diabetes, 134, 219, 222–227

diapers, 117

Diego Armando Maradona, 291

Dieste, Harmel & Partners, 100, 123–125

diet soft drinks, 174

digital camera, 234

digital divide, 233, 240

direct mail, 10

direct marketing, 245, 293

discount stores, 93, 149

Discovery en Español, 258

disposable income
household, 56
personal, 22

distrust of government, 224, 226

diversity in schools, 38, 86

divorce, 113, 132

Dominican Republic, 11

Dora the Explorer, 82, 260

Doritos, 98

double-entendres, 202

Dr. Aliza, 80

Dream Big! (book), 120

dropout rate, 36

drug stores, 149, 196–200
drugs, 134, 136
dry beans, 181
dry grocery, 185–188
dry soup mixes, 169
Dulce de Leche-Caramel candies, 92
durable goods, 127

early childhood education, 39
earnings gap, 42
e-commerce activity, 241
Ecuador, 11
education, 26, 35–39, 86, 95, 127
    attainment, 41–42, 72, 127
    materials, 86
    programs, 107
elected officials, 49
Election 2000, 125
    Florida, 50
El Diario/La Prensa, 267, 285
Elherald.com, 247
El Morro, 208
El Nuevo Herald, 247, 286
El Salvador, 11, 15, 250
El Sentinel (Orlando daily newspaper), 243
Emanon Entertainment, Inc., 291
emotional branding, 204–208
empanadas, 153
employment, 26, see Labor force
end displays, 182–184
English as a second language, xvii
entertainment, 32, 88, 96, 243
Entravision (EV) Commu-

nications, 261, 267, 278
entrepreneurs, 43–46, 115
EPM Communications, 97
Espera (pre-natal magazine), 81
ESPN, 103, 250, 258
ethnic foods, 179
European influences, 185
event marketing, 28, 89, 245, 295
eye care, 224
eye-level marketing, 89, 97, 199, 310
¡Exito! (Chicago weekly), 243, 286
experiential marketing, 89
extended families, 131, 255

familismo, 85, 104, 108, 137
family, 218, 228, 242
    relationships, 106
Fanta, 175
fashion, 118
fast food, 211–212
fatalism, 134, 219
feminine protection, 175–178
Ferraez Publications of America, 291
fertility rates, 5, 35, 58, 79, 117
Fiesta Broadway (event), 29, 222
Fiesta menu (McDonald's), 211–212
Figueroa, Arminda, 184
financial services, 114, 116, 129
First Chicago Bank, 129
Florida Marlins, 92
focus groups, 245

folic acid
    awareness, 83
    education campaign, 82
food, 31
    purchase behavior, 179–200
    preparation, 71, 158, 169, 209
    outlets, 149
    shopping behavior, 185
food and beverage industry, 92, 308
food away from home, 154
Ford Motor Company, 26
foreign-born Hispanics, 33, 59
Fortune 1000 companies, 47
Fox Sportsworld Español, 97, 104, 258–259
fragrances, 118,119
Francisco, Don, 100, 256
Franklin Electronic Publishing, 274–277
Fridenberg, Dr. Judith, 134
Frito-Lay, 97, 107
frozen waffles, 162–165
fruit-flavored beverages, 173
FuturaMente (sponsorship program), 39, 86
FuZion, 258

Galavision, 82, 89, 103, 258
Gamesa, 179
Garcia, Andy, 206
gatekeepers, 137
Gateway Computers, 125
GEMS (TV cable network), 103
general market, 255

Generation Ñ, 77, 93, 291

generational divide, 238

generations
    segmenting by, 60

GeoScape International, 130, 317

geo-segmentation, 182, 317

G.I. Joe, 92

gifts, 102

globalization, 12

Golden Globe Awards, 266

Gonzalez, Elian, 50

Gore, Al, 48, 50

Got Milk?, 210

Goya, 268

grandchildren, 131

grandparents, 136

grass-roots events, 206, 295, 310

grocery purchase decisions, 99

grocery stores, 144, 149

Growing Old in the Barrio (book), 134

Grupo Gigante Supermarkets, 285

Guatemala, 11

HBC (biggest Hispanic radio company), 267

HBO Español, 258

HIV/AIDS, 219

Häagen Dazs, 92

hair-care products, 118

Hallmark Cards, 256, 257

Harris Bank, 121

Harris Interactive, 233

Harvard University's Civil Rights Project, 95

Hasbro, Inc., 92

Hawaii, 229

Head and Shoulders, 102

HeadQuarters Advertising, Inc., 224, 318

health
    information, 242
    insurance, 134, 222–227
        Medicaid, 223
        Medicare, 223
        risk behaviors, 109

health and beauty care products, 196–199

healthcare, 32, 132, 133, 134, 219–227

HealthNet, 248

Healthy Families Program (HFP), 223–227

healthy living, 154. 174, 220

heart disease, 219, 222–227

Heineken, 203

hepatitis, 219

high cholesterol, 134

high-density markets, 109

high school, 36
    dropout rate, 107

higher education, 96

HispanicAd.com, 266, 243

Hispanic
    as consumers, 255
    as a market, 254
    audience, 254
    businesses, 43–47, 249, 250, 252
        women-owned, 251
    foreign born, 58
    majority, 20
    media, 253–301
    media watchers, 262–263
    women, 99

Hispanic advertising agencies, 254

Hispanic Association on Corporate Responsibility (HACR), 47–48

Hispanic Broadcast Corporation (HBC), 278

Hispanic Business, Inc., 108, 287

Hispanic Business Magazine, 128, 287, 297–299

Hispanic cable, 258–260

Hispanic Internet Tracking Studies (HITS), 235

Hispanic market, birth of, 255

Hispanic Opinion Tracker, the HOT Study, 118, 290

Hispanic population, 11
    by city, 19–21, 237
    by U.S. region, 14
    density, 87
    distribution by state, 16–19
    growth, 58
    size of, xvii, 3–4
    sub-group differences, 14

Hispanic Magazine Monitor, 288

Hispanic Market Weekly, 72, 264, 266, 243

Hispanic Media Directory, 283

Hispanic radio, 268–282

Hispanic Radio Network (HRN), 282

Hispanic Scholarship Foundation (HSF), 107

Hispanic Trends, 48

Hispanic TV, 254–266

Hispanic Television Network (NTVN), 259

"Hispanic" vs. "Latino", 6

HispanTelligence, 108, 249

Historic tourism, 229

Holahoy.com, 247

Hollywood Reporter, The, 265

home computer, 86

homeownership, 116, 129

home remedies, 224

home security system, 234

home theater systems, 235

Homerunazo scholarship campaign, 92

Honda, 109

Honduras, 11

hot dogs, 207

hot-sauce factor, xvii

household

    formation years, 113

    income, 22, 59, 62, 72, 128

    middle-class, 128–130

    operations, 32

    seniors, 134

    single-male, 169

    size, 30–31

    triple-decker, 131

household expenditures, 55–57

    by product category, 31–32

    on travel, 230

housing, 32

Houston, 181

Houston Astros, 92

Houston-Galvaston-Brazo-ria, 275

Hoy (New York daily news-paper), 243, 247, 285

Huggies, 81

Humphreys, Jeff, 22

Hyundai Motors America, 221

Ice Cream Patrol, 102

immigrants, 33–34, 50, 113, 119, 185, 228

immigration, 5, 10, 36, 59, 135, 223

Immigration and Natural-ization Service, 224

Impact Databank, 201

income, 42

    gap, 59

    household, 22, 59, 62, 72

infant mortality, 83

in-culture, 256, 259, 290, 291

    advertising, 272

    approach, 10

    market research, 255

    marketing, 68, 77, 143

    toys, 92

influencers, 205

insert targeting, 288

instant coffee, 158–161

insurance, 32, 129

integrated Hispanic-mar-ket strategy, 282

international shipping, 102

internet, 12, 82, 86, 102, 233–246

J.C. Williams Group, 184

Jack in the Box, 261

Jarritos (soft drinks), 173

Jennifer Lopez, 95, 292

jewelry, 252

jobs, service industry, 114

Johnson & Johnson, 81

JMCP (advertising agency), 82

Justice, Department of, xvii

KHCK in Dallas, 91

Kmart, 125

KMEX-Television, 285

Kellogg's, 89–90

Kline, Jeff, 282

Kool-Aid, 204

Kraft Foods North Amer-ica, Inc., 91, 203

Kravetz, Carl, 27

LATV, 261

LULAC (civil rights organi-zation), 125

La Agencia de Orci & Aso-ciados, 40, 109

La Copa Virtual (online's first ever soccer tour-nament), 102

La Estrella, 286

La Herencia (The Inheritance), 281

La Opinión (Spanish-lan-guage newspaper), 96, 243, 247, 285

Labatt USA, 201–203

labor force, 9, 26, 41, 59

    participation, 113, 127, 129

    women, 85

    teens, 94, 104

Lafley, A.G., 122

Lamaze Para Padres (mag-azine for new mothers), 82

language, 58, 87, 137, 260–263

    and media, 108

    barriers, 133

    preferences, 63, 153, 239–240, 267, 268, 270, 274–275, 283, 290

        by Gen Ñ, 95

    segmentation, 187–200, 255

    segmentation strategies, 64–70

    Spanglish, 239, 260

Lapis-Integrated Hispanic Marketing, 91

lard, 153, 181
Latin America, 102, 243
Latin
  boomers, 77, 126–130
  culture cross-over, 94
  music, 94, 100
  pride, 89, 106
Latin–Pak, 294
Latin-style foods, 94
Latina Magazine, 117, 287, 290
Latina Style! (magazine), 117, 287
Latinas, 84, 124, 175–178, 250
  as mothers, 81, 188
  boomers, 127
  immigrant, 290
  in management, 115
Latinos, see Hispanic
Latinos and Latinas, 77, 113–125
Latino Health Access (LHA), 133, 220
Latino Impact, 291
Latino Leaders, 291
"Latino Virtual Gallery" (http://latin.si.edu), 134
LatinWebMonitor, 246
laundry supplies, 194
leisure-time, 88
Leo Burnett USA, 91
Lifschitz, Dr. Aliza, 80
Lilly Endowment, Inc., 107
Lincoln Mercury, 26–29
lipstick, 119
liquor, 193
literacy, 137
Lizarralde, Carlos, 239
Llamas, Olivia, 104
Lopez, Jennifer, 95, 292
Lorge, Maritza, 277
Los Angeles, 74, 68, 143. 181

Dodgers, 92
  four-county area, 272
Los Bebés, 77,79
Los Grandes, 77, 131–138
Los Metiches (TV program), 103
Los Niños, 77, 86
Low calorie foods and beverages, 174
Low income families, 85
Lozano, Ignacio E., 247
Lucero (music artist), 100

M&M/Mars, 92, 268
MOCAICA, 222
MSN, 250
MSR&C Ethnic Market Report, 271
MTV-S, 258
McDonald's, 211–212
magazines, 287–292
  multimedia, 291–292
magnet areas, 129
Major League Baseball, 92
Major League Soccer, 203
malls, 93
Maney, Tom, 258
March of Dimes, 82, 83
margarine, 153–158
Maria Paradox, The (book), 120
Marie Clarie en Español, 288
Marc Anthony, 95
market research, 245
  companies, 254
  researchers, 109
marketing, 58
  cause, 282
  community, 109
  data, 244
  events, 28, 89, 245
  eye-level, 89, 97, 199
  experiential 89

  external marketing strategies, 306–307
  grass roots, 206
  in-culture, 68, 7, 313
  inserts, 288
  integrated planning, 305–327
  internal marketing, 311–314
  multicultural, 67
  one-to-one, 89
  online, 244, 249, *appendix*
  point of purchase, 149–152
  promotions, 108
  segmentation, 55
  to seniors, 136–138
  word of mouth, 88
Marketing to the Emerging Majorities newsletter, 97
Marketing Research Association, 245
Market Segment Group, The, 205, 271
marriage, 113, 132
Martin, Ricky, 95
Mattel, 92
mature market, 131–138
Maya and Viva TV, 96
Maya Communications, 104
Maxwell House, 204
meals, see food preparation
Mederma, 82
media, 81, 93, 103, 117
  bilingual, 103–104
  planning, 122
  spending, xv
  strategy, 72
  usage by Latino youth, 96
Media Audit, The, 286

media reps, 109

median age, 5, 9
  by country of origin, 15

MediaWorks, 202

median income, 23

Medicaid, 223

Medicare, 223

Medi-Cal for Children (MCC), 223–227

medical care, 219

medicine, 134, 165–168

men, 41, 232, 288, 291

Men's Fitness en Español, 288

menudo, (tripe), 171

merchandising, 182–184

Metro TV, 96

Mexican food, 251

Mex Grocer, 251

Mexican-Hispanic population, 10–15

Mexicans, 38, 46, 72, 74, 143

Mexico, xvi, 11, 201–203

Mi Casita, 82, 89

Miami, 181

Miami Herald, The, 286

microwave ovens, 127

middle class, 85, 128

military, 110, 223
  careers, 110

Minority Business Development Agency (MBDA), 249

mnemonics, 282–283, 293

model-search contests, 103

mom-and-pop stores, 185–200

money management, 127

money transfers, 12, 60

Moreno, Rita, 206

mortality rates, 134

mortgages, 114, 127

most watched programs, 264

mothers, 162–163, 204–208, 224
  Latinas, 81, 123
  new, 81

movies, 250

MujerFutura (Woman of the Future), 250

multicultural marketing, 67

Multi-Cultural Marketing News, 243

Mun2, 103, 258, 260

Mundos, 103

museums, 231

music, 203, 243, 250

myths, related to pregnancy, 80

NBC Network, 266

Nabisco, 203

nag factor, 82, 88

National Academy on Aging, 133

National Association for Hispanic Health (www.hispanichealth.org), 227

National Association of Hispanic Publications, 284

National Association of Latino Elected Officials (NALEO), 49

National Coalition for Hispanic Health and Human Services Organizations, (COSSHMO), 226

National Council of La Raza (NCLR), 206, 222, 226

National Geographic en Español, 288

National Health and Nutrition Examination Survey (NHANES), 221

National Hispana Leadership Institute (NHLI), 115

National Society of Hispanic MBAs, 116

National Telecommunications and Information Administration, (NTIA), 233

naturalization, 50

naturalized citizens, 34

Nestlé, 81, 158

New California Media Group (NCM), 271

New York City, 134, 181

New York Hispanic Federation, 222

New York Yankees, 92

news, 242, 243

newspapers, 283–286

Nicaragua, 11

Nickelodeon, 82, 260

Nielsen, see ACNielsen

Nielsen Media Research, Inc., 82, 246, 257, 259, 269, 272

Nielsen Hispanic Television Index (NHTI), 257

non-food items purchased in food stores, 194–196

North America Free Trade Agreement, 59

novelas (soap operas), 97, 108, 222

Nuevo Mundo, 286

nutrition, 83

O (magazine), 288

Obesity, 219
  childhood, 221

Olympic Games, 266

one-to-one marketing, 89
on-line
    advertising, 242–246, 249
    marketing, 249
    shopping, 102, 241–242
Orange Crush, 175
Orci, Norma, 40
Oscar Mayer, 203, 207
outdoor advertising, 245, 294
over-the-counter remedies, 165–168

PR agencies, 109
packaged goods, 121
Pampers, 123
Panama, 11
pancakes, 162
Pantene, 123
paper goods, 194
Pappas Telecasting Companies, 259
Paraguay, 11
parents and children, 105–107
parking lots, 183
Parranda 2002, 282
Peruvian Connection, 252
pensions, 133
Pennzoil, 249
People en Español (magazine), 117, 118, 287, 290
PepsiCo, 98–101, 107, 108
personal-care products, 32, 118
personal digital assistants (PDAs), 235
Peru, xvi, 11
pet-care products, 194
Pew Internet & American Life Project, 236

Pfizer Pharmaceuticals, 121, 136, 222
pharmaceutical
    companies, 222
    industry, 214
Philip Morris, 107
Phoenix-Mesa, 275
pizza, 91
Pizza Hut, 250
Playboy en Español, 258
Playtex, 82
Plaza Sesamo, 82
point of purchase (channels), 149–152, 179
    end displays, 182–184
    merchandising, 182–184
    signage, 182
    window displays, 182–184
politics, 48
Pollo Loco, 261
population, see Hispanic population
pornography, 237
portable people meter, 269
portals, 243
Posada, Julian, 184
Post, 204
pregnancy, 83
pre-natal care, 79
pre-school enrollment, 85
pre-schoolers, 82
prescription drugs, 133, 134, 196
Primeros Doce Meses, 82
Princess Cruises, 228
print
    advertising, 245
    magazines, 282–292
    newspapers, 282–292
Procter & Gamble, 102, 121–125
product categories, 153

product mix, 179
product sampling, 283, 294–295
professional workers, 59
promotion agencies, 109
promotional programs, 108, 207
public services, 133
public transportation, 232
Publicidad Siboney, 255
pudor (privacy), 219
Puente, Jr., Tito, 208
Puerto Rico, 4, 11, 123, 268
Puerto Ricans, 14, 15, 38, 46, 72, 74
Pulse (measurement service), 256
purchase behavior, 153

qualitative research, 245
quality of life, 220
    for seniors, 133
Quinceañera Barbie, 92
Quirk's Market Research Review, 245
Quiroz, Lisa, 290

Racial segregation, 95
radio, 80, 96, 267, 268–282
    advertising, 245, 276
    formats, 278–282
    market research, 270–271
RadioShack, 276
Radio Unica, 80, 277, 278, 281, 285
reading language, 67
ready–to-eat meals, 154
recreation, 88, 232
Regalos Sin Fronteras (Gifts without Borders), 102

relatives, 228

religious beliefs, 175

Republicans, 49

retail channels, 179–200

retirement, 133

reventón (slang for party), 99

Reuters, 242

Ricky Martin, 95

risk behaviors, 109

Robinson's-May, 221

Rodriguez, Paul, 29

Rodriguez, Ray, 260

role models, 120,121, 206–208

Roslow, Peter, 256

Roslow Research Group (RRG), 235, 256

Roy P. Benavidez, 92

Royal Crown Foods, 251

rum, 193

Sábado Gigante (Giant Saturday), 100, 256

Sabor (term for flavor), 99

salty snack, 98

sampling, 294–295

San Antonio, 181

Sanchez and Associates, 121

sandwiched generation, 126, 136

sanitary napkins, 175–178

Santiago Solutions Group, The, 22, 314–327

Saralegui, Cristina, 288

Saralequi, Xavier, 258

satellite-dish systems, 235

Saucedo, Xavier, 179

savings accounts, 94

Scantrack Ethnic Service, 154

scholarships, 36, 208, 249 funds, 107

schools, 127 enrollment, 35–36

secondary data, 245

segmentation by age, 77

country of origin, 71–76

generation, 60

length of residence, 59–63

model, 60

place of birth, 58–63

segmentation strategy, 55–57, 58–63

by language, 64–70

segregation by race, 95

Selig Center for Economic Growth, 22, 26

Selecciones (Reader's Digest), 288

Senorial, (soft drink), 173

seniors, 131–138, 232

September 11, 2001, 50, 85, 114

service industries, 132 jobs, 114

Service Merchandise, 276

share of heart, 40, 86, 89, 121, 134, 136, 222, 239, 282, 311

Shakira, 95

Shaw, Deborah Rosado, 120

shopping behavior, 179–200

shopping channel preferences, 185–200

shortening products, 153–158

Sí TV, 261

signage, 182

Simmons Hispanic, 290

Sinclair, John, 253

Sirius Satellite Radio, 278

sitcoms, 96

Six Flags theme park, 91

skiing, 232

Small-business-ownership, 115

small grocery, 185–200

Smithsonian, The, 134

soap operas, 108

soup, 168–171

soccer, 89, 97, 102, 103, 109, 203

Social Security, 9

soft drinks, 98, 171–175 diet 174

software, 242

Sour Skittles, 92

South America, 5, 11

South Americans, 15

South American countries, 10–12

Southern California Edison, 221

Spain, xvi, 11, 243, 268

Spanglish, 239, 260

Spanish Advertising and Marketing Service (SAMS), 255

Spanish Broadcasting System (SBS), 278

Spanish dominant, 270

Spanish Harlem, 134

Spanish International Communication Corporation (SICC), 254

Spanish International Network (SIN), 254

Spanish language 64, 95, see also Language advertisements, 97 media, 89

spending, see Household expenditures

sports, 103, 243

sports programs, 96

stereo system, 234

Staples, 276

StarMedia Network Inc., 249

Strategy Research Corporation (SRC), 235, 256, 274, 300

stroke, 226-227

styles, 118

suburban population, 20

supermarkets, 93, 144, 149. 185-200

Sylvia's La Canasta Mexican, 251

Taco Bell, 268

Taina (children's television show), 82

tampons, 175-178

Tecate, 201-203

technology, 114, 233-246

Teenage Research Unlimited, 93, 94

teens, 93-109
  health, 109
  stress, 109
  spending, 93-94
  buying power, 106

Teen en Español, 288

TeleFutura, 103, 259-261, 266

telemarketing, 292-293

Telemundo Internacional, 103, 255, 257, 260, 266

telenovelas, 257

telephone
  services, 12
  use, 60

Televisa, 256, 266

television, 80, 82, 96
  programming, 28
  sets, 127

tequila, 193

Terra.com, 102

Terra Compras, 102

Terra Lycos, 102, 243

The Barrio Games, 92

The Brothers Garcia (TV show), 103, 260

Tia Remedios, 225

Tide, 123

Times Mirror, 285

tobacco products and smoking supplies, 31

Tomás Rivera Policy Institute, 43, 48, 72, 128, 233

Tombstone Pizza, 91, 204

toothpaste, 199

Torres, Jannet, 64

tourism, 228-232

traditional behaviors, 116

transitionals, 60

transplants, 60

transportation, 32

Travel Industry Association of America, The, 229-232

Trejo, Stephen, 129

travel, 60, 228-232

triple-decker households, 131

Tucker, Sara Martinez, 107

TV Azteca, 259, 260, 267

TV Ñ, 96, 107, 108

USA Networks, 259

ulcers, 219

Ulloa, Walter, 261

Univision, 80, 103, 107, 256, 257, 260, 266
  online, 243, 246

upscale Hispanics, 26

upscale products, 129

urban influentials, 99

Urban Institute, 109

Urban Latino TV (news-magazine-style show), 96, 292

Urban Magazine, 285

urban population, 19

Urban Sofrito, 285

Uruguay, 11

USAirways, 104

U.S. Army, 110-112

U.S. Bureau of Labor Statistics, 23

U.S. Hispanic population, xvi

U.S. House of Representatives, 49

U.S. Soccer Player Award, 109

vaccine approach, 306

vaccine clinics, 89

vegetable oil, 153-158

vegetable shortening, 153-158

Velveeta, 204

Venevisión, 258, 266

Venezuela, xvi, 11

Verizon, 104

videogames, 235

VidaVision, 267

Vietnam, 92

Villar, Arturo, 264, 288

VISA 2001 study, 127

Vista Magazine, 288

volumetric data, 56

Vosberg, Mark, 91

voting, 48

WQHS, 266

Walt Disney Company, 103, 107

warehouse clubs, 149, 187-200

websites, 243, appendix
  www.elherald.com, 247
  www.espn.com, 250
  www.Holahoy.com, 247
  www.HispanicAd.com, 243
  www.HispanicBusiness.com, 108
  www.hispanichealth.

org, 227

www.laopinion.com, 285

www.loquesea.com, 239

www.Mex-Grocer.com, 251

www.terra.com, 243

www.terra.com/teen/, (Canal Teen), 103

www.TitularesProdu. com, 243

www.Todobebe.com, 82

www.Soloella.com, 82

www.univision.com, 236

www.peruvianconnec- tion.com, 252

www.nacersano.org, 82, 83

www.VilaWeb.com, 240

www. Yupi.com, 243

www.hispanichealth. org, 227

www.najp.org, 284

weekly earnings, 42

Wells Fargo Bank, 221

widows, 132

William Blair & Co., 265

win-win-win strategies, 121

window displays, 182–184

wine, 193

world wide web, see Inter- net and websites

women, 26, 41, 83, 85, 99, 115, 118, 124, 175–178, 205, 219, 223

senior, 133

Woodstock, 104

Wool, Abby, 257

word-of-mouth, 154

communications, 138

marketing, 88

workers, see Labor force

workforce, 26, 41–50

working mothers, 85

World Cup Soccer, 103, 109, 243

XM Satellite, 278

Yahoo! en Español, 243, 247, 250, 286

Yankelovich Hispanic Monitor, 104

young adults, 93

young singles, 113

youth, 238

Yupi/MSN, 249, 250

Zip Value Clusters, 130

Zoloft, 121, 223

Zoom Media Group, 291

Zubi Advertising, 92

ABOUT THE AUTHOR

 **M. Isabel Valdés** is a recognized pioneer in Hispanic marketing and founder of the in-culture movement. For more than 20 years, Ms. Valdés has conducted marketing research with unique culturally sensitive methods and state-of-the-art-techniques. Recently, Ms. Valdés founded Isabel Valdés Consulting (isabelvaldes.com). Her firm advises clients on a broad range of business-related issues in global and in-culture marketing. Ms. Valdés is a member of PepsiCo/Frito-Lay's Latino Advisory Board; a board member of Accion USA, a micro-lending institution; and a member of the Advisory Board for Consumer Trends Forum International.

Ms. Valdés has received numerous honors, including being selected by *Fortune Small Business* as a "Woman Entrepreneur Star," and Business Woman of the Year by the New York Hispanic Chambers of Commerce in 1995. In March 2000, she was named by *American Demographics* magazine as the "21st Century Star of Multicultural Research."

Presently a lecturer at Stanford University's Professional Publishing Course, Ms. Valdés is also a trustee of the Tomás Rivera Policy Institution, a member of the board of National Hispana Leadership Institute in Arlington, Virginia, and a board member for the Mexican Museum of San Francisco.

Ms. Valdés conducted communications research for Stanford University and was a member of the clinical faculty at Stanford University School of Medicine's Division of Family Medicine for six years. She earned an M.A. in Communications and an M.A. in Education from Stanford University. She also holds professional degrees in Communications, and Communications Arts and Advertising from two leading universities in South America. A seasoned entrepreneur, she was the founder of Hispanic Market Connections, president of Cultural Access Group, and co-founder and partner of Santiago & Valdés Solutions. She is now a senior advisor to its successor, The Santiago Solutions Group, and she runs her own consulting company, Isabel Valdés Consulting.

Ms. Valdés was born in Chile and recently became an American citizen. She is married to Dr. Julio Aranovich, a native of Argentina, and the mother of Gabriel, 24, and Clara, 16.